The Cartesian
Port Royal Logic

This book sets out for the first time in English and in the terms of modern logic the semantics of the *Port Royal Logic* (*La Logique ou l'Art de penser*, 1662–1685) of Antoine Arnauld and Pierre Nicole, perhaps the most influential logic book in the 17th and 18th centuries. Its goal is to explain how the *Logic* reworks the foundation of pre-Cartesian logic so as to make it compatible with Descartes' metaphysics. The *Logic*'s authors forged a new theory of reference based on the medieval notion of objective being, which is essentially the modern notion of intentional content. Indeed, the book's central aim is to detail how the *Logic* reoriented semantics so that it centered on the notion of intentional content. This content, which the *Logic* calls *comprehension*, consists of an idea's defining modes. Mechanisms are defined in terms of comprehension that rework earlier explanations of central notions like conceptual inclusion, signification, abstraction, idea restriction, sensation, and most importantly within the *Logic*'s metatheory, the concept of idea-extension, which is a new technical concept coined by the *Logic*. Although Descartes is famous for rejecting "Aristotelianism," he says virtually nothing about logic. His followers fill the gap. By putting to use the doctrine of objective being, which had been a relatively minor part of medieval logic, they preserve more central semantic doctrines, especially a correspondence theory of truth. A recurring theme of the book is the degree to which the *Logic* hews to medieval theory. This interpretation is at odds with what has become a standard reading among French scholars according to which this 16th-century work should be understood as rejecting earlier logic along with Aristotelian metaphysics, and as putting in its place structures more like those of 19th-century class theory.

John N. Martin studied philosophy at the University of California, received his doctorate from the University of Toronto, and spent his career teaching philosophy and logic at the University of Cincinnati. Research areas include formal semantics, philosophical linguistics, and the history of logic. Books include *Elements of Formal Semantics* (1987) and *Themes in Neoplatonic and Aristotelian Logic* (Ashgate 2004).

Routledge Studies in Seventeenth-Century Philosophy

The Idea of Principles in Early Modern Thought
Interdisciplinary Perspectives
Edited by Peter R. Anstey

Physics and Metaphysics in Descartes and in His Reception
Edited by Delphine Antoine-Mahut and Sophie Roux

Experiment, Speculation and Religion in Early Modern Philosophy
Edited by Alberto Vanzo and Peter R. Anstey

Mind, Body, and Morality
New Perspectives on Descartes and Spinoza
Edited by Martina Reuter and Frans Svensson

Locke's Ideas of Mind and Body
Han-Kyul Kim

Causation and Cognition in Early Modern Philosophy
Edited by Dominik Perler and Sebastian Bender

Leibniz's Legacy and Impact
Edited by Julia Weckend and Lloyd Strickland

Freedom, Action, and Motivation in Spinoza's *Ethics*
Edited by Noa Naaman-Zauderer

The Cartesian Semantics of the *Port Royal Logic*
John N. Martin

For more information about this series, please visit: www.routledge.com/Routledge-Studies-in-Seventeenth-Century-Philosophy/book-series/SE0420

The Cartesian Semantics of the *Port Royal Logic*

John N. Martin

LONDON AND NEW YORK

First published 2020 by Routledge

2 Park Square, Milton Park, Abingdon, Oxon OX14 4RN
605 Third Avenue, New York, NY 10017

Routledge is an imprint of the Taylor & Francis Group, an informa business

First issued in paperback 2022

Copyright © 2020 Taylor & Francis

The right of John N. Martin to be identified as author of this work has been asserted by him in accordance with sections 77 and 78 of the Copyright, Designs and Patents Act 1988.

All rights reserved. No part of this book may be reprinted or reproduced or utilised in any form or by any electronic, mechanical, or other means, now known or hereafter invented, including photocopying and recording, or in any information storage or retrieval system, without permission in writing from the publishers.

Notice:
Product or corporate names may be trademarks or registered trademarks, and are used only for identification and explanation without intent to infringe.

Publisher's Note

The publisher has gone to great lengths to ensure the quality of this reprint but points out that some imperfections in the original copies may be apparent.

Library of Congress Cataloging-in-Publication Data
A catalog record for this book has been requested

ISBN: 978-0-815-37046-8 (hbk)
ISBN: 978-1-03-233770-8 (pbk)
DOI: 10.4324/9781351249195

Typeset in Sabon
by Apex CoVantage, LLC

For Jane and Neil

Contents

Acknowledgments viii
Abbreviations ix

Introduction 1

1 The Semantics of Terms. Intentional Content 9

2 The Semantics of Terms. Signification and Extension 39

3 The Semantic of Terms. The Structure of Ideas 71

4 The Semantics of Propositions. Truth and Consequences 109

5 The Semantics of Discourse. Method 148

6 The Semantics of Discourse. Existential Import 184

Appendix 222
Index 238

Acknowledgments

The author gratefully acknowledges the research support over many years provided by the Charles Phelps Taft Research Center at the University of Cincinnati, and Jean-Yves Besiau's supporting role in fostering the biannual Congress of the Square of Opposition, which has provided a forum for the presentation and discussion of papers in the history of logic. The author also gratefully thanks his proofreaders, Mel Andrews, Kathleen Kidder, and Kathryn Lorenz of, respectively, the Departments of Philosophy, Classics, and Romance Languages at the University of Cincinnati, who have reduced somewhat the number of his transcription errors. He also acknowledges the permission by the *History and Philosophy of Logic* and its publisher Taylor & Francis Ltd. (www.tandfonline.com) for reprinting in portions of *Martin 2011*, *Martin 2013*, and *Martin 2016a*.

Abbreviations

Antoine Arnauld and Pierre Nicole, *Logique ou l'Art de Penser* in *Arnauld* is abbreviated *LAP*. The 2003, vol. V, edition by Elmar Kremer and Denis Moreau, is abbreviated *KM*. The English translation of *LAP*, *Arnauld 1996*, by Jill Vance Buroker, is abbreviated *B*.

Antoine Arnauld, *Des Vraies et des Fausse Idées* in *Arnauld 2003*, vol. I, is abbreviated *VFI*. Its English language translation, *Arnauld 1990* by Stephen Gaukroger, is abbreviated *G*.

René Descartes, *Œuvres de Descartes* from *Descartes 1897–1909*, edited by C. Adam and P. Tannery, is abbreviated *AT*. The original 17th-century spelling of *Arnauld 2003* is retained.

If not otherwise attributed, translations are those of the author.

For production reasons references are placed at the end of each Chapter.

Introduction

From the late 17th to the 19th centuries, the *Port Royal Logic* of Antoine Arnauld and Pierre Nicole was probably the most influential logic text in the western world.[1] Today, however, it is hardly known, even among historians of philosophy. The reasons for the neglect is clear. Its formal logic is Aristotelian, which is of little technical interest today. Because the text is technical and in its way arcane, even historians of philosophy when investigating Arnauld prefer his more discursive works, of which there are many. There have been several book-length studies of the *Logic* in French. These have mildly suggested that the *Logic* turns away from medieval logic and even in some ways anticipates Boolean algebra. Some have also suggested that because the *Logic* defines truth in terms of idea, it rejects a correspondence theory of truth. The interpretations in this book argue in the opposite direction. The Cartesians preserved a great deal of medieval logic, and advocated a clearer correspondence theory of truth. In English, the *Logic* has received some attention from linguists, but they have had little to say about logic as such. On the whole, the secondary literature on the *Logic* as logic is sparse.

This book is a study of the *Logic*'s metatheory. Its goal is to explain why its semantics should be of interest to modern logicians. To be sure, the *Logic* is not rigorous in the modern sense. On the other hand, it is principled and proceeds from basic to defined terms in an orderly manner. Among the items of formal interest are its recursively sound formulations of truth-conditions for categorical propositions and its characterization of syllogistic validity by a set of five rules and a "containment principle." Historically, the interpretations argued for here contend that the *Logic* is less a repudiation of its medieval antecedents than a reconstruction on Cartesian foundations of standard doctrines from earlier logic. In particular, it attempts to reconcile a version of

---

1 For a discussion of the historical influence of the *Logic* see *Auroux 1993* and *Kennedy 1995*.

the medieval correspondence theory of truth with Cartesian dualism. Descartes' followers rightly observed that there was a problem making dualism consistent with earlier accounts, which were usually based on causal connections between the soul and body. Throughout the book, the *Logic*'s particular doctrines are shown to have roots in earlier teaching. Philosophically, what is most interesting about the *Logic* is the role of intentional content. Because the authors needed a new way to explain the way words in mental language signify things in the world, they fashioned an explanation in terms of intentional content, a concept they reconstructed in what they took to be an ontologically neutral way from the medieval notion of objective being. Intentional content is, in various ways, at the heart of the *Logic*'s semantics, employed repeatedly for the solution of semantic problems.

The major interpretive claims of special interest in the book's chapters are these:

Chapter 1 argues that the *Logic* fashions a notion of intentional content from the medieval concept of objective being that is consistent with Descartes' substance-mode ontology and avoids assigning to objective being a special ontological status.

Chapter 2 argues that although the *Logic*'s notion of extension, in terms of which the truth-conditions for categorical propositions are defined, is a set of inferior ideas, containment and exclusion relations among extensions nevertheless track containment and exclusion relations outside the mind, with the result that the *Logic* espouses a genuine correspondence theory of truth.

Chapter 3 argues that although ideas and extensions possess the properties of parallel partially ordered structures, ideas are not dual to extensions and it is anachronistic to read into the *Logic* an early form of Boolean algebra. Its account of structure has more in common with the medieval theory of mental language and its associated tree of Porphyry.

Chapter 4 argues that the *Logic*'s truth-conditions for categorical propositions in terms of "universal term" is a non-circular abstraction from the medieval theory of distributive supposition, that its six general rules for the syllogistic provide a decision procedure for the valid moods, and that the valid moods are successfully characterized by the *Logic*'s so-called containment principle, which is much like the rule *dici de omni*.

Chapter 5 argues that the *Logic*'s account of analysis and synthesis draws from a long tradition of earlier syllogistic paradigms, and that although the formal logic it assumes is limited to the syllogistic, its analysis of the concept of "logical inference" is rule-governed and formal, similar to that of modern logic.

Chapter 6 argues that the *Logic* accepts sensation as a source of knowledge and with it a distinction between essential and contingent truth, in which the truth-conditions for essential affirmations do not carry existential import but those for contingent affirmations do.

Summary of the *Logic*'s Content

The book's exposition follows a traditional order modeled on the Organon. Part I concerns the logic of terms; Part II the logic of proposition; and Part III the logic of arguments. Part IV is devoted to method, a topic not directly discussed in medieval logic but of great interest in the 15th and 16th centuries. These four parts correspond to four basic mental operations: conception, judgement, reason, and ordering. Each is based on the one before. Method consists of deductions, formed from propositions, formed from terms.

Part I concerns the logic of terms. Terms are ideas, which are a variety of mental act. They are either innate or caused by the soul. If caused, it is by abstraction or restriction. They possess three basic semantic properties. The most fundamental is intentional content, which is construed in the *Logic* as a set of defining modes. Content, as the authors conceive of it, is a reformulation in Cartesian terms of the medieval notion of *objective being*. The next basic semantic concepts, in definitional order, are signification and extension. Both are defined in terms of intentional content. Their role is to explain how terms refer to the things outside the mind. The authors endorse a variety of occasionalism that rejects a causal connection between matter and the soul. Rejecting Aristotle's empiricism, they hold that an idea relates to the world because the modes in its intentional content are true of things outside the mind. God ensures a connection to the world. When the soul has a sensation of a material substance, God causes the soul to have a vivid awareness of modes. This "perception" is a kind of proto-idea, and modes constitute its "content." Some of these are material modes, like relative size and motion. God's providence ensures that they are true of the material substance currently affecting the body's sense organs. On the other hand, some of the modes in perception, like color, taste, and smell, are spiritual and true of the soul. By abstraction from the modes in perceptual experience, the soul forms ideas. In more technical language, by selecting modes for the content of the perception, the soul forms a new idea that has the selected modes as its new "content." Some ideas, like infinity, are innate. Once the soul has a supply of ideas, many of which are abstract, it can form narrower ideas by the operation of restriction. In restriction, a new idea is formed by taking the intersection of contents of two prior ideas.

Ideas constitute the terms of mental language. Part I introduces basic distinctions in grammar and semantics that are used throughout the book. It begins by acknowledging the existence of Aristotle's ten categories of being, but the distinctions among them play little role subsequently. More important are the traditional "predicables": genus, species, difference, property, and accident. These figure later in the *Logic*'s account of scientific knowledge, which is formulated in terms of genera and species.

Part I goes on to distinguish substantives and connotative terms, real and nominal definitions, and explicative and restrictive relative clauses—all distinctions drawn from medieval logic. Of Part I's fifteen chapters, the last seven concern difficulties arising from the misuse of intentional content, a concern throughout the book. Of particular importance to semantics is the notion of "false ideas," which is adapted from medieval logic and Descartes' *Meditations*. In the *Logic*'s version, a false idea is one that fails to signify anything in the world, for example, *golden mountain*. An affirmative proposition with a false idea as subject term cannot be true. False ideas figure prominently in Part IV as part of the claim that contingent affirmative propositions carry existential import.

Part II gives a detailed account of the parts of speech in mental language. "Significative" terms include nouns, pronouns, explicative and restrictive relative clauses, verbs, and other complex predicates. Propositional forms include the four categorical propositional types of the syllogistic, propositions with complex subjects, propositions that contain the alethic modalities, conjunctions, disjunctions, and conditionals. The distinctions are partly grammatical and partly semantic. Part II concludes with perhaps the most interesting technical part of the book, an analysis of the truth-conditions of categorical propositions in terms of the distributive properties of terms.

The first sections of Part III lay out the logic of the syllogistic and some of its simple extensions, and the latter sections discuss various fallacies and misuses of languages. Much of the content of Part III was regarded at the time as essential material in a logic textbook. The authors include an extended account of the syllogistic despite the fact that they regard it as trivial—nobody with elementary intelligence, they say, makes errors in syllogistic reasoning. Most of Part III's formal logic repeats well-known lore. From a modern perspective, the discussion of validity is rather an unsystematic mixture of concepts from syntax and semantics. Of some interest is a list of six rules for characterizing the valid moods. The list was taken up by Leibniz and has been repeated in Aristotelian logic textbooks since. On a syntactic reading, they amount to a decision procedure for the valid moods. The authors also advance suggestions for reducing complex syllogisms—those with complex subject terms—to standard moods. Of some interest is a "containment principle" for identifying valid moods. The final sections of Part III on traditional fallacies are of interest largely due to the importance the authors attach to mistakes in understanding intentional content.

Part IV is devoted to method. Although the topic as such was of little interest in the Middle Ages, method was vigorously investigated in the 16th and 17th centuries. Drawing on this literature, the *Logic* sets out its own version of the view that method divides into analysis and synthesis. These two aspects of method are explained as consisting of distinctive varieties of syllogistic reasoning: analysis is reasoning *to* scientific axioms, and synthesis is reasoning *from* scientific axioms. Axioms consist of real definitions and other general truths describing the nature of things. Axioms must be certain, either justified by clear and distinct ideas or arrived at by previous arguments that confer certainty. An axiom may also be a nominal definition, an *ad hoc* coinage of scientific terminology accepted by the scientific community. By borrowing from rule sets previously promulgated by Pascal and Descartes, the authors propose their own rules for discovering and disseminating scientific knowledge. Scientific knowledge, for example, as laid out in a scientific treatise, is formulated in demonstrations, which have as their underlying structure the syllogistic logic of Part III. Its propositions generally describe the genera and species that make up the natural world. The natural science the authors had in mind was largely Descartes' physics of material extension.

Part IV argues that it is possible to prove deductively that sensory knowledge and religious faith are, by and large, reliable. Sensation and religious teachings are reliable because God is not a deceiver. Of particular interest is the mechanism for sensory knowledge. The authors defend a version of direct perceptual realism. Their account combines occasionalism and the correspondence theory of truth, and it forms the core of a famous debate between Arnauld and Malebranche on whether ideas are representational entities standing between mental awareness and things in the world. The *Logic*'s position is that in perception the soul has a vivid awareness of material modes, like motion, and that these modes are truly instantiated in the individual affecting the body. There is no mediating entity between the mental event of the soul's understanding of the mode and the instantiation of the mode in a material substance.

Logically, the doctrine is important because it motivates the *Logic*'s distinction between necessary and contingent truth. Some contingent affirmations with subject terms abstracted from sensation are true because God ensures that the material modes experienced are actually instantiated in the material substance affecting the senses. Affirmations with false ideas as subject terms, however, are false because they have a content that is not true of anything whatever. On the other hand, essential definitions describe true natures. They are timelessly true. The *Logic* thus aligns itself with the medieval tradition that holds that there is a fundamental semantic distinction between essential and contingent truths: contingent affirmative categorical propositions carry existential import, but essential definitions do not.

Technical Logic

The *Logic* lays out its theory in a more or less definitional order, proceeding from the properties of terms to those of propositions, from propositions to arguments, and from arguments to scientific theory. It would be anachronistic, however, to expect modern rigor. Concepts are sometimes introduced before their defining terms. Concepts are sometimes introduced by what appears to be a definition but which turns out be a description of only paradigm cases, and often concepts are explained by just a few examples.[2] What are called rules and axioms are often just important principles, not part of a formal axiom system in the modern sense. On the other hand, the metatheory has a clear conceptual development. The discussion in the following chapters will generally follow this conceptual order, necessitating some jumping forward and backward in the *Logic*'s text. When a definition is missing or incomplete, an attempt will be made to give a formulation that captures the *Logic*'s intent.

At times the *Logic* makes use of the technical jargon of its period. Frequently this has parallels in modern logic. When this happens, it is useful to translate the historical view into modern terms. Once translated, what is being said is often clearer to a modern reader. Because of their formal clarity, modern terms also make it easier to see a doctrine's implications. Formal reconstructions in modern terms, like those in the Appendix, also enable comparison to modern theory and evaluation according to modern criteria.

At some points this sort of reformulation into modern terms is particularly useful. In Part I, for example, ideas emerge as having algebraic structure. Ideas, contents, and extensions form ordered sets, and these structures map into one another. Other commentators have remarked on similarities between the *Logic* and modern algebra, but as we shall see in Chapter 3, some of these are exaggerated.[3]

In the enthusiasm for formal reconstruction there is a danger that a modern formulation may not be justified by the exact wording of the text or that the modern view attributes anachronistic implications, which follow because the modern vocabulary is embedded in a broad framework, like Boolean algebra or set theory. To avoid ungrounded reconstruction, the discussion throughout the book will keep close to the text, perhaps tediously so. Nevertheless, we shall find that the *Logic* does describe some structure that closely conforms to algebraic relations, and that these are fundamental to how ideas correspond to things in the world. These algebraic properties are the topic of Chapter 3 on the structure of ideas.

---

2 Arnauld admits as much, *Arnauld and Nicole 1993*, p. 335, B 260:

> this *Logic* was augmented almost by half since the first essays, which were written in four or five days, no one should be surprised if the different passages added at different times, and even while it was being printed, are not always as well placed as they might have been if they had been inserted from the start.

3 See *Martin 2011, Martin 2013, Martin 2016c, Martin 2016b, Martin 2017*, and the discussion at various points in this book.

Perhaps the most technically interesting part of the *Logic* is its statement of the truth-conditions for categorical propositions at the end of Part II. The issue there is whether a term's "distributive" extension can be used in a non-circular way to define the truth-conditions of categorical propositions. Because the related notion of distributive supposition in medieval logic was defined in terms of truth, it could not have been used without circularity to define truth itself. But by analyzing distribution directly through a term's referential properties, the *Logic* liberates distribution from its definitional dependence on truth, thereby enabling a definition of truth in terms of distribution. The account is the subject of Chapter 4.

The *Logic*'s formal logic, which is set out in Part III, is limited to the syllogism and some of its simple extensions. Little of the material is technically new. An exception is the claim that syllogistic entailment is really a species of idea-containment. The claim is similar to the view sometimes advanced that Aristotle's syllogistic is founded on the so-called principle *de omni et nullo*. Chapter 4 explains how the *Logic*'s version is correct when formulated in terms of the monotonic properties of the categorical quantifiers as explained in general quantification theory.

Part IV discusses analysis and synthesis. The account is technical in that it makes subtle use of syllogistic logic. Chapter 5 explains the details. Of some interest is the seemingly paradoxical claims that in "analysis" a theorem can be used to prove its premises, and that it is possible to deduce from a description of a particular event a general law that explains it.

The Appendix provides formal definitions of technical terms introduced informally in the book, as well as, several formal reconstructions of parts of the *Logic*'s theory and a primer on syllogistic logic for those unfamiliar with it.

References

Arnauld, Antoine. 1990. *On True and False Ideas*, Manchester, Manchester University Press.

Arnauld, Antoine. 2003. *Œuvres Philosophiques d'Arnauld*, Bristol, Theommes Press. Kremer, Elmar and Denis Moreau (eds.).

Arnauld, Antoine and Pierre Nicole. 1993. *La Logique ou d'Art de Penser*, Paris, Librairie Philosophique J. Vrin. Clair, Pierre and François Girbal (eds.).

Arnauld, Antoine and Pierre Nicole. 1996. *Logic or the Art of Thinking*, Cambridge, Cambridge University Press. Buroker, Jill Vance (translator).

Auroux, Sylvain. 1993. *La Logique des Idées*, Montréal, Paris, Bellarmin, Vrin.

Descartes, René. 1897–1909. *Œuvres de Descartes*, Paris, Vrin. Adam, C. and P. Tannery (eds.).

Kennedy, Rick. (ed.). 1995. *Aristotelian & Cartesian Logic at Harvard*, Boston, Colonial Society of Massachusetts (distributed by University of Virginia).

Martin, John N. 2011. Existential Import in Cartesian Semantics. *History and Philosophy of Logic*, 32:2, 1–29.

Martin, John N. 2013. Distributive Terms, Truth, and *the Port Royal Logic*. *History and Philosophy of Logic*, 133–154.

Martin, John N. 2016a. A Note on "Distributive Terms, Truth, and the Port Royal Logic." *History and Philosophy of Logic*, 37:4, 391–392.

Martin, John N. 2016b. Privative Negation in *the Port Royal Logic*. *Review of Symbolic Logic*, 9, 23.

Martin, John N. 2016c. The Structure of Ideas in the Port Royal Logic. *The Journal of Applied Logic*, 19, 1–19.

Martin, John N. 2017. Extension in the Port Royal Logic. *South American Journal of Logic*, 3, 1–20.

1 The Semantics of Terms. Intentional Content

A Cartesian Challenge

Arnauld and Nicole inherited and sustained an immense logical tradition. As followers of Descartes, they rejected some of Aristotle's views, but with respect to much of earlier logic they were conservative. Although they de-emphasis scholastic material like the syllogistic and placed new emphasize on others like intentional content, they endorsed unchanged large parts of medieval logic. A major exception was the theory of reference or, as they called it, signification. Signification lay at the heat of the earlier logical tradition because it entered into the definition of many other ideas. The standard explanation of signification, however, which held that bodily modes travels to the soul, was undermined by dualism. The reconstruction of signification is set out in Part I of the *Logic*. This chapter describes how the account is built up out of two parts: standard distinctions from traditional logic plus a reworked concept of intentional content based on the medieval notion of objective being.

Cartesian Ontology

At several points the *Logic*'s the authors refuse to engage in metaphysics, which they regarded as a fruitless endeavor. They set aside as useless the problem of universals—the issue of whether universals exist, as they put it, *a parte rei*.[1] They also dismiss as "inconceivable" various Aristotelian concepts like substantial form, weight, and attractive powers.[2] Instead, they endorse Descartes' dualism and his quasi-geometric physics of extended matter. But their remarks that distance themselves from Aristotle are misleading. Their rebellion was selectively. Key to their distinctive views is a long list of Aristotelian concepts that had become orthodox in medieval logic.

---

1 *LAP, Discours* I, *KM* V 112–113, *B* 11–12.
2 *LAP* IV.6, *KM* V 380–381, *B* 249.

Perhaps their most fundamental Aristotelian commitment is to a substance-mode ontology. Part I endorses a long list of Aristotelian concepts that detail this ontology, which may be summarized here. The authors begin by partitioning Being into its two broadest species: substances and modes. This partitions is subdivided in the traditional way into Aristotle's ten categories: substance and nine species of modes: quality, quantity, relation, activity, passivity, place, time, position, and state.[3] Modes are also called attributes and qualities. The distinction between substances and modes is explained in the orthodox way. Substances have independent existence, but modes exist only as instantiated in substances. Modes are cross-classified into Porphyry's five predicables: genus, species, difference, property (*proprium*), and accident.[4] Predicables are distinguished from one another by the degree to which a mode is instantiated necessarily. Every species and genus has a necessary nature, whereas properties are necessary but not definitive, and accidents are contingent.

A species' nature or essence is described in a real definition, which is a necessarily true proposition that affirms of the species its genus and difference. As a result of their natures, species fall into a finitely branching finite tree-hierarchy that is headed by the highest genus, Being. Scientific knowledge consists primarily of essential definitions and their consequences.[5] All of these are thoroughly orthodox Aristotelian views. We shall see, however, that the authors give them a distinctive Cartesian cast.

The *Logic*'s main departure from Aristotelian ontology is its dualism. The category of substance, it claims, is partitioned into "mind and body." These "are the two species of substance."[6] Although most medieval logicians would concur that there exists a fundamental difference between spiritual and material substance, what is distinctive in the *Logic* is the additional principle that the two species of substance cannot share modes. Modes that inhere in minds cannot inhere in bodies, and material modes cannot inhere in spirits. Although the principle has a ring of plausibility given dualism—indeed one wonders why ancient ontologists were not more troubled about spirits and minds sharing properties—it has devastating implications for the foundations of medieval metalogic. The inability of material modes to affect the mind vitiates what was then the standard account of signification, and along with signification other parts of the theory which were defied in terms of signification, for example, the definitions of truth and validity.

---

3 *LAP* I.3, *KM* V 137–138, *B* 33–34. The authors describe the distinctions among the nice varieties of modes as "fairly useless." With the exception of relations, they seldom refer to them.
4 *LAP* I.7, *KM* V 146–150, *B* 40–44.
5 *LAP* I.6, 7, and 12.
6 *LAP* I.6, *KM* V 148, *B* 42.

The standard theory had turned on the premise that material modes travel to the soul. As logic developed in the 13th century, it became accepted that, in the first instance, language is mental. Ontologically, language was believed to consist of accidental modes of the soul or "mental acts." These were thought to have a structure or grammar. Basic mental acts, which were called concepts, were understood to be signs for things in the world, or to be "significative." They could represent any category of being, whether material and spiritual. Concepts in turn were parts of, or causal preliminaries to, more complex acts called propositions. Propositions took various grammatical forms. Of these the four categorical propositions of the syllogistic were basic. Concepts served as their terms. A proposition was true or false depending on whether the world was "as its terms signified." A series of ordered propositions, in turn, formed a yet more complex structure called an arguments. An argument was valid or invalid depending on whether its inference preserved truth. There was an immense logical lore spelling out the details. It was not the purpose of the *Port Royal Logic* to overthrow this body of theory. The *Logic* is more accurately described as reworking elementary parts of medieval logic in a way that made it consistent with Descartes' philosophy. Providing a new analysis of signification was a major challenge.

Medieval Theories of Signification

Theories varied, but Aquinas' account of signification is representative. As a true Aristotelian, Aquinas understood concept formation to be empirical: "there is nothing in the intellect that was not first in the senses."[7] He conceived sensation to start with a physical process in which sensible properties, called a "sensible species," are conveyed through a sensible medium, like air and the sense organs, to be ultimately instantiated in the brain. Once the properties leave the body, they were thought to have a special ontological property: they did not affect—they were not "true of"—the medium in which they were instantiated. When a rose is seen, its redness travels through the air to the eyes without making either the air or the eyes red. A property in this state was said to be "intentional" in the sense that although it is instantiated in a subject, it is not true of the subject. The property is then conveyed from the body to the soul by the passive faculty of imagination, through which the soul experiences what Aquinas called a "phantasm," a state of awareness of

---

[7] For Aquinas see *Summa theologiae* 1.1a, qq. 84 and 85, specifically q. 84, aa. 1, 2, 6, and 7, and q. 85, a. 1. The quotation is from *De veritate*, q. 2, a. 3, arg. 19. *Thomas Aquinas 2006 [1970]*: Nihil est in intellectu quod non sit prius in sensu.

the properties of the individual being sensed. This set of properties was called the perceived individual's "sensible species." In Aquinas' view the very properties previously instantiated in the body outside the mind were instantiated in the soul but in what he called an "immaterial" and "immobile" way. It is this transfer of properties from the body to the soul that Arnauld and Nicole rejected. For dualists, a material property cannot be instantiated in the soul even "intentionally."

According to Aquinas, imagination is an intermediate stage of concept formation. Imagination is followed by "abstraction." From the panoply of the individual's particular properties experienced as part of the phantasm, the active intellect separates out one or more properties. The selected properties are then instantiated as a unit separately in the soul, again in an intentional manner. The actualization of this separate property instantiation is a mental act called a "concept," the ancestor of what the Cartesians would later call an idea.

Aquinas' causal process requires both the phantasm, as a "material cause," and the agent intellect, called an "active cause" because it acts upon the material cause to form a concept. Aquinas also holds, somewhat mysteriously, that the intellect may abstract from the sensible species the properties that constitute object's essential nature—its "quiddity" or "intelligible species"—which he says is generally non-sensible or "invisible."[8]

The doctrine of sensation and abstraction is directly relevant to medieval semantics because the process is supposed to explain why concepts are "significative." The concept, which is a property instantiated in the soul, is the same property that was that was formerly instantiated in an individual outside the mind. The property in the soul, albeit instantiated intentionally, is supposed to be numerically identical to the property instantiated in object outside the mind. Nominalists, who denied that numerically the same property can be instantiated in more than one individual, would say that the property-instance in the soul is "similar" to the instance in the individual. In either case, the property in the soul, the so-called concept, possesses signification in two ways: descriptively and causally. Descriptively, it signifies all individuals that possess that property or, if you are a nominalist, it signifies all individuals that instantiate similar property-instances. Causally, it signifies all individuals that could have caused a phantasm from which the property concept could have been abstracted. In the passage below Aquinas refers to both the descriptive and causal properties of the concept, and

---

8 For more detailed accounts along the same line see Ockham, *Reportatio* II, q. 13 in *William of Ockham 1981*; John Buridan, *Commentary on Aristotle's De Anima II*, q. 9, Chapt. 35, in *John Buridan 1984*, pp. 495–512, and *Questions on Aristotle's De Anima*, q. 8, in *John Buridan 1989*, pp. 288–311.

speaks of the relation of the concept to its cause as one of similarity (*aedequatio*):[9]

> Moreover all cognition is accomplished by the assimilation [*assimilation*] of the cognizing thing to the thing cognized, so that assimilation is called the cause of cognition: as vision knows color through by being ordered by the species of color. Therefore the primary way in which being compares to the intellect is that being agrees with the intellect, which agreement indeed is called equality [*aedequatio*] of the intellect and the thing, according to which conformity, as it is said, cognition follows the thing. So therefore the being of a thing precedes the conceptualization [*ratio*] of truth, but cognition is a certain sort of veridical effect [*quidam veritatis effectus*].

Some like Olivi, Suárez, and Malebranche later reject the causal transfer of properties from matter to the soul because they subscribe to an Augustinian view that the direction of causation is the other way around, from spirit to matter. Nevertheless, they retain the descriptive part of the doctrine holding that concepts were properties of the soul similar to those of their *significata*.[10]

---

9 *De veritate*, Thomas Aquinas 2006 [1970] [51577] q. 1, a. 1, arg. 7:

> Convenientiam vero entis ad intellectum exprimit hoc nomen verum. Omnis autem cognitio perficitur per assimilationem cognoscentis ad rem cognitam, ita quod assimilatio dicta est causa cognitionis: sicut visus per hoc quod disponitur secundum speciem coloris, cognoscit colorem. Prima ergo comparatio entis ad intellectum est ut ens intellectui concordet: quae quidem concordia adaequatio intellectus et rei dicitur; et in hoc formaliter ratio veri perficitur. Hoc est ergo quod addit verum super ens, scilicet conformitatem, sive adaequationem rei et intellectus; ad quam conformitatem, ut dictum est, sequitur cognitio rei. Sic ergo entitas rei praecedit rationem veritatis, sed cognitio est quidam veritatis effectus. Secundum hoc ergo veritas sive verum tripliciter invenitur diffiniri. Uno modo secundum illud quod praecedit rationem veritatis, et in quo verum fundatur; et sic Augustinus definit in Lib. Solil.: *verum est id quod est*; et Avicenna in sua Metaphysic.: *veritas cuiusque rei est proprietas sui esse quod stabilitum est ei*; et quidam sic: *verum est indivisio esse, et quod est*. Alio modo definitur secundum id in quo formaliter ratio veri perficitur; et sic dicit Isaac quod *veritas est adaequatio rei et intellectus*; et Anselmus in Lib. de veritate: *veritas est rectitudo sola mente perceptibilis*. Rectitudo enim ista secundum adaequationem quamdam dicitur, et philosophus dicit in IV Metaphysic., quod definientes verum dicimus cum dicitur esse quod est, aut non esse quod non est. Tertio modo definitur verum, secundum effectum consequentem; et sic dicit Hilarius, quod *verum est declarativum et manifestativum esse*; et Augustinus in Lib. de vera Relig.: *veritas est qua ostenditur id quod est*; et in eodem libro: *veritas est secundum quam de inferioribus iudicamus*.

10 On Olivi see *John Buridan 1989*, qq. 72 and 73. On Buridan see *John Buridan 1989*, Appendices C1 and C2, pp. 485–621. On Suárez see *De Anima* IV in *Suárez 1856–1878*, 2.17, p. 721; 8.13, p. 745; 2.13, p. 719; 4.1, p. 731; 2.12–13, pp. 719–720, as well as pp. 740 and 528. On Malebranche see the discussion in Chapter 5 below. For a general discussion of these issues see *Tachau 1988* and *Pasnau 1997*.

Arnauld and Nicole cannot accept any of these accounts because, in their view, ideas, which are modes of the soul, are not in any sense, not even "intentionally," be modes of bodies. Material modes cannot be transmitted to the soul through sensation. They explain:[11]

> It is thus false that all our ideas originate in the senses. On the contrary, one can say that no idea in the mind originates in the senses, although motions in the brain, which is all the senses can bring about, may provide the occasion for the soul to form various ideas that might not have been formed without this occasion. Indeed, even these ideas almost never resemble what is in the senses and the brain. Furthermore, it would be absurd to attribute the many ideas that have nothing whatever to do with corporeal images to the senses.

The authors adopt instead a version of occasionalism. In their view, on the occasion in which a material substance affects the body's sense organs, God causes there to be in the soul a sensory perception. This perception is a mode of the soul. It has not been caused by any alterations of the body. There is no property transfer. It remains true on their view, however, that during the experience, the soul is vividly aware of modes. Some of these like extension, motion, and relative position are in fact the very same modes that are true of the material substance currently affecting the body's sense organs. Others, like color and taste, are true only of the soul, even though ordinary folk think they are true of material things outside the mind.

The authors, however, retain part of the medieval account. The modes that is experienced on the occasion of sensation, which Aquinas called the sensible species, provide the material for subsequent abstraction and the formation of abstract ideas. But at this point the authors face an explanatory problem. How can a perception, which is a mode of the mind, convey awareness of other modes like extension that are true of objects outside the mind? How is it, in other words, that a perception has a content that consist of modes distinct from those of the soul itself, some of which are material and some mental? The same problem carries over to ideas formed by abstraction. If an abstract idea is mode of the soul, how can it be an idea of something that possesses modes different from those of the soul and its modes? How can an idea have a "content"?

---

[11] *LAP* I.1, *KM* V 132–133, *B* 29–30; I:9. See also *LAP Discours* II, I.3, *KM* V 122, *B* 33; I.9, *KM* V 157, *B* 49–50; *KM* V 168–170, *B* 58–60; *VFI* 6, *KM* I 204, *G* 71–71; 27, *KM* I 349–350, *G* 208; and Chapt. 28 of *VFI* generally. On Descartes' rejection of causation from bodies to souls see Descartes, *Notae in Programma*, AT VIIIb, 358,20–359,12; and *Garber 1993*. For a more general discussion of these issues in Descartes and Arnauld see *Nadler 2011, Nadler 1989*, and *Garber 1993*.

An idea cannot literally be the same mode as one that occurs in its content, as it was in medieval descriptive theories. Nor is a causal account possible. The idea is not causally connected to what it stands for. How then does an idea signify? The *Logic*'s theory of reference provides the answer to this question. At its center is a notion of intentional content. Explaining the solution requires a review the *Logic*'s particular account of intentional content.

Contrary to what is sometimes said, intentionality in philosophy did not start with Brentano. It is a medieval concept and fundamental to the *Logic*'s semantic. The particular sense the *Logic* employs derives from the medieval notion of objective being. Objective being is probably most familiar to modern students from its appearance in Descartes' *Meditation* III, but earlier versions had been used in explanations throughout the Middle Ages. The *Logic*'s authors accepted some of its earlier properties and reject others, ending up fashioning a concept suited to their particular explanatory purposes. In earlier accounts objective being was a *sui generis* explanatory entity with an ontological status distinct from both spirit and matter. The version that emerges in the *Logic*, however, is one that is ontologically neutral but nevertheless suitable for its role in semantics. To understand the *Logic*'s particular view of intentional content, it is necessary to review how it accepts some and rejects others of the medieval versions of the notion that preceded it. This review of the history of objective being leading to the *Logic*'s particular version will be the first of several such explorations of the roots of key concepts in the *Logic*.

Objective Being as "What Is Understood"

The task before Arnauld and Nicole was to rebuild on Cartesians lines the foundations of signification theory. A causal account was closed due to dualism. On the other hand, a descriptive theory was possible. Their version turns on objective being. Objective being had occurred frequently enough in earlier logic that it merited short explanations in 16th- and 17th-century logic textbooks. The details of its earlier versions differed somewhat depending on the problem it had been introduced to explain. Common to all accounts was that objective being is an "object of understanding." Exactly what this meant depending on the kind of understanding in question. One kind understanding was that of an abstract concept or common noun. In this case objective being was identified with "what we understand" when we understand the term. Another kind of understanding was that associated with perceptual illusions. In this case objective being was identified with "what it is we sense" when we experience an illusion. Objective being was also said to explain God's understanding prior to creation. In this case objective being was identified with the "exemplar causes" God referred to in the act of creation or with the "essence" or real definition that he knew to be true of species prior to creation. Usually, objective being was understood to occupy a special ontological status distinct from spirit and matter. More importantly for the history of the *Logic*, in some later accounts objective being was identified with a second-order mode of a concept, as a mode of a mode in the soul.

Duns Scotus (1266–1308) provides one of the earliest examples of objective being as an explanatory entity. Scotus explains God's understanding of creatures prior to creation as relation that holds between God and an exemplar cause. This cause is described as "the thing as understood by him." A creature prior to its creation did not exist in reality, but God nevertheless understood it. What he understood at creation is the same as what he understands now and in the future. His understanding is eternal. The object of this understanding, "the thing understood," has a special kind of being, which he referred to as *esse cognitum* or *esse diminutum*. It is this entity that is the object both of divine and human knowledge when it is understood as part of an essential truth. Its special status explains why descriptions of essences are non-contingent and eternally true. Scotus explains the view as follows:[12]

> Therefore I say that a thing from eternity did not have a true essential or existential being, but grounded an ideal relation according to diminished being which it has from eternity (which is true being, distinct from essential and existential being, as is evident from Metaphysics IV): as if it were posited that I had existed from eternity and that from eternity I had understood a rose according to its essential and existential being [*esse essentiae et esse exsistentiae*]; and although it did not have anything but cognized being [*esse cognitum*],

---

[12] *John Duns Scotus 1966*, vol. XVII, Lectura I, Dist 36, q. unica, pp. 468–469:

> [p. 468] Responsio propria: Ideo dico quod res ab aeterno non habuit esse verum essentiae vel exsistentiae, sed fundat relationem idealem secundum esse deminutum, quod habuit ab aeterno (quod est esse verum, distinctum contra esse essentiae et esse exsistentiae, sicut patet ex [p. 469] VI *Metaphysicae*): sicut si ponatur quod ego fuissem ab aeterno et quod ab aeterno intellexissem rosam, ab aeterno tunc intellexi rosam secundum esse suum essentiae et secundum esse exsistentiae; et tamen non habuit esse nisi cognitum, sicut si modo rosa omnino nihil esset, intelligo rosam et secundum esse essentiae et exsistentiae, et tamen neutrum habet. Unde terminus intellectionis est esse essentiae vel esse exsistentiae,—et tamen illud quod obicitur intellectui, tantum habet esse deminutum in intellectu.
>
> Ex isto autem patet illud quod supra dictum est in quaestione praecedente, quomodo intellectus divinus producit lapidem in esse intelligibili: non enim tantum producit relationem, sed totum producit ad esse deminutum, quod est esse verum et cognitum.

See the discussion in *Normore 1986*. Compare Scotus, *Ordinatio* II, d. 3, p. 1, q. 1 in *John Duns Scotus 1987*.

as if in a way the rose were entirely nothing, I understand the rose both according to essential and existential being, even though it has neither. While the terminus of intellection is essential or existential being, what is objectified in an intellection [*quod obicitur intellectui*] has only a diminished being [*esse deminutum*] in the intellect.

From this moreover what was said in the preceding question above is evident, in whatever way the divine intellect produces a stone, it exists in intelligible being [intelligible being]: for it does not just produces a relation but produces a whole thing in diminished being [*esse dimiutum*], which is true and cognized being [*esse verum et cognitum*].

Scotus here refers to a feature of *esses cognitum* that later writers came to think of as a defining characteristic of objective being, but one that Arnauld and Nicole later reject. An objective being is a *relatum* distinct from God and things in the actual world. It is apart from the mind. As such, it seems to have a special ontological status distinct from matter and spirit. Arnauld and Nicole later rejected this view as postulating superfluous entities. As we shall see, objective being for them is spiritual; it is a property of ideas.

There is a second feature of Scotus' view only implicit in the text but drawn out by later writers. The object of knowledge is understood as possessing properties or, in Cartesian language, as possessing modes. Today we would say that objective being has a descriptive content. The descriptive aspect is key to various explanatory applications of objective being, and remains the core of *Logic*'s later version.

Although William of Ockham later rejected objective being, in his earlier work he proposes a version that draws on its descriptive content.[13] As in Scotus' account, this entity is "the object of understanding." In Ockham's case it is the object of understanding an abstract idea. He calls it a "fiction" or *fictum*.[14]

> the universal is not something real having subjective being, neither in the soul nor outside the soul, but only has objective being in the soul, and is a certain fiction [*fictum*], having such being in objective being as an external thing has in subjective being. And this is so in the way that the intellect, seeing some thing outside the soul, fashions a consimilar thing in the mind, such that, if [the intellect] were to have productive power as it has fictive power, it would produce such a thing in subjective being outside [the soul] numerically distinct from

---

13 For his later rejection of *ficta* as unnecessary see *Ouodlibet* 4, q. 35 in *William of Ockham 1991*, vol. II, p. 387.
14 Ockham, *Ordinatio* 1, d. 2, q. 8 in *William of Ockham 1987*, pp. 3–4.

the former [thing], and [that which is produced] would be proportionately similar [to that former thing], as it is for the architect.

Here Ockham says outright that a fictum has descriptive content. It is "consimilar" to what it represents. It exhibits the very modes possessed by the things it stands for. Moreover, he is clear about its ontological status. This entity is not a thing in the material world because it is abstract. Nor does it fall in the category of mode, spiritual or otherwise. For this claim he has an argument. The object of understandings, albeit abstract, may fall in any of Aristotle's ten categories. Therefore, it cannot simply be a mode, which would have to fall exclusively in the category of quality: "a fictum can be of any category [of being] but a mental mode is only a quality. Hence the two are different."[15]

Ockham hypothesizes *ficta* to explain the object of abstract understanding. About the same time Peter Aureol (1275/80–1322) postulated objective being to explain illusions. According to Aureol when experiencing an illusion, we cannot be sensing a real being in the world outside the mind. He reasons that nevertheless we sense something. In some sense the object of an illusion exists. He says it exists "objectively":[16]

> When one is carried on the water, the trees existing on the shore appear to move. This motion, therefore, which is objectively in the eye [*in oculo objective*] cannot be posited to be the [sense of] vision itself; otherwise vision would be the object seen, and vision would have been seen, and vision would be a reflective power. Nor can it be posited to be really in the trees or in the shore, because then they would really have moved. Nor can it be posited to be in the air because it is not attributed to the air but to the trees. Therefore, it is only intentionally [*tantum intentionaliter*], not really, in seen being and in judged being.

It is clear for Aureol that objective being has an ontological status distinct from the mind and the material world. Ex hypothesis, because it the object of an illusion, it does not exist in the actual world. Nor is it in the soul because the properties exhibited by the object of an illusions, for example, the movement of trees on the sea shore, are not in general properties of the soul. While the object of perception exhibit locomotion, the soul itself is not the sort of thing that "moves."

Although Ockham, the nominalist, ultimately rejected *ficta* as unnecessary, others embraced them. Franciscus Toletus (1532–1596), for

---

15 Ibid., p. 4.
16 Peter Aureol, *Scriptum in I Sentarium*, lat. 329, d. 3, s. 14, a. 1; II:696, quoted in *Brown 2007*. See also *Tachau 1988*.

example, expanded on Scotus' view that identified the object of abstract understanding with objective being. Toletus makes explicit that that objective being is distinct from both the intellect and its properties, on the one hand, and objects in the world, on the other. As evidence he cites what were then called "beings of reason." We can understand, he points out, a non-existent non-mental entity, like a chimera. These exist neither in the mind nor outside it:[17]

> [the] thing that the intellect understands is said to be in the intellect objectively. This is why the soul, which the intellect understands, is said to be objectively in the intellect, not because these things inhere but because they are understood through its operation. Accordingly, a thing that is outside the intellect, it is said to be objectively in the intellect when is it is understood. Therefore, of those that are objectively in the intellect some have being in themselves, apart from the being by which they are understood. For example, man, animal, and whiteness have both objective being in the intellect and being in themselves, since they are no less separate for being understood; some do not have being in themselves when understood, and these are said to have only objective being, like a Chimera.

Others, notably Francisco Suárez (1548–1617) and Nicolas Malebranche (1638–1715), go beyond Toletus to regard an objective being as a quasi-Platonic entity in the tradition of Augustine. They expand on Scotus' view that God stands in a relation to objective being. In their accounts not only does objective being fall in a special category of entity distinct from both the soul and the matter, it constitutes an eternal exemplar in God's mind, which God referred to as a model when he created the world. These had to exist in God's mind eternally because he always knew their essential properties. Not only do they explain God's knowledge of essences prior to creation, they also account for our own knowledge of essential truths. Suárez espoused a correspondence theory of truth, even for cases in which what is described does not exist in the world. An essential truth, like a species definition, is true

---

17 *Prooemium*, Quest. III, p. 15 in *Toletus 1580*:

> aliquid dicitur esse in intellectu objective, illud scilicet quod ab intellectu cognoscitur, quo pacto omnia, quae intellectus cognoscit, dicuntur, esse objective in intellectu, non quod ipsi inhaereant sed quod per ipsius operationem intelligantur. unde res, quae est extra intellectum, quando cognoscitur, dicitur esse objective in intellectu. Horum igitur, quae objective sunt in intellectu, quaedam habent esse in se, licet non eo modo, quo intelliguntur, ut homo, animal, albedo, habent esse objective in intellectu & in se, quamvis non sint separata, sicut intelliguntur; quaedam non habent aliud esse in se, quam cognosci, & ista dicuntur habere solum esse objective in intellectu: sicut Chimera.

because it corresponds not to the facts in the world outside the mind, but to the descriptive features of an objective being.[18] The fact that essential truths are necessary and eternal, moreover, is explained by the fact that these entities do not change.

In this account objective being has a semantic role. It functions as a mediator between a term in mental language, which is a mode of the soul, and that term's *significatum* outside the mind. This mediation is effected by means of the descriptive content. We know that exemplars in God's mind carry descriptive content because creatures are made in their likeness. Similarly, the signification of a term in mental language is explained by objective being's descriptive content. A mental term represents an entity possessing objective being's properties—Frege would say the term expresses its "sense"—and signifies in the world those creatures made to conform to that representation. In the texts below Suárez describes the various properties of objective beings: their eternal nature, their role as exemplars, and their status as the grounds for knowledge of necessary essential truths:[19]

> Now briefly, it is responded, with St. Thomas (I, q. 10, a. 3, ad 3) that truth was not in these propositions [essential truths] from eternity except to the degree that they existed objectively in the divine mind, for they did not exist in themselves either in reality or subjectively, nor were they objectively in another intellect. For to be true knowledge by which God knew from eternity that man is a rational animal, it is not necessary that the essence of man have from eternity

---

18 Johannes Caterus (1590–1655) adopts the standard defense of the causal origin of Scotus' objective *esse*. This view holds that qua objects of idea, *esse objectivum* has no being apart from an idea itself as part of God's intellect caused by God as the *causa sui* of his own nature (a view that, if true, would vitiates Descartes' argument that the idea of God needs an efficient cause more perfect than Descartes himself). See *Wells 1990*.
19 *Metaphysical Disputations* XXXI.2.8 in *Suárez 1856–1878*, XXVI, p. 231:

> Nunc breviter respondetur cum D. Thoma, I, q. 10, a. 3, ad 3, ab aeterno non fuisse veritatem in illis propositionibus, nisi quatenus erant obiective in mente divina, quia subiective seu realiter non erant in se, neque obiective in alio intellectu. Ut autem vera esset scientia qua Deus ab aeterno cognovit hominem esse animal rationale, non oportuit essentiam hominis habere ex aeternitate aliquod esse reale in actu, quia illud esse non significat actuale esse et reale, sed solam connexionem intrinsecam talium extremorum; haec autem connexio non fundatur in actuali esse, sed in potentiali. Dices per illam scientiam non cognosci hominem posse esse animal rationale, sed necessario esse animal rationale; ergo solum esse potentiale non est sufficiens fundamentum eius. Respondetur negando absolute consequentiam, quia illa necessitas non est absoluta essendi secundum aliquod esse reale in actu, sed quoad hoc est possibilitas tantum; includit tamen necessitatem conditionalem, quia, nimirum, si homo producendus est, necessario futurus est animal rationale, quae necessitas nihil aliud est quam identitas quaedam obiectiva hominis et animalis.

some real being in act because that *being* [i.e. the being of essence] does not signify real and actual being, but rather only the intrinsic connection of such extremes [e.g. in species definitions]. This connection, moreover, is not founded in the being of an actual thing, but in that of potential things [*in potentiali*]. You reply that what is to be known through this knowledge is not that man *can* be a rational animal, but that he *necessarily* is a rational animal, therefore potential being [*esse potetiale*] alone is not sufficient for founding this knowledge. To this is to be responded by negating absolutely the consequence [viz. that potential being is sufficient for grounding necessary knowledge of essences], for that is not a being's absolute necessity relative to some real being in act, [*illa necessitas non est absoluta essendi secundum aliquod esse reale in actu*] but is due only to it being the case that this thing [i.e. a man] is a possibility [*quoad hoc est possibilitas*]. It embraces, moreover, a conditional necessity [*necessitatem conditionalem*] for, without question, if a man is to be produced, he will necessarily be a rational animal, which necessity is nothing other than an objective identity of man and animal [*identitas quaedam objectiva hominis et animalis*].

Thus, objective beings, Suárez says, ground essential truths, which are true eternally or, more accurately, timeless. They report the modes that form the descriptive content of an objective being. Truth here, however, is not the ordinary contingent truth of a report about the actual world. Rather essential truth is only "possibly truth"—a view later found in the *Logic*—because although it is possible for an essence to be instantiated in the world, it is not always actualized. There was a time when there was nothing but God. Similarly, imaginary things or so-called beings of reason do not exist. Nothing matches their descriptive content. They nevertheless possess objective being:

> However, a nature is said to be "credible" or "possible" [*creabilis vel possibilis*] inasmuch as in itself it is a real thing [*realis*], apt for existence [*apta ad existendum*], and a real exemplar in the same way can inhere in God, for these do not always represent an actual being [*actuale ens*], but also [may represent something] that is possible. And thus in the same way, the sciences, which consider a thing as abstracted from existence [*abstrahendo ab existentia*], are not about beings of reason [*entia rationis*], but rather are about real things [*realibus*]....[20]

---

20 *Metaphysical Disputations* XXXI.2.10, ibid. XXVI, p. 232:

> Dicitur tamen illa natura creabilis vel possibilis, quatenus secundum se realis est et apta ad existendum, et eodem modo potest habere in Deo reale exemplar; hoc

Therefore, if being in the sense of existence is excluded, essence still can retain the being of essence [*esse essentiae*], for it does not possess being on account of existence, but in itself, and therefore, if the extrinsic efficiency appropriate to [the creation of] any thing is excluded, essence possesses the such being of essence and consequently does so from eternity.[21]

Therefore, what is normally and rightly defined as a being of reason is *that which has being only objectively in the intellect* or is *that which is thought by reason as being, even though it has no entity in itself*.[22]

Descartes falls within this tradition. He too appeals to objective being as an explanatory entity, most famously in *Meditation* III. Unfortunately, he is less than clear about its ontological status. Nor does he says anything about its semantic role as a possible mediator in signification. He does, however, follow the early Ockham, Scotus and Toletus when he refers to objective reality as the object of understanding or, as he puts it, "the being of the thing represented":[23]

> By objective reality I understand the entity/being of a thing represented [*entitatem rei repraesentatae*] by that thing to extend that it is in an idea; in the same way it can be said to be an objective perfection or an objective artifact, etc. For whatever we perceive only in the object of ideas these are in these ideas objectively.

Descartes is here suggesting that objective being has a distinctive ontological status. At several places in the *Meditations*, for example, he says

---

> enim non semper repraesentat actuale ens, sed etiam possibile. Ac denique eodem modo, scientiae, quae considerant res abstrahendo ab existentia, non sunt de entibus rationis, sed de realibus.

21 *Metaphysical Disputations* XXXI.2.6, ibid. XXVI, p. 230:

> ergo, seclusa existentia, adhuc potest essentia retinere esse essentiae, nam hoc non habet ab existentia, sed ex se; ergo, seclusa omni efficientia extrinseca, habet tale esse, et consequenter ex aeternitate illud habet.

22 *Metaphysical Disputations* DM LIV.1.6. See *Doyle 1987*, p. 53:

> Et ideo recte definiri solet ens rationis esse illud, quod habet esse obiective tantum in intellectu, seu esse id, quod a ratione cogitatur ut ens, cum tamen in se entitatem non habeat. Undo recte dixit Comment. VI Metaphys., comment. 3, ens rationis solum posse habere esse obiective in intellectu.

23 Descartes, *Secundae Responses, Rationes, Definitiones*, AT VII, p. 160:

> III. Per realitatem objectivam ideae intelligo entitatem rei repraesentatae per istam ideam, quatenus est in ideâ; eodemque modo dici potest perfectio objectiva, vel artificium objectivum, &c. Nam quaecumque percipimus tanquam in idearum objectis, ea sunt in ipsis ideis objective.

of objective reality that although it may be imperfect in the sense that it is not actualized, it nevertheless is "not nothing" [*nec . . . nilil esse*].[24]

In his argument for the existence of God in *Meditation* III he is somewhat clearer. There he first offers an ontologically neutral argument that turns on the fact that the idea of God is not a "false idea." False idea is a technical distinction from medieval semantics. As we shall see in Chapter 6, the concept plays an important role in the *Logic*'s semantics. A false idea is one that fails of reference. In the language of the day, it is an idea that fails to signify anything that actually exists. Standard examples of false ideas are *golden mountain* and *chimera*. Descartes holds that a clear and distinct idea is automatically "true."[25] More precisely, his view is that a subject-predicate affirmation is known to be true if its subject term is a grasped by the soul as a clear and distinct idea and its predicate is the "content" of that idea. In his view, God allows the soul to apprehend clearly and distinctly the content of an idea only if the associated affirmation is true. His argument for God's existence, then, turns on fact that the idea of God is clear and distinct idea, and therefore true.[26] Because the idea of God is a true and represents God as have the highest degree of reality, it follows that the proposition *God exists* is actually true:

> III. 25 The idea of God . . . contains in itself more objective reality than any other. . . . It is likewise clear and distinct in the highest degree, since whatever the mind clearly and distinctly conceives as

---

[24] *Meditations* III, AT VII, p. 41, 26–29. "Atqui quantumvis imperfectus sit iste essendi modus, quo res est objective in intellectu per ideam, non tamem profectò plane nihil est, nec proinde a nihilo esse potest."
 Meditations V, AT VII, p. 64, 6–9: "invenio apud me innumeras idea quarumdam rerum, quae, etiam si extra me fortasse nullibi existans, non tamen dici possunt nilil esse. . . . Ut cum, exempli causa, triangulum imaginor." See also *Meditations* V, AT VII, p. 65, 2–6.

[25] Arnauld and Nicole will later hold that a proposition is automatically true in a timeless and necessary way if it affirms of a clear and distinct idea the content of that idea, but as we shall see, their view allows for cases like essential definitions in which that idea, although clear and distinct, does not refer. Unlike contingent truths that must have a referring term as subjects, they hold that essential truths do not have that presupposition. It follows in the *Logic*'s semantics that Descartes' argument from the fact that the idea of God is clear and distinct to his existence fails.

[26] Chapter 6 explains that according to the *Logic* there are two types of truth, essential and contingent. The subject terms of essential affirmations do not carry existential import, but those of contingent affirmations do. In principle it is possible to have a clear and distinct idea of an essential truth of an empty subject. In these cases although there is a clear and distinct idea, the subject term does not signify anything in the world. The predicate *existence*, however, is an exception. Because *existence* is predicate of God in "the highest degree," *God exists*, it seems, is not only possibly true, but also eternally true. See the text in note 28 and the discussion in Chapter 6.

real or true, and as implying any perfection, is contained entire in this idea.

Descartes, however, goes on to suggesting an additional reason in support of God's existence, one more relevant to the *Logic*'s semantics. This argument turns on a metaphysical principle that assumes that objective reality occupies a special ontological kind distinct from that of the soul and substances outside the mind. This principle in question is this: the reality of any mode represented in the objective reality of an idea must have as its actual cause an entity that possesses that mode to the same degree.[27]

> III. 27 ... I conceive God as actually infinite, so that nothing can be added to his perfection. And, in fine, I readily perceive that the objective being of an idea cannot be produced by a being that is merely potentially existent, which, properly speaking, is nothing, but only by a being existing formally or actually.
> ...
> 33 ... there must at least be as much reality in the cause as in its effect; and accordingly, since I am a thinking thing and possess in myself an idea of God, whatever in the end be the cause of my existence, it must of necessity be admitted that it is likewise a thinking being.

The reality of God represented in the objective being of God's idea cannot be merely a property of a human soul, or a fortiori of a human idea because neither the soul nor its ideas, neither in actual nor objective reality, have the exceptional properties that hold of God. Objective reality, therefore, is distinct from spirit and matter. Because the objective reality of God's idea represents him as having reality to the highest

---

[27] *Meditations* III, 27 and 33, Descartes 1901 [1641], www.wright.edu/~charles.taylor/descartes/meditation1.html. At the risk of over-simplifying, the argument runs like this. There are three kinds of entities (not a view the *Logic* accepts): souls, material substances, and entities possessing objective being. These have causes. These causes possess modes. Modes come in degrees. In modern jargon, they are gradable properties and consist of the instantiation to a degree of a "mass" quantity. In this case the mass quantity in question is "being." Moreover, causation conforms to a venerable principle: there is as much being in the cause as the effect. The cause of the idea of God is God—he is the cause of everything, especially innate ideas. The objective being of the idea of God possesses the mode existence to the highest degree. Therefore, the cause of the objective being of the idea of God possesses existence to the highest degree. The semantics of gradable modes is discusses at greater length in Chapter 3 and in the Appendix.

degree, the argument goes, its cause must likewise have reality in the highest degree.

To be sure, Descartes does not draw out his views about objective being so as to explain its role in logic or the semantics. His disciples in the *Logic*, on the other hand, make extensive use of it. In doing so, however, they reconceive the notion to shed from it any distinctive ontological status. For them objective being is conceived as a property of an idea, as a second order-mode. The modes in its objective content are instantiated, if at all, in real entities that fall in one of the ten categories of being. Although Arnauld does not explicitly endorse Descartes' argument that the proposition *God exists* follow from the clear and distinct idea of God as necessarily existing,[28] he does agree that necessary existence is included in the content of the idea of God.

While the *Logic*'s authors accept many of Descartes' views, it is probably more accurate to attribute the specifics of Arnauld's views on objective being to his dispute with Malebranche. Both Arnauld and Malebranche were disciples of Descartes. They agree that ideas have objective being and that they possess descriptive content, but they develop their views in opposite ways. Malebranche was ontologically generous while Arnauld was parsimonious. Malebranche endorsed the view that objective being is a distinct order of existence from the soul and matter; Arnauld reduced objective being to spiritual and material substance. Probably the best way to understand Arnauld's view is to read it as a reaction to Malebranche views that objective being has a special ontological status that allows it serve as a representational entity in perception mediating between the soul and the material world.

Malebranche was forthrightly a Christian Platonist in the tradition of Augustine. Ideas in God's mind, he thought, mediate between the human soul and the sensible world. He held that ideas, in the strict sense, and objective being are identical; the same thing is "la *réalité*

---

28 *VFI* Chapt. 6, *KM* I.206, *G* 73:

> Or l'existence nécessaire est manifestement enfermé dans l'idée que nous avons tous de l'être infiniment parfait.

The *Logic*, however, endorses Augustine's and Descartes' *cogito*, *LAP* IV.1, *KM* V 356, B 228. Existence cannot be separated from the clear and distinct idea of myself as a thinking thing. Therefore, I exist. Although in general the clear and distinct idea of species definition is sufficient evidence that the definition is an essential truth, the subject term of a true essential definition does not in general carry existential import. The case of the predicate existence appears to be an exception. A clear and distinct idea of *S* as existing seems to ensure that *S exists* is actually true. See the discussion of essential and contingent truth in Chapter 6.

objective, ou l'*idée*."[29] He distinguishes between perceptions and ideas. Perceptions are modes of the soul; but ideas have a special status and exist in God's mind. Human perceptions, however, are causally linked to ideas. In a process called "illumination" (adapted from Augustine) God causes the soul to "see" or "understand" ideas. Part of this understanding consists in understanding the modes that make up an idea's objective being. As in the *Logic*, mental language is made up of terms and these terms are modes of the soul, in this case "perceptions." An essential truth is a mental proposition formed of mental terms that describes a relation among God's ideas in God's mind. If the soul is appropriately illuminated so that it understands the ideas causally linked to the perceptions making up the essential proposition, the soul "sees" that descriptive content of the corresponding ideas and that the proposition is true. Malebranche takes his inspiration from Augustine:[30]

> It must be as St Augustine has said in five hundred places, ideas are eternal, immutable, necessary, and common to all minds, in order for there to be certain truth and falsehood, justice and injustice, eternal truths and laws, and that our minds are enlightened by these same ideas in consequence of their union with the universal reason which contains them all in its substance, which alone is the life and light of all The use to which objective being was put that most concerns us, however, is in attempts to spell out a full blooded Augustinian position that objective being is no less than ideas in God's mind, and that it is these that the terms in necessary truths stand for. The expositor of this view that most influenced Malebranche was Suárez. Suárez held not only that a universal affirmative about natures is equivalent to the conditional described above, but also that its subject matter is objective rather than actual being and that this objective being consists of God's eternal thought that are a necessary part of his nature.

Because perceptions are modes of the soul, they have "formal being," Ideas, aka objective being, on the other hand, exists only in God's mind. Malebranche is clear that mental terms (which Arnauld calls ideas) are distinct from ideas, which exist in God's mind. The argument that they are different is similar to Aureol's that concepts are distinct from objects of illusion. Perceptions and ideas are distinct because they possess different

---

29 *Réponse* I:vi, *Malebranche 1959–66*, 6.58. See also *Search* III.2.i, *Malebranche 1962*, 1:414–5, *Malebranche 1997*, pp. 217–218; and *Trois lettres de l'auteur De la Recherche de la Vérité* I, *Malebranche 1959–66*, 6.217.
30 *Réponse, Malebranche 1959–66*, 9.933, *Nadler 1992*, p. 104.

properties. Knowledge, for example, is general while mental modes are particular:[31]

> Our knowledge is general, and the terms we use to express it are abstract. But the soul, however it might sense itself, does not know either itself or its modifications, the soul which is a particular being, a very limited and imperfect being. Certainly it cannot see in itself what is not there in any way at all. How could we see in one species of being all species of being, or in a finite and particular being a triangle in general and infinite triangles?

Mental modes are also contingent, mutable, and temporary, but ideas are not:[32]

> All knowledge, which is through God's ideas, is necessary, immutable, and eternal.

Malebranche also argues that mental modes are distinct from ideas in God's mind by invoking points similar to those in Descartes' *Meditation III*. The idea of God possesses infinity in its objective being, and therefore the idea cannot be caused by the human soul:[33]

> since the objective reality of idea of my thought, is the infinite, when I think it, it is not possible that this reality, or the idea I have of the infinite could be a modification of my soul.

From the fact that mental modes and ideas are different, Malebranche concludes that "what we know" is an idea in the mind of God. Ideas, moreover, are a necessary and eternal part of God's nature.

The semantics of mental language is explained by the dual role of ideas, both as emanant causes of things in the world and as the objective being understood by the soul. Ideas with their descriptive content are emanant causes of material substances in world. The doctrine is Platonic. Ideas in God's mind possess properties. They function as seminal causes because God causes a material substance to "imitates" or "participates in" the idea that is its seminal cause. In a Neoplatonic way, the material

---

31 *Elucidation* X, Malebranche 1959–66, 3.149, Malebranche 1997, p. 625. See also *Search* I.4.i, Malebranche 1959–66, 1.66, Malebranche 1997, p. 16; *Search* I.1.2, Malebranche 1959–66, 1.48, Malebranche 1997, p. 5.
32 *Trois lettres de l'auteur De la Recherche de la Vérité* I, Malebranche 1959–66, 6:199–200; Malebranche 1997, pp. 217–221.
33 *Réponse* VI:vi, Malebranche 1959–66, 6.199–200, 6.58:

> puisque la réalité objective ou l'idée de ma pensée, c'est l'infini, lorsque j'y pense, il n'est pas possible que cette réalité, ou l'idée que j'ai de l'infini, soit une modification de mon âme.

substance that imitates its cause possesses the same being as the cause, and hence its properties, but in a diminished way.

At the same time, an idea is what the soul understands. A term in mental language is a perception. In illumination God causes the soul to understand an idea associated with the term. This understanding includes an understanding of the modes that make up the idea's objective being. These modes are a kind of descriptive content. The relation of signification between terms in mental language and things in the world is, then, the "composition function" that first maps terms to ideas, and then ideas to the material substances that imitate the ideas. A perception signifies those material substances that instantiate by exemplification the modes in the objective being of the idea the soul grasps in illumination.

Arnauld's rejection of Malebranche's views is most fully developed in *On True and False Ideas*, which is the first of several polemics in their dispute about the representational properties of ideas. This work appeared in 1983, many years after the *Logic*'s first edition of 1662. In it Arnauld fills in details left implicit in the *Logic*. He categorically rejects the view that ideas are mediating representations between the soul and the material world:[34]

> I am astonished that the majority of philosopher have reasoned ... *that the soul can only perceive objects which are present to it*, and *that bodies can be present to it only through particular representations called ideas or species which, being similar to them, take their place and are in immediate contact with the soul in place of them.*

Here Arnauld espouses a variety of direct perceptual realism. He unambiguously reject the independent existence of representations between the soul and the external world:

> [T]hey could not help noticing two things about this vision. First, if we are to see the object it must be before or Present to our eyes, and because of this they regard the presence of the object as a necessary condition of seeing. Second, one also occasionally sees visible objects in mirrors or in water or in other things which represent them to us, and in this case it is thought, erroneously, that what we see is these same bodies but their images.[35]
>
> ...

---

34 VFI Chapt. 4, KM I.193, G 61–62.
35 VFI Chapt. 1, KM I.190, G 58:

> ils [i.e. tous les hommes] n'ont pu s'empécher de remarquer deux choses dan cette vue. L'une, qu'il falloit que l'objet fût devant nos veux, afin que nous le pussions voir: ce qu'ils ont appellé *présence*, &c c'est ce qui leur a fait regarder cette présence de l'objet comme une condition nécessaire pour voir. L'autre, qu'on voyoit aussi quelquefois les choses visibles dans les miroirs, ou dans l'eau, ou d'autres chose qui nous les représentoient; & alors ils ont cru, quoique par erreur, que ce n'etoit pas les corps même que l'on voyoit, mais leurs images.

They [wrongly] imagine that our eyes only perceive objects via images which they call intensional species [*especies intentionnelles*]. . . . [These are] "damnable" . . . "not true."[36]

The *Logic*'s account of perception is discussed in detail in Chapter 6. Here it suffices to note that Arnauld rejects Malebranche's representations [*êtres representatives*], which are supposed to be "distinct from ideas taken as perceptions."[37] He calls them superfluous [*superflues*][38] and useless [*inutiles*].[39]

Arnauld's alternative, which underlies the semantics of the *Logic*, employs a version of objective being that cleaves to an ontology of spirit and matter. He, nevertheless, explains signification by its descriptive content. The view was not entirely new. It was not uncommon in the 15th and 16th centuries for philosophers to vacillate when describing objective being. Sometimes they commit themselves to an entity distinct from soul and matter, but at other times they adopt a new way of speaking in which objective being is a property of concepts. If objective being is a property, albeit a second-order property, it falls within the constraints of the Arnauld's ontology of spirit and matter. This gradual change from a third kind of entity to a second-order mode led to the *Logic*'s version of intentional content.

The mixed view is illustrated by texts in Suárez despite the fact that he was a Platonist of an Augustinian variety. At times, he refers not to "objective being" but to "an objective concept that possesses formal being." The latter language is a way of describing the being of a concept as a mode of the soul:[40]

> That thing or idea [*ratio*] which is uniquely and immediately known or represented by means of the formal concept is called an objective concept.

Peter Fonseca (1528–1599) likewise refers to an objective concept rather than objective being:[41]

> [I]t should be posited that a concept is twofold: one formal, the other objective. . . . A formal concept is nothing more than the actual

---

36 *VFI* Chapt. 4, *KM* I.193, *G* 61.
37 *VFI* Chapt. 5, *KM* I.199, *G* 66.
38 Ibid.
39 *VFI* Chapt. 6, *KM* I.207, *G* 74.
40 *Disputationes Metaphysicae* II.1.1.25–26, *Wells 1990*, p. 41:

> Conceptus objectivus dicitur res illa, vel ratio, quae proprie et immediate per conceptum formalem cognoscitur seu repraesentatur. . . . Homo autem cognitus et repraesentatus illo actu dicitur conceptus objectivus.

41 *Fonseca 1615* q. ii, section 1. See *Cronin 1966*, p. 34:

> ponatur duplicem esse conceptum: formalem unum, alterum objectivum . . . conceptus formalis nihil est aliud quam actualis similitudo rei, quae intelligitur, ab intellectu

similitude to a thing, which is understood by the intellect, constructed for the purpose of expressing that thing . . . it represents the thing as having that form or nature through which it is conceived. . . . An objective concept is the thing that is understood according to that form or nature through which the formal concept is conceived.

As in medieval theories of signification, Fonseca is saying that a concept is formal inasmuch as it is part of the "form" of the soul or, in other words, one of the soul's modes. Objective being also has descriptive content because it is similar to the object it signifies—it is *actualis similitudo rei*. He says that the objective "concept" is "the thing as understood." It is to this thing that the concept is similar. Fonseca could be clearer. He does not, for example, explain how a concept can be similar to a thing—something the *Logic* will attempt to do.

Charles François d'Abra de Raconis (1580–1646) uses similarly ambiguous language. He too distinguishes between a formal and objective concept. A formal concept is a mode of the soul that carries descriptive content because it is similar to its *significatum*. Rather than speaking of an objective *being*, however, he uses the terminology objective *concept*, which suggests he is referring to a mental entity. On the other hand, like earlier logicians, he also describes objective being as "the thing as understood":[42]

> A formal concept is an actual similitude to a thing expressed by the intellect through understanding; by others it is called an action of the mind, and it is *de facto* an offspring of it, and informs it, and is accordingly called formal; it is an active intention, an intention certainly because by it stretches out [*intendit*] to perceive its intellective

---

> ad eam exprimendam producta. . . . cur dicatur formalis: nempe, quia repraesentat rem sub ea forma seu natura, secundum quam intelligitur . . . conceptus objectivus est res quae intelligitur, secundum eam formam naturamve quae per formalem concipitur.

42 *Raconis 1651*, *De Principiis entis*, a. 3, *De essentia et conceptus entis*, sectio 1a, *De nomine conceptu et existenti*, p. 827:

> Formalis conceptus est actualis similitudo rei ab intellectu per intellectionem expressa: ab aliis vocatur actio mentis estque de facto eius proles, ac eam informat unde formalis nucupatus est, et intentio activa: intentio quidem quia per eam intendit intellectus objectum suum percipere: activa vero ad distinctionem posterioris conceptus qui dicitur objectivus, vocaturque etiam intentio, sed passiva, quia est id quod terminatur ipsa activa mentis intentio. Dicitur autem conceptus non proprie sed cum addito, nempe objectivus, eo quod sit objectum conceptum et per actionem mentis expressum. Uterque conceptus facili exemplo explicari potest: aliquis propositi sibi animalis conceptum et naturam formet, ratio illa quam de eo per suam intellectionem exprimet seu verbum, ut loquuntur, efformatum, vocabitur, formalis conceptus, animal vero ipsum cognitum, objectivus.

object; indeed it is active to distinguish it from the latter concept which is called objective, which are also called intention, but passive, because it terminates the active mental intention. Moreover, it is not called merely a concept, but a concept with the qualification "objective"; this because it is the object conceived and expressed through the action of the mind. This concept can be explained by a simple example. Somebody forms for himself a concept and nature of a proffered animal. This ratio which expresses it through its intellection or, as they say, informed word, is called the formal concept. The real understood animal is itself the objective concept.

Eustachio de S.-Paulo (1573–1640) likewise distinguishes between formal and objective concepts. He understands a formal concept to be mental act, a mode of the soul, and to carry descriptive content because it is similar to its *significatum*. He also uses ambiguous language when describing the entity as "objective." On the one hand, he refers to an objective concept which suggests it is a mental entity. On the other hand, he identifies the objective concept with "the thing represented by the formal concept":[43]

> a formal concept is an actual similitude to a thing. . . . However, the objective concept, which is a formal *ratio*, is the thing that is represented to the intellect by the formal concept. . . . The objective concept, which is nothing other than the thing represented by the formal concept, corresponds to the formal concept.

The tendency towards describing objective being as a concept, rather than as something distinct from the soul and matter, prepares the way for Arnauld. Having little liking for metaphysics,[44] he rejects objective being as a distinct entity either as a "thing understood" or as a perceptual intermediary distinct from soul and matter. He retains that part of the view that is crucial to his explanatory purposes, namely, that objective being has a descriptive content.

His account makes appeal only to souls, material substances, and their modes. An idea is a mode of the soul. As such an idea is what Fonseca and others called a formal concept. Second, an idea contains objectively "what is understood." As such an idea is also what others called

---

43 *Eustachio de S. Paulo 1648*, in *Cronin 1966*, p. 35:

> Est autem formalis conceptus actualis similitudo rei quae intelligitur ab intellectu, . . . Objectivus autem qui dicitur etiam ratio formalis, est res quae per conceptum formalem intellectui repraesentatur, . . . Cum formali cuique conceptui respondeat objectivus, qui nihil aliud est quam res formali conceptu repraesentata.

44 See note 1.

an "objective concept," possessing descriptive content that consists of modes, some of which are spiritual, some material:[45]

> I have said that I take *perception* and idea to be the same thing. It must nevertheless be noted that, while this thing is single, it stands in a twofold relation, to the soul that it modifies, and to the thing perceived in so far as this latter is objectively in the soul, and the word "perception" more directly refers to the former relation, the word "idea" to the latter. Thus the *perception* of a square has as its most direct meaning the square in so far as it is *objectively* in my mind.

Here an idea is described as a mode of the soul—it "modifies" the soul. On the other hand, an idea is representational. In more technically language, an idea signifies things outside the mind by means of its objective being or descriptive content. The following passage describes what it is to "sense the sun" and to "understand a square." Both the sensation of a material thing and the understanding of an abstract idea have a content:[46]

> since every perception necessarily represents something and for this reason is called an *idea*, it cannot be essentially reflective upon itself [in such a way that] its immediate object is not this *idea*, i.e. the *objective reality* of the thing that my mind is said to perceive. For example, if I think of the sun, the objective reality of the sun, which is present to my mind, is the immediate object of this perception; and the possible or existing sun, which is outside my mind, is so to speak its mediate object. It is clear from this that, without invoking *representations* distinct from perceptions [as Malebranche does], it is true in this sense that, not only in the case of material things but generally in regard to all things, it is our ideas that we see *immediately* and which are *the immediate objects of our thought*, which does not prevent us from also seeing the object by means of the ideas which contain formally only what is in the idea objectively,[47] for example my conceiving the formal being of a square which is *objectively* in the idea or perception that I have of a square.

Thus, the idea of a square "contains the formal being of the square." In more technical jargon, the idea has an intentional content. That content

---

45 *VFI* Chapt. 5, *KM* I.198, G 66.
46 *VFI* Chapt. 6, *KM* I.204, G 71–72. Sensation is discussed in detail in Chapter 6.
47 The text here reads "ce qui n'empesche pas que nous ne voyons aussi par ces idées l'objet, qui contient formallement ce que n'est qu'objectivement dans l'idée" (author's translation).

includes the formal being of the square. In other words, the content consists of the modes that are true of the square.

As the passage suggests, there are important difference in the ways objective being functions in conception and sensation. Conception is the *Logic*'s term for the instantiation in the soul of an abstract idea. In conception we "understand" an abstract idea. This was the sort of case that concerned Ockham. When we conceive an idea clearly and distinctly, Arnauld holds, we are immediately aware of its content and are justified in believing the proposition that affirms of the idea its content. What is important here is that we are aware of the content. In the passage above Arnauld is saying that the clear and distinct conception is a sufficient condition for knowledge. In a sense, the act of conception causes the resulting epistemic state. Conception is logically prior if not prior in time. In addition, the process is self-reflexive. We are aware that we are experiencing the idea with its content. The issues here are discussed in more detail in Chapter 6.

Ontologically, the entities postulated are minimal and consistent with Cartesian substance-mode dualism. The process requires only three things: the soul, which is a substance; an idea, which is a mode of the soul; and the idea's content, which also consists of modes—some spiritual, some material. The idea is said to "contain" the modes that make up its content. The text uses the language of relations. It says that the idea, which is a mode of the soul, stands in the containment relation to the modes that make up its content, which may be either spiritual or material. The soul also stands in the relation of "understanding" to this content. The explanation, however, cannot go deeper. These facts about the nature of thought are simply fundamental—there is no further explanation. Ideas stand in a containment relation to material and spiritual modes; the soul is aware of ideas; and the soul understands the modes the ideas contain, even in the cases in which these modes are instantiated in material things outside the mind. The theory does not postulate a distinct category of objective entities like Suárez' exemplars or Malebranche's ideas in God's mind. The only entities required are the soul, the material world, and their various spiritual and material modes.

In the case of sensation—the sort of case that concerned Aureol—the soul experiences a perceptual state caused by God on the occasion of motions within the body's sense organs and brain. Ontologically, the perceptual state consists of the instantiation in the soul of a spiritual mode. Like conception, this state has a content of which the soul is self-reflexively aware. Again, as in conception, this content consists of modes. If the sensation is of something in the material world, some of the modes making up this content are material, like variations in extension, movement, relative position, and size. Some are properties of the soul itself, like color, taste, heat, and pain.

Sensation differs from conception in two ways. First, it is vivid. The awareness of a mode in sensation, like redness or motion, is much more vivid than the awareness associated with understanding in conception of the abstract ideas, like *redness* or *motion*. Secondly, the set of modes in sensation is detailed and particularized. If it is perception of something outside the mind, the material modes experiences characterize an individual in the world. If it is a sensation of an internal state, the modes characterize a particular psychological event. Three facts about sensation are fundamental: sensory experience has a modal content consisting of both material and spiritual modes; the soul is aware that it is experiencing the sensation; and the experience is vivid, even when its content contains material modes. As in the case of conceptualization, the process does not involve intermediate representations like Malebranche's ideas. It is simply a basic fact about sensation, says Arnauld, that God causes the soul to be vividly aware of a particularizing set of modes, some of which are material modes true of an object outside the mind.

In conjunction with his ontological shift from extra-mental entities to second-order mental modes, Arnauld also alters the terminology of objective being. In particular, he prefers "containment" and "being in" as terms referring to the relation between ideas and what is understood or sensed:[48]

> [objective reality] is not really distinct from our thoughts or perceptions but is rather our thought itself [*c'est notre pensée même*] insofar as it contains [*contient*] *objectively* what is formally in the object.
> . . .
> everything that I perceive clearly as being in the idea of a thing can correctly be asserted of that thing.[49]
> . . .
> For in the case of ideas we mean that the things we conceive are *objectively* in our mind and in our thought [*que nous concevons sont objectivement dans notre esprit & dans notre pensée*]. And this *way of being objectively in the mind* [*cette maniere d'être objectivement dans l'esprit*] is so peculiar to the mind and to thought, since it is what specifically gives them their nature, that one seeks in vain anything similar outside the mind and thought.

He also refers to the object of thought and its modes as "what is understood" and "what is conceived":

> When I say that the idea is the same as the perception, I understand by perception all that my spirit conceives, whether it be by the first

---

48 *VFI* Chapt. 5, *KM* I.199, G 66.
49 *VFI* Chapt. 6, *KM* I.206, G 73: "tout que je vois clairement être enfermé dans l'idée d'une chose, eut avec vérité être affirmé de cette chose." Compare the axioms in Part IV.

apprehension that it has of some things, by the judgment it makes of them, or by what it discovers through reasoning.[50]

I maintain that a thing is *objectively* in my mind when I conceive it. When I conceive of the sun, a square or a sound, then then sun, the square, or the sound are objectively in my mind, whether or not they are external to my mind.[51]

Although a thing is understood or senses in conception and sensation, that does not mean that what is understood is something apart from substance-mode ontology. In veridical sensation, there is an actual material substance that is sensed as having modes. If the sensation is non-veridical, the soul does not understand anything. When the soul conceives an abstract idea, what is understood are the properties of the objects that the idea signifies if there are any. The special case of "empty terms," idea that fail to signify anything that actually exists, has important implications for the *Logic*'s theory of truth and are discussed in Chapter 6. In such cases understanding is conditional or counterfactual. The soul understands what those things would be if they existed.

These passages detailing Arnauld understanding of objective being are drawn from *On True and False Ideas*, which is a more technical work philosophically because in it Arnauld is engaged in a direct argument with Malebranche about the mechanisms of thought and perception. Tellingly, he reverts to the technical Latinate vocabulary of *réalité objectif* and *être objectif*. In the *Logic*, however, which was directed to a larger audience, the departure from the Latin technical vocabulary is pronounced. Writing in the vernacular, its authors employ new terminology for its reformed version of objective being, one that avoids unwanted connotations of earlier terms. The new notion is called *comprehension*. The concept is very close to, and a progenitor of, the modern notion of intentional content:

> I call the *comprehension* of an idea the attributes that it contains in itself, and that cannot be removed without destroying the idea. For example, the comprehension of the idea of triangle contains extension, shape, three lines, and the equality of these three angles to two right angles, etc. . . . none of these attributes can be removed without destroying the idea.[52]

An idea's comprehension consist of those modes that characterize or define it. This group of modes is essentially a set in the modern set

---

50 *VFI* Chapt. 5, *KM* I.199, *G* 67.
51 *VFI* Chapt. 5, *KM* I.198, *G* 66.
52 *LAP* I.6, *KM* V 144, *B* 39.

theoretic sense, and it will be convenient in what follows to refer to it as such, with cautions that will be spelled out in Chapters 2 and 3 on the structure of ideas.

Within the *Logic*'s wider metalogic, comprehension is a primitive idea. That ideas have comprehensions is a fundamental principle that has no deeper explanation other than it is so ordained by God: every idea has a comprehension that consists of a set of modes. Similarly, it is a basic principle that every sensory experience has a content consisting of modes. The contents of sensations are similarly caused by God. Abstract ideas are either innate or caused by the soul. The comprehension of an innate idea is caused directly by God. The comprehension of a soul-generated idea is caused by the mental operations that cause the idea. These operations consist primarily of abstraction or restriction applied to the comprehensions of prior ideas, and are discussed more fully in Chapter 3. In all such case, however, an idea's comprehension or "content" is unique to it and determines its identity conditions: one idea is identical to another if, and only if, the two have the same comprehension.[53] It follows that there is no ambiguity in mental language—a common view in medieval logic—because no two distinct ideas have the same comprehension. Moreover, as explored in Chapter 3, comprehensions determine the structure of ideas. One idea is contained in a second if the comprehension of the second contains that of the first. For example, the idea *man* "contains" the idea *animal* because the modes definitive of *animal* are included in those of *man*. Algebraically, as discussed in Chapter 3, if comprehensions are regarded as sets, the set-inclusions relation defined on comprehensions induces an isomorphic partial ordering on idea "containment."[54]

Comprehension, then, is what remains in the *Logic* of the medieval notion of objective being. It is the *Logic*'s notion of intentional content. Strictly speaking comprehension only attaches to ideas that function as are substantives in mental language, i.e., to "common nouns." As explained in Chapter 2, adjectives too have an intentional content that consists of modes. This content identifies adjectives and structures them in the same way that comprehensions structure substantives. As will be

---

[53] *LAP* I.6, *KM* V 145, *B* 40:

> there is nevertheless this difference between the attributes it includes and the subjects to which it extends: none of its attributes can be removed without destroying the idea, as we have already said, whereas we can restrict its extension by applying it only to some of the subjects to which it conforms without destroying it.

Because the *Logic* eschews discussions of the problem of universals, the authors do not discuss whether two instances of the same idea in two different souls are identical, whether your idea of human and mine, which have the same intentional content, are identical.

[54] See the Appendix for a summary of the technical concepts from the set theory that are sometimes mentioned.

evident throughout the chapters that follow, intentional content is an explanatory "work horse"—when there is something to explain, intentional content is invoked. Not only does content determine the identity conditions of ideas and gives them structure, it contributes to the explanation of an array of other basic concepts. These include signification, real and nominal definitions, genera and species, necessary truth, abstraction, restriction, syllogistic entailment, and method. Chapter 2 details the way content determines signification, and Chapter 3 how content determines the structure of ideas and extensions. Subsequent chapters point out the role of content in semantics of progressively more complex parts of speech: propositions, arguments, and discourse.

References

Aquinas, Thomas. 2006 [1970]. *De veritate (Textum Leoninum Romae)*, Fundación Tomás de Aquino OCLC nr. 49644264. Roberto Busa, S.J. and Enrique Alarcón (eds.).

Brown, Deborah. 2007. Objective Being in Descartes: That Which We Know or That by Which We Know? In: Lagerlund, Henrik (ed.) *Representation and Objects of Thought in Medieval Philosophy*, Ashgate, Aldershot.

Buridan, John. 1984. On the Soul and Sensation, Book II. In: Sobel, Peter G. (ed.) *John Buridan on the Soul and Sensation: An Edition of Book II of His Commentary on Aristotle's Book on the Soul*, Ann Arbor, MI, University Microfilms.

Buridan, John. 1989. Question on Aristotle's De Anima. In: Zupko, John Alexander (ed.) *John Buridan's Philosophy of Mind: An Edition and Translation of Book III of His "Questions on Aristotle's De Anima (Third Redaction)," with Commentary and Critical and Interpretative Essays*, Ph.D. Dissertation, Ann Arbor, MI, Cornell University. University Microfilm.

Cronin, T. J. 1966. *Objective Being in Descartes and Suárez*, Rome, Gregorian University Press.

Descartes, René. 1901 [1641]. *Meditations*. www.wright.edu/~charles.taylor/descartes/meditation1.html. Veitch, John (ed.).

Doyle, John P. 1987. Suarez on Beings of Reason and Truth. *Vivarium*, 25, 47–75.

Duns Scotus, John. 1966. *Opera Omina*, Civitatis Vaticana, Typis Polyglottis Vaticanis.

Duns Scotus, John. 1987. *Ordination II d. 3 p. 1 q. 1*, unpublished typescript. King, Peter (ed.).

Eustachio de S. Paulo. 1648. *Summa philosophiae quadripartita, de rebus dialecticis, ethicis, physicis et metaphysicis*, Cantabrigia [Cambridge], Rogerus Danielis.

Fonseca, Petrus. 1615. *Commentariorum Petri Fonsecae lustrani, doctoris, theologi socieatatis iseu in liboros metaphysicoeum Aristotelis stagirita*, Cologne, Lazarus Zetznerus.

Garber, Daniel. 1993. Descartes and Occasionalism. In: Nadler, Steven M. (ed.) *Causation in Early Modern Philosophy*, University Park, PA, Pennsylvania State University Press.

Malebranche, Nicolas. 1959–66. *Œuvres complètes de Malebranche*, Paris, Vrin. Robinet, A. (ed.).

Malebranche, Nicolas. 1962. *Recherche de la Vérité*, Paris, Vrin.
Malebranche, Nicolas. 1997. *The Search After Truth*, Cambridge, Cambridge University Press. Lennon, Thomas M. and Paul J. Olscamp (eds.).
Nadler, Steven M. 1989. *Arnauld and the Cartesian Philosophy of Ideas*, Manchester, Manchester University Press.
Nadler, Steven M. 1992. *Malebranche and Ideas*, New York, Oxford University Press.
Nadler, Steven M. 2011. *Occasionalism: Causation Among the Cartesians*, Oxford, Oxford University Press.
Normore, Calvin. 1986. Meaning and Objective Being: Descartes and His Sources. In: Rorty, Amélie Oksenberg (ed.) *Essays on Descartes' Meditations*, Berkeley, University of California Press.
Pasnau, Robert. 1997. *Theories of Cognition in the Later Middle Ages*, Cambridge, Cambridge University Press.
Raconis, C. F. d'Abra de. 1651. *Tertia pars philosophiae seu physicae, quarta pars philosophiae seu metaphysicae. Totius philosophiae, hoc est logicae, moralis, physicae et metaphysicae, brevis et accurata, facilique et cara methodo disposita tractatio*, Lugdunum [Lyon], Irenaeus Barlet.
Suárez, Francisco. 1856–1878. *Opera Omina*, Paris, Ludovicum Vivès. Editio Nova, D. M. André.
Tachau, K. 1988. *Vision and Certitude in the Age of Ockham*, Leiden, Brill.
Toletus, Franciscus. 1580. *Commentaria, una cum questionibus, in universam aristotelis logicam*, Venice, Juntas.
Wells, Norman J. 1990. Objective Reality of Ideas in Descartes, Caterus, and Suárez. *Journal of the History of Philosophy*, 28, 31–61.
William of Ockham. 1981. Reportatio. In: Etzkorn, Girard J. (ed.) *Opera Philosophica et Theologica*, St Bonaventure, NY, Franciscan Institute.
William of Ockham. 1987. *Odinatio 1, d.2*. http://individual.utoronto.ca/pking/translations/OCKHAM.Ord1d2q8.trns.pdf. King, Peter (ed.).
William of Ockham. 1991. *Quodlibetal Questions, Vol. I, Quodlibets 1–4*, New Haven, Yale University Press.

2 The Semantics of Terms. Signification and Extension

Signification of Substantives and Adjectives

This chapter explores semantics in Morris' sense of the term: the study of the relation of words to things.[1] Two concepts prove to be fundamental to the *Logic*'s semantics: signification and extension. The more basic is signification. The term *signification* bears its meaning on its face. It is the sign-of relation, the relation a sign bears to what it stands for or represents. In accord with medieval logic, Arnauld and Nicole hold that the association is sometimes natural and sometimes conventional. Gestures and vocalizations are examples, both of which can be natural or conventional signs. A groan, for example, is a natural sign of discomfort. Facial expressions too are natural signs of emotions or "movements in the soul."[2] Most signs in language, however, are fixed by convention. Grammatically simple vocalizations, which the *Logic* calls "words," have their association fixed by convention. They signify in the first instance not things in the world but concepts in the mind, or what the *Logic* calls ideas. This is signification in the sense of a word-to-idea relation. The conventional rules that fix the association are traditionally called *nominal definitions*. A recurring theme in the *Logic* is the misunderstanding of nominal definitions, because mistakes in pairing words with ideas lie at the root of many fallacies in natural science and ordinary morality.[3]

A second and more important sense of signification is the relation from ideas as terms in mental language to the entities they represent. This the idea-to-thing relation. This is the *Logic*'s primary reference relation. The "things" an idea may refer to may fall in any one of Aristotle's ten categories of being. As this relation is understood in the *Logic*, however,

---

1 *Morris 1939.*
2 *LAP* II, *KM* V 139–140, *B* 35.
3 For a discussion of the medieval doctrine that vocalizations are signs for concepts see, for example, Peter of Spain, *Tractatus*, 1.1–6, and the Gulia Klima, Introduction to Buridan *Summulae*. The *Logic* sets forth its version of the standard doctrine at I.4 and discusses nominal definitions at I.12–13, and in Part 4.

reference must be to actual entities. In restricting signification to actual things, the *Logic* departs from much of medieval logic, in which concepts were generally understood as signifying possible entities. Typical of a general disdain for metaphysics, however, Arnauld denied the existence of possible entities and gives them no role in his semantic theory.[4]

Although the word-to-idea relation is generally explained by a conventional rule, the idea-to-thing relation is explained by the nature of ideas themselves. Every idea possesses an intentional content. This content not only uniquely characterizes the idea; it also determines the things it signifies in the world. In addition to the word-to-idea relation and the idea-to-thing relation, there is the word-to-thing relation, which, to use set theoretic vocabulary, is the composition relation of the two. All three relations are at various times called "signification": spoken word W signifies thing T in the world if, and only if, W signifies idea I in the soul and I signifies thing T:[5]

> It follows that we can express nothing by our words when we understand what we are saying unless, by the same token, it were certain that we had in us the idea of the thing we were signifying by our words, although this idea is at times more clear and distinct, and at others more obscure and confused, as we shall explain below.

This triple sense of "signification" was common in medieval logic. Context in the *Logic* usually makes clear which is intended.

In keeping with its informal use of technical terms, the *Logic* uses a variety of synonyms for *signify*: *represent, express, apply to,* and *is true of*. In this book, however, *signification* will refer to the idea-to-thing relation if not otherwise noted. Complicating matters is the inferiority relation. This is the relation that holds between an idea and its "inferiors," which are other ideas. This relation, which is between ideas, is likewise referred to by various verbs including *signifies, expresses,* and *applies*. In this book it will be referred to only as the *inferiority relation*. Exactly what is meant by "inferior idea," however, is a long story, which will be taken up shortly.

There is, therefore, a plethora of relations to keep straight: the three signification relations, the inferiority relation, the various relations described in Chapter 1, which included the set-inclusion relation among comprehensions, the containment relation among ideas, and the relation

---

4 See Letter "Arnauld to Leibniz," May 13, 1686, *KM* VI, pp. 31–32. As a result of this skepticism there is really no discussion in the *Logic* of the truth-conditions of alethic modalities or of the medieval doctrine of ampliation according to which terms in modal contexts stand for possible entities. See *Stencil 2016*.
5 *LAP* II, *KM* V 129, B 26.

that pairs ideas in a one-to-one with their comprehension. Still to come is the notion of extension and the relations it bears to ideas and things in the world. In preparation for what is ahead, it will be useful to summarize some of this structure.

The various relations detailed in the *Logic* conform to a definitional order. This order is in some instances also a causal order. A causal prerequisite in creation is also conceptually prior. First are ideas and their intentional contents. Contents are called *comprehensions* if the idea is a "substantive." We shall see below that adjectives too have intentional content. In both cases contents are essentially sets of modes. It is appropriate to interpret contents as sets in the modern sense because contents share with sets at least two properties: contents are identical if they have the same members, and contents are ordered by set-inclusion—one content is included in another if, and only if, all the modes in the first are in the second. Moreover, because an idea is identified by its content, contents and ideas stand in a one-to-one correspondence. This correspondence in turn "induces" an ordering on ideas called containment, which corresponds to the set-inclusion order on contents: idea A is contained in idea B if, and only if, the content of A is a subset of that of B. The *Logic* has no fixed term for the relation that holds between an idea and its content. In addition to these relations, there is the word-to-idea relation already described. The word-to-idea relation is many-many because speech conventions are both ambiguous and redundant. The same word is often paired with more than one idea, and more than one word may be paired with the same idea. All of the relations so far described in this brief summary obtain at the level of speech and ideas. Nothing as yet has been said about relations to things in the world.

The *Logic*, however, also posits mutual relations between spoken words, ideas, and things. Chief among these are the three versions of the signification relation mentioned earlier in the chapter: words-to-ideas, ideas-to-things, and words-to-things. Of these, ideas-to-things is basic reference relation. It is explained by the prior ideas-to-contents relation. Idea I signifies thing T if, and only if, all the modes in the content of I are true of T. As already explained, the word-to-thing relation can then be defined as a composition relation: word W signifies thing T if, and only if, W signifies idea I and I signifies thing T.

At this point it is possible to introduce the concept of extension. Signification determines an idea's "extension." Extension is one of the more important concepts in the *Logic*'s metatheory because it plays a central role in the statement of truth-conditions in Part II. As we shall see, extension is defined in terms of the inferiority relation, and thus the inferiority relation is also important. As one might expect, the truth-conditions of categorical propositions are a function of the inclusion and exclusion relations among the extensions of terms. As we shall see, the *Logic*'s analysis of extension in terms of inferiority is not straightforward.

42 Signification and Extension

On the surface, extension has a rather simple definition: an idea's *extension* is the collection of its inferior ideas. The more difficult concept is inferiority. Its interpretation requires some discussion, which we will turn to next. To complete this preview, however, we will simply declare at this point that inferiority is defined in terms of idea-to-thing signification: idea A *is inferior to* idea B if, and only if, all the things A signifies B also signifies. The definition of extension is then clear. The extension of an idea is the collection or set of its inferior ideas; it is the set of ideas that signify only things that the idea itself signifies. The use of "set" terminology here is justified because extensions, like contents, obey the same identity and ordering conditions as sets. Two extensions are identical if, and only if, they have the same inferiors, and one extension is included in another if, and only if, all the inferiors of the first are inferiors of the second.[6]

An example will help visualize this relational spaghetti. The spoken word "human" signifies the idea *human*. This idea has (the tradition says) as its comprehension the set of modes {*rationality, animality, self-motion, life, corporality, being*}. The idea and the word thus signify those things that instantiate these modes. The extension of the idea *human* is the set of its inferior ideas. This is the set of all ideas that have comprehensions that are true only of things that are rational, animal, self-moving, alive, corporal, and existent.

As may be clear, the account posits several different ordering relations: set-inclusion on intentional contents, which are sets of modes; set-inclusion on extensions, which are sets of inferior ideas; and the containment relation on ideas, which is induced by set-inclusion on contents. The various orderings, moreover, mirror one another. These orderings invite analysis in the terms of modern algebra. The temptation is increased by the fact that elsewhere the *Logic* defines "operations" on ideas. The operations the *Logic* is referring to are mental acts by which the soul makes new ideas: abstraction, restriction, and privative negation. Chapter 3 explores the degree to which it is profitable to describe any of the operations in the terms of modern algebra, a somewhat disputed subject among modern interpreters. But before trying to reformulate the views in modern terms, it is necessary first to set them out clearly in the *Logic*'s own terms.

The mechanism of signification varies depending on an idea's grammatical type. Ontologically, terms and propositions are mental acts, which are modes of the soul. They also have a "grammar" or structure.

---

6 Like comprehensions as sets of modes, extensions as sets of ideas are sets in a minimal sense. It is clear from the texts that both comprehensions and extensions as collections possess the identity conditions and ordering properties of sets, but these readings are not to suggest that the *Logic*'s authors brought to bear on them any broader properties of set theory.

The grammar presupposed for "mental language," perhaps not surprisingly, is much like that of the syllogistic and its various simple extensions. It is the logician's regimented and simplified version of ordinary language. The propositional forms discussed in the *Logic* are mainly the four categorical propositional forms augmented by relative clauses, modal adverbs, tenses, and truth-functional connectives. Although terms and simpler propositions are described as "parts" of more complex expressions, the *Logic* does not attempt to lay down rules of grammar or to define the grammatical "part-of" relation. There is no suggestion of generative rules for a syntax in the modern sense. It is probably best to understand the notion of "grammatical part" as it was in medieval logic. Two accounts of "part" were common. The first takes the meaning of part literally. It assumes that there is a "spiritual" sense in which one mental act or mental mode can be an integral part of another. A second view is ontologically simpler. It understands "grammatical part" causally. One act is a part of another in this sense if the first is a causal preliminary to the second. In this sense one expression is part of another because the soul must first instantiate the former before it can instantiate the latter.[7]

Although the *Logic* says little about grammar rules, it does divide terms into parts of speech in the manner of classical and medieval grammar. The terms that serve as subjects and predicates of simple propositions are divided into concrete nouns, abstract nouns, and adjectives, which are distinguished from one another by their semantics. Concrete nouns stand for substances, and may be singular or general. Abstract nouns signify modes. Adjectives, which are also called connotative terms, stand for things that possess a mode:[8]

> Everything we conceive is represented to the mind either as a thing, a manner of a thing, or a modified thing.
> ...
> When I think of a body, my idea of it represents a thing or a substance, because I consider it as a thing subsisting by itself and needing no other subject to exist.
> But when I think that this body is round, the idea I have of roundness represents only a manner of being or a mode which I conceive as incapable of subsisting naturally without the body whose roundness it is.
> Finally, when I join the mode to the thing and consider a round body, this idea represent a modified thing.

All three types—concrete, abstract, and adjectival nouns—share the same general semantic mechanism for signification. Each term has an

---

7 See the discussion by Klima in his introduction to Buridan's *Summulae*.
8 *LAP* I.2, *KM* V 134–135, *B* 30–31.

intentional content consisting of modes that determine what it signifies. A term signifies those things that satisfy the modes in its intentional content. Although all three conform to this paradigm, largely for historical reasons the terminology of signification differs for the three types.

Of the three, signification for concrete substantives, like "earth," "sun," and "God," is the most straightforward. Substantives "represent to the mind" or, in more technical terms, "signify" things in the world as individuals or groups of individuals. These individuals or groups, fall into the category of substance. Like "Gabriel" and "angel," they sometimes signify spiritual substances.[9]

The fact that substantives signify things in the material world, however, poses a problem for dualism. On the one hand, the standard medieval theory of truth was a correspondence theory. It defined truth by reference to signification. A proposition is true, it was said, if "howsoever it signifies so it is." On the other hand, true propositions and their terms are mental entities, which are causally removed from the material world. Part of the *Logic*'s task was to explain how correspondence between the two kinds of substances was possible. The solution put forward appeals to signification as the relation that bridges soul and matter. The new concept of extension provides a correlate, albeit one consisting of ideas, which corresponds to what a term signifies. Extension is defined in terms of signification: the extension of an idea is the set of its inferiors, and an idea's inferiors are those that signify only what the idea itself signifies. With this definition it is possible to define truth. The resulting truth-conditions are fully discussed in Chapter 4. The case of the universal affirmative will serve as an example here: *every S is P* is true if, and only if, the extension of S is a subset of that of P.[10]

As Arnauld and Nicole define extension, it was a concept new to the logical theory. Because Cartesianism is not taken very seriously by modern logicians, the *Logic*'s notion of extension is almost entirely unknown to logicians today. In the *Logic*, however, it is central.

To avoid misunderstanding it is important to stress that what the *Logic* calls "extension" is not what modern logicians understand by the term. In modern logic, and even in Leibniz, a term's extension is the set of things in the world that a term refers to or, in earlier terminology, that it signifies. The *Logic* has no technical term for extension in the modern sense, but it will be quite useful to adopt one here. Let us call the set of entities that an idea signifies its *significance range*. Depending on the

---

9 *LAP* II, *KM* 5.134, *B* 30.
10 This is an approximation. The details are explained more fully in Chapter 4. The definition is actually given equivalently in terms of exclusion rather than set inclusion: *every S is P* is true if the intersection of the extensions of S and P is the same as that of S.

idea, the entities signified can be in any one of Aristotle's ten categories of being.

An idea's extensions as defined in the *Logic* is, therefore, distinct from its significance range. Extensions in the *Logic* always contain just ideas, but significance ranges may contain material or spiritual substances or their modes, depending on what entities the idea signifies. Extensions and significance ranges, however, are defined in such a way that they track each other. This linkage is due to the fact that extension is defined in terms of the inferiority relation:

> I call the *extension* of an idea the subjects to which this idea applies. These are also called the inferiors of a general term, which is superior with respect to them. For example, the idea of a triangle in general extends to all the different species of triangles.[11]

Here the notion of inferiority occurs in the *definiens* of extension: the extension of an idea is the set of ideas inferior to it. Unfortunately, the *Logic* does not provide an explicit definition of inferiority. This is one of those cases in which the *Logic* fails to conform to modern standards of rigor. Although the concept of inferiority lacks an explicit definition, it is possible to abstract its meaning from examples and from its use in the context of the overall theory.

Examples go part of the way. In medieval logic a species was often said to be inferior to its genus,[12] and the *Logic* often cites species-genus pairs as examples of inferiors. In the preceding excerpt, for example, the various species of triangle are cited as inferiors of the genus triangle. But the reading of inferiors as an idea's subspecies is too narrow. First of all, the species-genus relation is one of necessity. This necessity regulates that natural world and is the object of scientific study, as explained in more detail below in Chapter 6. In the authors' correspondence theory of truth, however, an idea's inferiors are often contingent. In the discussion of classification, in particular, they are clear that an idea may be divided into inferiors that are not species but are only "accidental." The issue is discussed in detail later in this chapter.

More generally, the significance range of an idea may be divided into contingent subsets in many ways, some of which are accidental groupings. For example, although *man* is an example of a necessary inferior

---

11 *LAP* I.6, *KM* V 145, *B* 40:

> J'appelle étendue de l'idée, les sujets à qui cette idée convient, ce qu'on appelle aussi les inférieurs d'un terme général, qui à leur égard est appelé supérieur, comme l'idée du triangle en général s'étend à toutes les diverses espèces de triangles.

12 Cf. *John Buridan 2001*, pp. 110, 117, 148, 149, 625.

of *animal* because it is a species of *animal*, the idea *thief* is an accidental inferior of *man* and the idea *the great train robbers* is an accidental inferior of *thief*. Thus, although both *every man is an animal* and *all the great train robbers are thieves* are true, the former is necessary but the latter is contingent. Arnauld and Nicole intend that all three ideas *man*, *thief*, and *great train robber* be included in the extension of *animal*, and that *the great train robbers* be included in that of *thief*.

These examples show that inferiority should be defined in term of signification: idea A *is inferior to* idea B if, and only if, everything that A signifies B signifies. Because an idea's extension is explicitly defined as the set of its inferior ideas, it follows that a term's extension is the set of all ideas that signify only those things that the term signifies. Extension may then be characterized directly in terms of comprehension: the extension of idea A is the set of all ideas B such that for any x, if all the modes in the comprehension of B are true of x, then all the modes in the comprehension of A are true of x. It then follows, as will prove important in Chapter 4, that the intentional content of terms combines with the contingencies of the world to determine what propositions are true.

The technical fact that there is a one-to-one correspondence between extensions and significance ranges ensures that truth can be defined in terms of relations among extensions, which are sets of ideas, yet nevertheless be about things in the world. The proof of this correspondence is given in Chapter 3, and it is assumed in account of truth-conditions in Chapter 4. What is important to appreciate at this point is the coordination between signification and extension. A substantive has as its comprehension a set of modes, and these determine its signification. It signifies all those entities that satisfy the modes in its comprehension-set. It then follows by the definition of extension that a term's extension is the set of ideas that signify only entities in its significance range.

What has just been sketched is the semantics of what the *Logic* calls *substantives*. These are concrete nouns like *the sun* and *planets* that signify substances, either singly or collectively. *Abstract nouns* form a second type of non-adjective. These are terms like *round* and *prudence* that signify modes, which may fall in any one of the nine Aristotelian non-substance categories:[13]

> Nouns that signify modes primarily and directly, such as "hardness," "heat," "justice," and "prudence," are also called substantives or absolutes because their signification has some relation to substances.

Like substantives, an abstract noun's signification is determined by its comprehension. It is, however, a second-order term. It signifies a mode

---

[13] *LAP* I.2, *KM* V 134, *B* 30.

because its comprehension contains a mode that is true of modes. *Whiteness* and *prudence* are examples. Although the authors have little to say about second-order modes, they do comment on what we would call metalinguistic terms. These are terms that signify terms, like *noun* and *adjective*. Because a term in mental language is an idea and an idea is a mode of the soul, these are a variety of abstract noun. Following the medieval tradition, they are called nouns of *second intention*.[14]

Terms that are neither concrete nor abstract are adjectives. On the one hand, concrete and abstract nouns, the authors say, directly signify their subjects. Adjectives, on the other hand, signify "things as modified." A species name, for example, has an essential or "real" definition. In semantic terms, it has a comprehension that is fixed by nature. When we are speaking, however, we are usually not actively thinking of a term's comprehension. We may not even know what it is because, as Part IV emphasizes, discovering the true comprehension of a species—its real definition—is the task of natural science. When we use an adjective, on the other hand, we betray by the word itself the mode by which we are signifying things in the world. The adjective draws attention to the mode used to fix the entity that the adjective signifies in the world. In the technical language of medieval logic, an adjective is a "connotative term":[15]

> Nouns that signify things as modified, indicating the thing primarily and directly although more confusedly, and the mode indirectly although more distinctly, are called adjectives or connotatives. Examples are "round," "hard," "just," "prudent."

In this passage the *Logic* embraces the medieval analysis of adjectives as "connotative terms." The doctrine is an example of a general tendency within the *Logic* to carry further parts of traditional logic that fit its purpose. In the *Logic*'s vocabulary, an adjective signifies a mode "distinctly and secondarily" and the subjects in which the mode inheres "confusedly and primarily." Thus far, the doctrine is standard medieval logic. What the *Logic* adds is an explanation of signification in terms of intentional content. In its semantics the "secondary signification" of an adjective is made up of modes, and these modes determine the adjective's "primary signification," just as the comprehension of a concrete or abstract noun determines what it signifies.

That the mechanism of signification for adjectives is intended to be essentially the same as that of concrete and abstract nouns is shown by the *Logic*'s classifying adjectives as connotative. In medieval logic, a connotative term was understood to be a term in spoken rather than mental

---

14 *LAP* I.2, *KM* V 136, *B* 32.
15 *LAP* I.2, *KM* V 134–135, *B* 30–31.

language that functions as an abbreviation for a complex predicative expression in mental language formed of abstract nouns. The semantics of the mental terms that adjectives signify (in the word-to-idea sense) was a special case of the semantics of abstract nouns. Ockham explains the relation of adjectives to concrete and abstract terms this way:[16]

> But a connotative name is one that signifies something primarily and something secondarily. Such a name does properly have a definition expressing what the name means. And often you have to put one [term] of that definition in the nominative and another [term] in an oblique case. This happens for the name "white." For "white" has a definition expressing what the name means, in which one word is put in the nominative and another one in an oblique case. Thus, if you ask what the name "white" signifies, you will say that [it signifies] the same as [does] the whole expression "something informed by a whiteness" [*aliquid informatum albedine*] or "something having a whiteness" [*aliquid habens albedinem*]. It is clear that one part of this expression is put in the nominative and another [part] in an oblique case.

The distinction was still current at the time of the *Logic*, as Fonseca makes clear:

> A connotative noun is one that signifies something of the sort that is conjoined to something else as being conjoined to something, for example, "white," "clothed," "blind," and "unseeing," for "white" signifies whiteness that is conjoined with a swan, papyrus, or some other white thing. "Clothed" signifies clothes that are conjoined to a man.[17]

Ockham uses the same terminology as the *Logic*: a connotative term "signifies primarily" an entity or group of entities in one of Aristotle's nine categories of being, and it "signifies secondarily" a mode.[18] For example, *white* signifies primarily white things in the world and signifies

---

16 *Summa Logica* I.10, Spade translation, *William of Ockham 1995*.
17 Fonseca 24, p. 68:

> Nomen connotativum est, quod significat aliquid adiacens quasi adiacens alicui: ut candidum, Vestitum, Caecum, Nonvidens. Candidum enim significat candorem, qui adiacet cygno, papyro, et caeteris rebus candidis: Vestitum, significat vestem, quae adiacet homini: Caecum, negationem aspectus, quae adiacet animali ad videndum apto, et haec una dictio Nonvidens, negationem aspectus, quae adiacet omnibus non videntibus sive [illa entia sint, sive non] sint.

18 The order terminology of "primary" and "secondary" derives of Aristotelian ontology. The subject of an adjective is ontological prior because in general it exists independently

secondarily the quality *whiteness*. Ockham applies this doctrine to connotative terms in the passage quoted. The spoken adjective corresponds to a mental substantive. A spoken subject-predicate proposition affirms or denies an adjective in an oblique case (genitive, dative, or ablative case) of a subject in the nominative case. (There are no case endings in mental language.) This corresponds to a mental proposition in which the adjective is replaced by an abstract noun. The spoken proposition is synonymous with a longer spoken proposition in which the adjective is replaced by a noun in the nominative or accusative case (e.g. *aliquid*), that corresponds to the same abstract term in mental language as the adjective. This synonymous spoken proposition says of the subject that it is "informed" by that mode (e.g. *informatum albedine, habens albedinem*). Similarly, the *Logic* says that *Socrates is human* is short for *Socrates possesses humanity* ("*habens humanitatem*"), a proposition that lacks adjectives.[19]

The dependence of connotative terms on non-adjectival nouns, and their eliminability in their favor, is further supported by a second medieval doctrine. Traditionally connotative terms were classified as "denominative." These are terms that are derived from non-adjectival nouns in the nominative case. Buridan makes the distinction as follows:[20]

> We should note that here those terms are described which cannot be predicated of their subjects essentially, but denominatively. Now,

---

of its modes. The *Logic* describes this priority this way (*LAP* I.2, *KM* V 135–136, *B* 31–32):

> Thus it is the nature of a true mode that one can clearly and distinctly conceive the substance of which it is a mode without it, while not being able, conversely, to conceive the mode clearly without conceiving at the same time its relation to the substance without which it could not exist naturally. It is not impossible to conceive the mode without paying distinct and explicit attention to its subject. But the fact that we cannot deny this relation of the mode without destroying our idea of it shows that the relation to the substance is included at least confusedly in the idea of the mode. On the other hand, when we conceive two things or two substances, we can deny one of the other without destroying either idea.
>
> For example, I can easily deny prudence without paying distinct attention to someone who is prudent, but I cannot conceive prudence while denying its relation to some person or other intelligent nature having this virtue.

On the one hand, substances are ontologically independent of other substances, and modes of other modes. This independence is reflected in the fact they are not identical to one another or, as the *Logic* puts it, that "the denials of their identities are true": *Socrates is not Plato, animals are not cows,* and *prudence is not chastity.* On the other hand, a mode cannot exist unless it is instantiated in its subject, as reflected by the fact that the denial *Socrates is not mortal* is false.

19 *LAP* I.2, *KM* V 134–135, *B* 30–31.
20 Buridan, *Summulae* 3.1.3, *John Buridan 2001*, pp. 146–147.

> for a term to be properly predicated denominatively, one [condition] is required on the part of the utterance and another on the part of the intention. For on the part of the utterance, a denominative term has to be concrete, deriving in its formation from its abstract form, as "white" from "whiteness." ... And we should note that the grammarian reasonably derives "whiteness" from "white," namely, the abstract [form] from the concrete. For we have the concept of "white" or of "just" naturally prior to the concept of "whiteness" or of "justice," as should be observed from elsewhere. Therefore it is understandable that the names "white" and "just" were the ones earlier imposed to signify.

Buridan makes clear that on the level of mental language, which is occupied by ideas or what he calls "intentions," abstract nouns are prior to adjectives ontologically and semantically. An adjective "derives its formation from" the abstract noun that signifies a mode directly. Such "derivations" are part of the medieval doctrine that connotative terms have nominal definitions. The connotative term is derived from the abstract noun because it is a spoken abbreviation for a longer expression in mental language that contains only substantive, non-connotative terms. In Buridan's theory, strictly speaking, there is no need for a semantic account for adjectives in addition to that for concrete and abstract nouns because adjectives do not occur in mental language.

The *Logic*, however, does not endorse the view that connotative terms are eliminable by nominal definitions in favor of non-adjectives. Rather, it freely employs adjectives as predicate in many of its examples of categorical propositions, both in the logical theory of Part III and in the natural science of Part IV. Rather, it seems to admit adjectives into mental grammar with a special semantics of their own. Concrete nouns signify substances, and abstract nouns signify modes, both as a function of the term's comprehension. When these terms are used in speech, however, language does not betray the content of their comprehensions. The user may not even be particularly clear about what they are. Adjectives differ from both concrete and abstract nouns by exhibiting their intentional content. They mention the mode in terms of which they signify things in the world. An adjective signifies primarily those things in the world that its secondary signification—its intentional content—is true of.

The authors refer to this difference in distinguishing three levels or degrees of abstraction: first concrete nouns, second adjectives, and third abstract nouns. During perception, say of a football game, the soul may abstract the concrete noun *ball* by noticing that the ball is round. It forms the idea, which has the mode roundness in its comprehension among others. This idea signifies balls in part because they are round. The soul may also attend to the mode roundness as it is instantiated in the ball and then go on to abstract the adjective *round*. This idea signifies round things by alluding to the fact that they are round. In more technical terminology, its signifies secondarily roundness and primarily round things. To say it signifies a mode secondarily means that it expresses the fact that its intentional contains the mode roundness, and indicates that this content determines what it signifies in the world. Finally, the soul may attend directly to the mode roundness itself and notice its characteristic second-order properties. It may then abstract the abstract noun *roundness* that contains these properties in its comprehension. *Roundness* then signifies the mode roundness because roundness possesses these second-order properties. The *Logic* describes the process as follows:[21]

> when what is in itself a substance or a thing comes to be conceived in relation to some subject, the words signifying it this way become adjectives, such as "human" and "carnal." When we strip the adjectives formed from these substantive nouns of this relation, we make new substantives out of them. So after having formed the adjective "human" from the substantive word "man," we form the substantive "humanity" from the adjective "human."

Although the *Logic*'s authors do not endorse the medieval view that adjectives are spoken abbreviations for complex mental abstractions, adjectives clearly have an intentional semantics functionally parallel to that of concrete and abstract nouns. The authors employ both the terminology of connotative term and of primary and secondary signification to explain this parallel semantics. An adjective signifies in a double sense—it is connotative—because it signifies primarily those entities that possess the mode or modes that it signifies secondarily. Moreover, just as comprehension serves as the intentional content of concrete and abstract nouns, secondary signification functions as the intentional content of adjectives. As with concrete and abstract nouns, an adjective's identity is determined by its intentional content: two adjectives are identical if, and only if, they have the same secondary signification. Also as in the case of concrete and abstract nouns, intentional content determines what an adjective signifies in the world: an adjective signifies primarily those entities that instantiate the mode or modes that it signifies secondarily. Secondary signification also determines an adjective's inferiors. An adjective's inferiors are the ideas that signify only subjects that the adjective itself signifies primarily. An adjective's extension, therefore, is the set of these inferior ideas. In short, an adjective's secondary signification is functionally equivalent to the comprehension of other nouns.

In sum, all substantives, whether they be concrete or abstract nouns, and all connotative terms have a similar semantics, governed by intentional

---

21 *LAP* II.1, *KM* V 188, B 74.

Species

The *Logic*'s authors are selective in what parts of traditional logic they think are important and are then conservative in what they accept. In retaining parts of earlier logic, however, they must remain consistent with Descartes' metaphysics and epistemology. There is perhaps no better example than their retention of Aristotle's doctrine of species. Although the Cartesian external world consists fundamentally of vortices of material corpuscles, the authors continue to hold basic tenets of Aristotelian science: nature is divided into genera and species; species have necessarily true essential definitions; and discovering essential definitions is the main goal of natural science. The world of Descartes, of course, was not Aristotle's. The examples of material things the *Logic* cites are not plants and animals, but extended physical objects like the earth and the sun. The species it mentions are populated by the creatures of mechanics and geometry that make up Descartes' physics, for example, triangles and matter in motion. But what is relevant to the semantics of terms are not the physics they invoke but the structure attributed to genera and species as terms of language.

Early in Part I the authors divide existents into Aristotle's ten categories. Equally important, they endorse Porphyry's division of terms into the "predicables": genus, species, difference, property (traditionally *proprium*), and accident. The text is explicit that predicables are to be regarded as ideas: they are the "five kinds of universal idea."[22] Ontologically, as ideas, predicables are modes of the soul, but they are also terms in mental language. As terms they have semantic properties, in particular intentional content and signification. Grammatically, the five predicables fall into two types: genera and species, which are concrete or abstract nouns; and *differentiae*, properties, and accidents, which are adjectives.

The semantics of genera and species as set forth in the *Logic* is relatively straightforward. Both are common nouns, and as such they possess a structure determined by their comprehensions:

> For when general ideas represent their objects as things and are indicated by terms called substantives or absolutes, they are called *genus* or *species*....
>
> An idea is called genus when it is so common that it extends to other ideas that are also universal, as the quadrilateral is a genus with respect to the parallelogram and the trapezoid....

---

22 *LAP* I.7, *KM* V 146, *B* 40.

> Common ideas that fall under a more common and general idea are called species, just as the parallelogram and the trapezoid are species of the quadrilateral, and body and mind are species of substance.[23]

The semantic subordination of species to genus has immediate consequences for the truths of science. The reason a species "falls under" or "contains" a genus is that its comprehension includes that of the genus. It follows that anything that satisfies the modes in a species' comprehension necessarily satisfies the modes in the comprehension of its genus. Moreover, because everything that is signified by a species is also signified by its genus, it follows that a species-idea falls in the extension of its genus.

The semantics of differences, properties, and accidents, on the other hand, is more complex, as are its consequences for the theory of truth. All three are adjectives:[24]

> By contrast, if ideas that represent their objects as modified things, and that are indicated by adjectival or connotative terms, are compared with the substances these connotative terms signify confusedly although directly, then they are called not genera or species, but *differences, properties*, or *accidents*. This is true whether in fact these connotative terms signify essential attributes, which are actually only the thing itself, or true modes.

Because they are adjectives, differences, properties and accidents are connotative terms. They differ semantically, however. The *Logic* explains these differences by appealing to traditional theory, in this case the theory of essential or "real" definitions. A real definition (*definitio rei*) is a necessarily true universal affirmative proposition that predicates of a species its genus modified or "restricted by" its difference. The genus is a common noun. The difference is an adjective; as such it "signifies secondarily" a mode. In the definition the subject term is the species, and the predicate is the genus modified by the difference. In the *Logic*'s jargon, the mode signified secondarily by the difference holds necessarily of the things the species signifies. A real definition:

> explains the nature of a thing by its essential attributes, of which the common one is called the *genus*, and the proper one the *difference*.[25]
> These ideas are called differences when their object is an essential attribute distinguishing one species from another, such as extended, thinking, and rational.[26]

---

23 *LAP* I.7, *KM* V 146–147, *B* 40–41.
24 *LAP* I.7, *KM* V 147, *B* 41.
25 *LAP* II.16, *KM* V 243, *B* 126.
26 *LAP* I.7, *KM* V 144–147, *B* 41.

The species' difference together with the differences of the species' higher genera make up the species' comprehension. That they do so is a consequence of the fact that essential definitions impose a tree structure on species. This structure is a Cartesian version of the medieval tree of Porphyry.[27] Viewed as a tree, species and genera occupy or "label" its nodes. The (inverted) tree branches descends downward from a highest genus through subordinate species. Each branch terminates in a finite number of steps with a proper name. With the exception of the highest genus, which the *Logic* calls *being* or *substance*, every species is the direct descendant of the genus that defines it. With the exception of proper names, which are direct descendants of lowest or *infimae species*, every species is a genus with respect to its immediate descendant, which is the species it defines. Within this scheme, the *Logic* classifies proper names as general terms, and thus as a kind of degenerate case of species.[28] Algebraically, the tree is finite and finitely branching, each nodes is labeled by species, and each descent is labeled by a difference. The authors describe the structure as follows:[29]

> Thus the same idea can be a genus with respect to the ideas to which it extends, and a species when compared to another, more general idea. For example, body is a genus with respect to animate and inanimate bodies, and a species with respect to substance. The quadrilateral is a genus compared to the parallelogram and the trapezoid, and a species with respect to shape.
>
> But there is another notion of the word "species" that applies only to ideas that cannot be genera. This occurs when an idea has under it only individuals and particular, just as the circle has under it only individual circles, which are all of the same species. This is called the lowest species, *species infima*.
>
> There is also a genus that is not a species, namely the highest of all genera. Whether this genus is being or substance is unimportant, and it is more a question for metaphysics than logic.

Because every genus with the exception of the highest has its own definition, repeated applications of definitions unpack the entire set of a

---

[27] Although the authors of the *Logic* do not cite Porphyry, on the basis of linguistic similarities between the *Logic* and the commentary of Julius Pacius, Auroux argues that they were familiar with Pacius' edition of the *Isogoge*. See *Auroux 1993*, p. 68, and *Auroux 1992*.

[28] The *Logic* holds that proper nouns count as a special case of common nouns. This view follows from its classification of particular affirmative propositions as a special case of universal affirmatives (*LAP* II.3 and III.9). It follows that a particular affirmative has a universal term as subject.

[29] *LAP* I.7, *KM* V 146–147, *B* 41.

species' defining modes. When the differences labelling all the descents leading to a species are combined into a group, this group makes up the species' comprehension. This content constitutes the species' "essence" and determines its "nature." Moreover, because this content is determined by God and is unchanging, any proposition that ascribes these defining modes to a species is necessarily true. As Part IV explains, a primary goal of natural science is to discover these real definitions.

Because ideas signify things in the world, these subordination relations also impose structure on things outside the mind. When a genus contains a species, it is necessarily true that those things in the world signified by the species possess all the species' defining modes. In more technical terms, the significance range of the species is a subset of the significance range of its genus.

The division of the three remaining predicables into difference, proprium, and accident is an exhaustive partition of the set of adjectives. Differences are distinguished from properties and accidents by the fact that they occur in real definitions. A difference "signifies secondarily" a mode that is necessarily true of the things it signifies primarily. This mode is part of the comprehension of the species it defines.

A proprium is an adjective that is necessarily true of a species but not definitive of it. More precisely, it signifies secondarily a mode that is necessarily true of the members of a species' but not part of the species' essence or comprehension. The property may hold for reasons of either logic or nature. Accordingly, a proprium is necessarily true of the things the species signifies primarily.

An accident, on the other hand, is an adjective that is "not necessarily connected to the idea of a thing." That is, it is an adjective that signifies secondarily a mode that is only contingently true of the things it signifies primarily. The adjective *prudent* is an example. Whether someone is prudent is a contingent fact or, as the *Logic* puts it, we can conceive of a person who is not prudent.[30]

Although in Part I the authors do not explain the epistemology relevant to identifying accidents, it is significant that the authors recognize the existence of accidents at all. The *Logic* does indeed defend a kind of rationalism. According to its metaphysics, essential truths regulate the world and do so according to God's determinations of conceptual containments. But not all truth is conceptual. As discussed in Chapter 6, Part IV of the *Logic* holds that many propositions about history, culture, and morality are contingently true. The *Logic*'s early recognition of accidents in Part I is a preview of its later explanation of the conditions underlying contingent truth and the possibility of empirical knowledge.

---

30 *LAP* I.7, *KM* V 150, B 43–44.

Built into the tree structure of genera and species as determined by essential definitions is an assumption that may strike the modern reader as odd. This is the view that the same difference cannot enter into the definition of more than one species. No two species of distinct genera can have the same difference. A difference is true of only a single species. This restriction dates to Aristotle. In *Parts of Animals*, for example, Aristotle maintains that *two-footed* must be considered ambiguous when it occurs in the definitions of *two-footed human* and *two-footed bird*.[31]

Although the *Logic*'s version of genera and species and its associated theory of real definition conform in most ways with earlier logic, there is a key respect in which it is simpler. Earlier logic did not classify differences as adjectives or connotative terms. According to the traditional doctrine, adjectives are only correctly used in accidental predication. In the *Logic*'s terminology, they would secondarily signify an accident and primarily signify things in the world that possess that accident. According to the *Logic*, on the other hand, a difference is an adjective, and when it occurs in a real definition it is not an accident. In the terminology of the day, a species and its difference are "convertible." Every man is rational, and every rational entity is a man. (Angels are rational in another sense.) Semantically, these defining adjectives function like their associated species, which is a substantive. A difference signifies in the world precisely the individuals that make up its species, which are exactly those entities that possess the species' defining mode. The tradition held that differences are not connotative terms because they lack a characteristic feature of connotative terms, namely, that they do not have nominal definitions. More technically, it held that the predication of a difference of a subject cannot be expounded into a conjunction in which one conjunct assigns the subject to a genus and the second conjunct says of the subject that it possesses a property referred to by an abstract noun.[32]

---

31 For Aristotle's version see *Parts of Animals* 3, 642b20–643a20.
32 For a detailed account of the traditional view see Buridan, *Summulae* 2.4.2 and 2.5.2, Klima 123–124, 127–128. *Summulae* 8.2.4, Klima p. 639:

> And difference is defined thus: a difference is that which is predicated of many things differing in species in response to the question "What is it like?" [*in eo quod quale*], as "rational" is predicated of man and of God, who differ in species, and [is predicated] *in quale*, because if it is asked: "What is a man like?," it is appropriate to reply: "rational." This definition is certainly in need of exposition and supplementation. For the term "white," which is not a specific difference, but an accident, is suitably predicated of many things differing in species in response to the question "What is it like?" [*in quale*], posed in respect of a man and a horse. Therefore Porphyry correctly says that to this definition it has to be added that [a difference] "leads to essence [*esse*]," that is, that it is predicated essentially, as opposed to denominatively, which involves some extrinsic connotation, as in the predication of property and accident. And then the definition has to be supplemented thus: "a difference is what is predicated essentially of many things ... etc." And "essentially" is put there to exclude property and

The authors of the *Logic* do not accept this earlier characterization of adjectives as terms subject to this sort of "exposition." They have instead a simpler semantic definition. A term is connotative if it secondarily signifies a mode and primarily signifies those things that possess that mode. All three—difference, property, and accident—count as connotative on this definition.

The convertibility of a species and its difference—that the two have the same extension—is guaranteed by the distinction between comprehensions and extensions. A species and its difference are distinct terms. The one is a common noun, and the other is an adjective. Moreover, they have different intentional contents. A species has as its comprehension the collected differences true of its higher genera. The difference, on the other hand, has as its intentional content its secondary signification. This is the mode characteristic of it. For example, the species *man* has as its comprehension the set of modes {*rationality, self-movement, life, corporeality, substantiality*}, while the difference *rational* has as its secondary signification the simple set {*rationality*}. Hence, the two ideas are distinct. On the other hand, the *Logic* holds that *man* and *rational* have the same extension:[33]

> it is clear that the *difference* constitutes the species and distinguishes it from other species, *it must have the same extension* as *the species*. Thus they must be able to be said reciprocally of each other, for example, that everything that thinks is mind, and everything that mind thinks.

Because the two have the same extension, the subject and predicate of the proposition *every man is rational* are convertible, making the proposition equivalent to *every rational creature is a man*.

At several points the *Logic* allows for an exception to the general rule that a species' difference is mode. These are cases in which a difference is a privative negation. Thus, the genus divides into two species, one of which suffers an essential privation relative to the other. Accordingly, one species is differentiated by an adjective that signifies a mode that makes up its essence, but the definition of collateral species employs the privative negation of this mode. This privation is signified by an adjective that signifies secondarily the lack of this mode. The genus *animal*, for example, is said to divide into the species *human* with the difference *rational* and the species *brute*, which is defined by the privative difference

---

> accident, and in response to the question "What is it like?" [*in eo quod quale*] is put there to exclude genus and species, which are predicated in response to the question "What is it?" [*in quid*].

33 *LAP* I.7, *KM* V 147–148, *B* 42.

irrational.[34] The degree to which the *Logic* envisioned a privative negation operation on ideas is discussed in Chapter 3.

Extension as Defined by Signification

The central role of extension in the *Logic* is clear. A term's extension is defined as the set of its inferior ideas. An idea is in a term's extension if, and only if, it signifies only things the term does. The truth-conditions of categorical propositions are stated in terms of inclusion and exclusion relations on extensions. The formulation of truth-conditions in terms of extension ensures that truth amounts to a correspondence between proposition and facts in the world. Extension, in short, lies at the center of the *Logic*'s truth theory. The texts supporting this interpretation of extension in terms of signification, however, are difficult, scattered, and imprecise. They center on the definition of inferiority in terms of signification. Because extension is central to the work, the remainder of this chapter will review the textual basis for these interpretative claims.

Historically, the use of the term *extension* (*extensio* in Latin, *étendue* in French) as a technical term in semantics was new to the *Logic*. The term *extensio* (*megethos* in Greek) had had a long history in physics, and the term continued to be used in this sense in Descartes' metaphysics and physics as the name for the essential property defining material substance. It had not, however, been used previously as an abstract noun to name the semantic value of a term in truth-theory, nor as the name for the set of a term's "inferior" ideas.

In the commentary tradition, cognates of extension had occasionally been used to describe the semantic properties of terms. For example, in reference to Porphyry's remark that a genus is "more of a collection" (*magis id quod genus*) than a species,[35] Scotus comments that Porphyry is saying that the genus is "extended to the many" (*extenditur ad plura*).[36]

---

34 Texts that refer to privative negation of ideas are *LAP* I.7, *KM* 148, *B* 42; and II.15, *KM* 242, *B* 124.

35 De speciem 12, *Isagoge a Boethio translate* in *Porphyry 1995*, [02] II:

> Descendentibus igitur ad specialissima necesse est diuidentem per multitudinem ire, ascendentibus uero ad generalissima necesse est colligere multitudinem (collectiuum enim multorum in unam naturam species est, et magis id quod genus est, particularia uero et singularia semper in multitudinem e contrario diuidunt quod unum est; participatione enim speciei plures homines unus, particularibus autem unus et communis plures; diuisiuum enim est semper quod singulare est, collectiuum autem et adunatiuum quod commune est).

36 *John Duns Scotus 1999*, III, 7–8.23:

> Ad aliud dico quod genus non est magis uniuersale, quia "magis" dicit intensionem formae eius cui adiungitur, sed quodammodo maius uniuersale, quia extenditur ad plura, sicut quaternarius est maior numerus binario, non magis. Sicut etiam una

Commenting on the same text, Cajetan and Toletus say that "more" is being used by Porphyry "extensively" (*extensive*).[37]

As explained earlier, the *Logic* provides a definition of extension. It is the collection of a term's inferior ideas:[38]

> I call the *extension* of an idea the subjects to which this idea applies. These are also called the inferiors of a general term, which is superior with respect to them. For example, the idea of a triangle in general extends to all the different species of triangles.

The interpretive difficulty lies in the fact that the authors do not define what they mean by "inferiors." In their *History of Logic* Kneale and Kneale remark that the *Logic*'s use of the term "inferior" is ambiguous and that this ambiguity affects the meaning of extension, which is defined in terms of inferiority:

> according to Arnauld and Nicole, the extension of a general term is the set of its inferiors, but it is not clear whether the inferiors of which they speak are supposed to be species or individuals. When working out their example they say that the idea of triangle in general extends (*s'étend*) to all the various species of triangle, but in the next paragraph they make the point that the extension of a term, unlike its comprehension, might be cut down without destruction of

---

species specialissima non dicitur magis species quam alia, licet habeat plura contenta sub se.

37 *Caietanus 1936*, p. 56:

> Ad hoc breviter dicitur, quod esse magis collectivum multorum potest intelligi dupliciter. Uno modo intensive; et sic species est magis collectiva, quia magis unit adunata, ut ratio adducta probat. Alio modo extensive; et sic genus est magis collectivum, quia multo plura sub sua adunatione cadunt, quam sub speciei ambitu. Unde species et genus se habent sicut duo duces, quorum alter habet exercitum parvum, sed valde unanimem, alter exercitum magnum, sed diversarum factionum. Porphyrius autem loquebatur hic de extensiva collectione, et ideo dixit genus est magis collectivum.
>
> Hic notandum est dupliciter aliquid posse dici magis collectiuum; ut notat Caietanus: priori modo id quod est magis unum, quod dicitur magis collectiuum intensive; altero modo id, quod plura comprehendit, & sic dicitur magis collectiuum extensive: Iuxta hoc intellige minus universale esse magis collectiuum intensive; quia magis sunt unum quae in minus universali conveniunt, quam quae solum in magis universali: at magis universale est magis collectiuum extensive quia sub se plura continet; & sic loquitur Porphyrius.

Compare also *Toletus 1985 [Köln 1615/16]*, Caput II, p. 53.

38 *LAP* I:6, *KM* V 145, *B* 40:

> J'appelle *étendue* de l'idée, les sujets à qui, ce qu'on appelle aussi les inférieurs d'un terme général, qui à leur égard est appellé supérieur, comme l'idée du triangle en général s'étend à toutes les diverses espèces de triangles.

the idea ("*on peut la reserrer quant à son étendue . . . sans que pour cela on la détruise*"), and this is not true of the set of species falling under a genus. . . . The confusion of their exposition seems to be due to their use of the word "inferiors," which is itself metaphorical and unclear. It will be remembered that in medieval representations of Porphyry's tree individuals such as Socrates, Plato, and Brunellus were often mentioned at the bottom of the table in which all the other entries were general terms.[39]

Since the *Logic*'s authors do not define the inferiority relation, its meaning must be gathered indirectly from its usage in different passages, from the role it assumes within the wider theory, and from the occasional examples the authors provide. In particular the Kneales raise the issue of whether inferiors are individuals or ideas, and if ideas, whether they are they limited to species.

As will be clear in the following discussion, the *Logic*'s examples of inferiors show that they are ideas, not individuals. The texts cited below provide a number of examples of inferior ideas: species of triangles; those stars that are self-illuminating and those that are not; nobles and commoners; people who communicate just with speech and those who also use writing; and Platonic and non-Platonic philosophers.

What is somewhat less clear in the text is what sort of ideas count as inferiors. Are they just species or can any idea be an inferior? The issue is important for understanding the *Logic*'s account of truth because truth-conditions for categorical propositions are defined in terms of extensions. The issue is also important historically because some commentators, most importantly Jean-Claude Pariente, have interpreted the inferiority relation as consisting only of species.[40] On Pariente's reading, it is only genera that have inferiors, and their inferiors consist of its species and their subspecies. It would follow that an idea's extension consists of all the ideas that are defined in its terms or, in the language of the *Logic*'s metatheory, an idea's inferiors are all those that have an intentional content that includes the content of the idea itself. An immediate consequence of this reading is that truth is entirely conceptual and determined solely by relations of containment on comprehensions. Because a universal affirmative is true if, and only if, the extension of the subject is included in that of the predicate, *every S is P* would be true if, and only if, the comprehension or secondary signification of *P* were a subset of that of *S*. This "intentional" reading of inferiority relation, therefore, interprets the *Logic* as advocating a kind of extreme rationalism in which truth is solely a function of intentional content.

---

39 *Kneale and Kneale 1962*, pp. 318–320.
40 *Pariente 1985*, Chapt. 8, pp. 227–258.

Signification and Extension 61

As a matter of usage, it must be acknowledged that it was common in medieval logic to use the term inferior to stand for the species of a genus. Buridan's usage is typical. For example, in discussing the "said of" relation from Aristotle's *Categories*, he remarks that a genus is affirmed essentially of a species and refers to the subject as an "inferior" of the predicate. Two examples will illustrate this usage. In these texts from the *Summula*, Buridan uses *inferior* to refer to the relation of species to its genus:[41]

> And then it follows that every universal term is said of a subject, because it has an inferior term under it of which it can be predicates essentially.
>
> . . .
>
> But the philosopher has frequently spoken about beings *said of* a subject . . . namely . . . those that are predicated of its inferiors, which we called *said of* a subject.

Aristotle himself sometimes appears to treat species as the objects of reference or, more precisely, as the semantic values over which quantifiers ranges in a subject-predicate affirmation. For example, the cases he cites as confirming the proposition *some animals are viviparous* are not individuals but the species *man, horse*, and *camel*.[42] In the *Logic*, because inferiors make up the subject term's extension, if categorical quantifiers were understood to range only over inferior species, truth would emerge as a purely intentional attribute. It is clear, however, from both the *Logic*'s texts its broader theory, that the intentional reading of the inferiority relation is too limited.

Although the authors do not provide a formal definition of the inferiority relation, they do discuss it. There are, in all, five passages that refer to an idea's "inferiors." In none are inferiors limited to species. There is only one example in which it is a species. This occurs in the definition of extension quoted above, in which the example of the inferiors of the idea triangle are its species. In two of the five texts, the examples cited explicitly describe inferiors are accidents rather than species. The most transparent text is the discussion of classification in Part II. The purpose

---

41 *John Buridan 2001*, 3.1.5, p. 149:

> Tunc ergo sequitur quod omnis terminus uniuersalis dicitur de subiecto, quia habet sub se terminum inferiorem, de quo est praedicabilis essentialiter.

and 3.2.2, p. 155:

> Quia locutus est saepe Philosophus de dici de subiecto . . . scilicet . . . inter ea quae praedicantur essentialiter de suis inferioribus, quae diximus dici de subiecto.

42 See *Thompson 1995*.

of the passage is to distinguish various types of classification. The third and fourth types are varieties of classification "by accidents." It is the longest text in the *Logic* to mention inferiors, and it provides the best examples of inferiors as accidents:[43]

> The third [type of classification] occurs when we classify a common subject by the opposing accidents it may have, either in terms of its different inferiors or in terms of different times, such as: Every star is luminous in itself or only by reflection. Every body is in motion or at [162] rest. Every Frenchman is a noble or a commoner. Every person is healthy or sick. Every nation expresses itself either only by speech or by writing as well as speech.

---

43 *LAP* II.15, *KM* V 240, *B* 124. There are just four additional passages in the *Logic* mentioning inferiors. They are quoted below. It is clear in the text that in some cases they are intended to be understood as accidents and not species. The first text is the definition of extension quoted earlier, *LAP* I.6, *KM* V 145, *B* 40:

> I call the *extension* of an idea the subjects to which this idea applies. These are also the inferiors of a general term, which is superior with respect to them. For example, the idea of a triangle in general extends to all the different species of triangles.
>   Although the general idea extends indistinctly to all the subjects to which it applies, that is, to all its inferiors, and the common noun signifies all of them.

LAP I.7, *KM* V 147–149, *B* 42–43:

> Hence the primary essential attribute which each species includes over and above the genus is called its difference. Our idea of it is a universal idea because one and the same idea can represent this difference everywhere it is found, that is, in all the inferiors of the species.
>   . . .
>   Because it [i.e. a property, *proprium*] is signified by a connotative term, we attribute it [the property] to the species as its property. And because it also applies to all the inferiors of the species, and the sole idea we have of it, once formed, can represent this property everywhere it exists, it is considered the fourth of the common and universal terms.

LAP I.7, *KM* V 149, *B* 43:

> *Example.* Having a right angle is the essential difference of the right triangle. Since it is a necessary consequence of the right angle that the square of the hypotenuse is equal to the squares of the two sides which enclose it, the equality of these squares is considered a property of the right triangle, applying to all and only right triangles.

LAP II.10, *KM* V 221, *B* 105–106:

> Exceptives are propositions in which we affirm something of an entire subject with the exception of some of the inferiors, using an exceptive particle to show that this thing does not apply to them. Obviously these propositions contain two judgments and are thereby compound in meaning. For example: No ancient philosophers, except the Platonists, recognized God's incorporeality. This means two things: first, that ancient philosophers believed God was corporeal; and second, that the Platonists believed the contrary.

The fourth is classifying an accident into its different subjects, such as classifying goods into mental goods and corporeal goods.

Here there are four explicit examples of accidental inferiors:

- *Stars.* Cartesian authors would likely regard stars as a species. It possesses two inferior ideas: stars that are self-illuminating luminous in themselves and stars that are not self-illuminating.
- *Frenchmen.* This is accidental inferior of *humanity*. It has two accidental subordinates: *nobles* and *commoners*.
- *Humanity.* This is a species that is divided into two accidental classes: *those that express themselves by speech only* and *those that express themselves by speech and writing*.
- *Goods.* This is an accident that is divided into two accidental inferiors: *mental goods* and *corporeal goods*.

Elsewhere in a description of the proposition type known as exceptives (*every S is P except those that are Q*), the text cites as examples of inferiors of the accident *philosopher* the non-species *Platonists* and *non-Platonists*.[44]

In multiple ways, the broader theory the *Logic* proposes also requires that an idea's inferiors include accidents. It is important to be clear in advance what place the inferiority relation would occupy in the theory's definitional order. It is one of several concepts in terms of which the concept of extension is defined. The definitional order is as follows: intentional content is a primitive; signification is defined in terms of intentional content; inferiority is defined in terms of signification; and extension is defined in terms of inferiority:

> *Intentional content*, as a set of modes, is an undefined primitive, called *comprehension* in the case of nouns and *secondary signification* in the case of adjectives.
>
> An idea *signifies* exactly those things that instantiate all the modes in its intentional content.
>
> One idea *is inferior to* another if, and only if, anything that the first signifies the second also signifies.
>
> An idea's *extension* is the set of its inferior ideas.

It follows, then, that an idea's extension is not limited to its subspecies, nor to the ideas defined in its terms. Rather an idea's inferiors include any idea that signifies only what the idea itself does, whether this happens for reasons of definition or due to contingent matters of fact.

---

44 *LAP* II.10, *KM* V 221, *B* 105–106.

Although the details are described in the chapters that follow, it will be helpful to preview the main ways in which accidents figure the *Logic*'s broader metatheory. We have already discussed that the *Logic*'s doctrine of the predicables, which includes accidents as possible elements of an idea's extension. Accidental inferiors are also an important part of the *Logic*'s commitment in Part IV to contingent truth. A mode contingently true of a subject is by definition an accident. Accidents also figure prominently in the *Logic*'s doctrine of false ideas. False ideas are one that fail of existential import. True ideas do not. The requirement that they do not fail of reference applies only to contingent propositions that affirm accidents as predicates. In each of these roles accidents are included in the extensions of ideas. Each, therefore, requires an interpretation of the inferiority relation in which accidents count as inferiors.

Consider first the commitment to accidents as a type of predicable. An accident is a mode "that is in no way necessarily connected to the idea of a thing, so that one can easily conceive the thing without conceiving the mode." The example the *Logic* cites is *prudence*.[45] If the affirmative *Peter is prudent* is true, it is true because the inferiors of *Peter* are a subset of the inferiors of *prudent*. *Prudence*, on the other hand, is an accident, and thus its comprehension is not included in that of *Peter*. It follows that relation of extensional-inclusion does not coincide with that of comprehension-inclusion.

Next consider contingent truth. In Part IV the *Logic* makes a clear commitment to contingent truth as a category distinct from necessary truth. Although the *Logic* holds that the most important component of scientific knowledge is conceptual and concerns essential definitions, it also assigns a subordinate role to contingent truth:

> The first reflection is that it is necessary to draw a sharp distinction between two sorts of truths. First are truths that concern merely the nature of things and their immutable essence, independently of their existence. The others concern existing things, especially human and contingent events, which may or may not come to exist when it is a question of the past. I am referring in this context to the proximate causes of things, in abstraction from their immutable order in God's providence, because on the one hand, God's providence does not preclude contingency, and on the other, since we know nothing about it [i.e. contingent creation], it contributes nothing to our beliefs about things.
>
> For the other kind of truth [viz. of essential natures], since everything [of this sort] is necessary, nothing is true that is not universally

---

45 *LAP* I.7, KM V 150, B 43–44.

true. So we ought to conclude that something is false if it is false in a single case.⁴⁶

Examples of contingent truths cited in various places include:⁴⁷

The king of China has converted to Christianity.
Constantine was baptized by St. Sylvester.
St. Peter was in Rome.

Although real definitions capture essences and natures, they do not include information about which individuals actually exist, nor the details of individual events in history and their "proximate causes." In order for these contingent facts to be known, it must be the case that the extensions of the terms in question include non-necessary inferiors. *St. Peter was in Rome* is true because all the ideas inferior of *St. Peter*, including accidents like *the apostle who denied Christ* and *the brother of Andrew*, are included among the inferiors of the predicate *those who were in Rome*. As explained in Chapter 6, the *Logic* holds that a sensation is a generally reliable source of knowledge. Moreover, much of the knowledge gleaned from sensation is of contingencies.

Further evidence that inferiority is defined in terms of signification is found in the truth-conditions for categorical propositions from Part II. These only make sense if the inclusion and exclusion relations among extensions are understood to include accidental inferiors. It will suffice here to consider just the truth-conditions for universal negative propositions.⁴⁸ Sylvain Auroux has pointed out that the "intentional interpretation" of extension as subordinate species yields incorrect truth-conditions.⁴⁹ The axioms in Part II (II.17–19) lay out the truth-conditions for negative universal propositions in terms of an exclusion relation between term extensions: *no S is P* is true if, and only if, the intersection of the extensions of *S* and *P* is empty. On the intentional interpretation, the extension of an idea would contain only ideas defined in terms of it. The extension of idea *A* would be the set of all ideas *B* such that all the modes in the comprehension of *A* are modes in the comprehension of *B*.

---

46 *LAP* IV.13, *KM* V 398, *B* 263. In the first edition of 1662 the text continues:

On the contrary, possibility [i.e. even a single possible instance, a *possibilium*] is a sure mark of the truth with respect to what is recognized as possible, whenever it is a question only of the essence of things. For the mind cannot conceive anything [concerning essences] as possible unless it conceives it as true according to its existence.

47 *LAP* IV.13, *KM* V 398–400, *B* 263–265.
48 For a full account of the truth-conditions of all four categorical propositions see *Martin 2013* and *Martin 2016*.
49 *Auroux 1993*, p. 135.

But intuitively the truth of a universal negative is not a function of the definitions of ideas, but turns rather on facts in the world.

For the sake of argument, suppose that *no doctor is a thief* is true but *no doctor is a poet* is false. The reason is not that the idea *doctor-thief* does not exist, but that the idea of *doctor-poet* does. Rather, both are definable and exist as ideas. It is possible to cause both ideas to exist by "restriction" (i.e. by combining the comprehensions of their component ideas). Under the intentional interpretation, one restricted idea would be in the extensions of *doctor* and *thief*, and the other would be in extensions of *doctor* and *poet*. The reason one proposition is true but the other false is not related to the definitions of these ideas. Rather, it is a function of facts outside the mind. The significance range of *doctor-poet* is non-empty, but that of *doctor-thief* is empty. As we shall see in Chapters 4 and 6, similar considerations apply to the truth-conditions of the other three categorical propositions.

The final theoretical reason supporting the reading of extension as defined in terms of signification turns on the doctrine of false ideas. One of the *Logic*'s objectives was to make clear the implications of Descartes' dualism for epistemology and morality. The authors argue that because we misinterpret the data of sensation as children, we come to think that emotional and sensory properties of the soul are caused by material things. We misidentify spiritual modes as material. As a result we form so-called false ideas by mixing material and spiritual modes into the single comprehension of a single idea. Because some of these modes are spiritual and some material, they cannot in principle be instantiated together in any existing substance. Simply put, a false idea is one that has an intentional content that is not true of any existing thing.

The consequences of this tendency are important for philosophy because it leads to errors in ontology and epistemology. It also has consequences for morality because false ideas mislead us into thinking that moral properties are tied to material things. False ideas play an important role in the *Logic*'s semantics of contingent propositions. This is explained in detail in Chapter 6. Here, however, it is appropriate to give a preview to show how a commitment to false ideas requires accidents as elements of extensions.

It had been standard since Aristotle that propositions—not sensations, concepts, or ideas—are the correct bearers of truth and falsity. According to Aristotle, a proposition, whether it be an affirmation or denial, is a combination that is true if it corresponds to "what is," and false otherwise.[50] This view was endorsed throughout medieval logic.[51]

---

50 *Prior Analytic* I, 16a13–19, Aristotle 1989.
51 See, for example, Aquinas' approval of a similar view of Augustine's: *De veritate*; OCLC nr. 49644264, http://worldcatlibraries.org/wcpa/oclc/49644264, *Aquinas 2006 [1970]*.

Ideas, however, were said to be false in a sense that derives from the prior use of falsity as a property of propositions. Descartes famously appeals to false ideas in the *Meditations*. An idea, he says, may possess "material falsity" (*falsitas materialis*) if it represents something unreal as if it were real (*cum non rem tanquam rem repraesentant*).[52] He cite the idea *goat* as a true and the idea *chimera* as false. The *Logic* makes the distinction as follows:

> If the objects represented by these ideas, whether of substances or modes, are in fact such as they are represented to us, one calls them true. If they are not such, then, in the manner in which they could be, they are false. [*si ils ne sont pas tels elles sont fausses en la maniere qu'elles les peuvent être*], and this is what one calls in the schools beings of reason, which consist ordinarily of the assemblage that the soul makes out of two ideas real in themselves, but which are not joined in truth to form a single idea, as that which one can form of a mountain of gold is a being of reason because it is composed of two ideas, of mountain and of gold, which it represents as unified though they really would not be so.[53]

---

52 Descartes explains a false idea as follows (*Meditations* III.19–20; *AT* 7.43, 45–47):

> 19 ... caetera autem, ut lumen & colores, soni, odores, sapores, calor & frigus, aliaeque tactiles qualitates, nonnisi valde confuse & obscure a me cogitantur, adeo ut etiam ignorem an sint verae, vel falsae, hoc est, an ideae, quas de illis habeo, sint rerum quarundam ideae, an non rerum. Quamvis enim falsitatem proprie dictam, sive formalem, nonnisi in judiciis posset reperiri paulo ante notaverim, est tamen profecto quaedam alia falsitas materialis in ideis, cùm non rem tanquam rem repraesentant: ita, exempli causâ, ideae quas habeo caloris & frigoris, tam parum clarae [44] & distinctae sunt, ut ab iis discere non possim, an frigus sit tantùm privatio caloris, vel calor privatio frigoris, vel utrumque sit realis qualitas, vel neutrum. Et quia nullae ideae nisi tanquam rerum esse possunt, siquidem verum sit frigus nihil aliud esse quàm privationem caloris, idea quae mihi illud tanquam reale quid & positivum repraesentat, non immerito falsa dicetur, & sic de caeteris.
>
> 20. Quibus profecto non est necesse ut aliquem authorem a me diversum assignem; nam, si quidem sint falsae, hoc est nullas res repraesentent, lumine naturali notum mihi est illas a nihilo procedere, hoc est, non aliam ob causam in me esse quàm quia deest aliquid naturae meae, nec est plane perfecta; si autem sint verae, quia tamen tam parum realitatis mihi exhibent, ut ne quidem illud a non re possim distinguere, non video cur a me ipso esse non possint.

53 *LAP* I.2, *KM* V 136, *B* 32:

> Que si les objets représentés par ces idées, soit des substances, soit des modes, sont en effet tels qu'ils nous sont représentés, on les appelle véritables: que s'ils ne sont pas tels elles sont fausses en la manière qu'elles les peuvent être; & c'est ce qu'on appelle dans l'école êtres de raison, qui consistent ordinairement dans l'assemblage que l'esprit fait de deux idées réelles en soit, même qui ne sont pas jointes dans la vérité pour en former une même idée, comme celle qu'on se peut former d'une montagne d'or, est un être de raison, parce qu'elle est composée des deux idées de montagne & d'or, qu'elle représente comme unies, quoiqu'elles ne le soient point véritablement.

A true idea represents things as they are; one that is false does not. In more technical terms, a false idea is one that through abstraction and restriction the soul has constructed by combining incompatible modes into a single intentional content. What makes it false is that the modes in the combination's intentional content are not jointly instantiated in any actually existing thing. Some ideas like *golden mountain* are even impossible. It is impossible in nature to instantiate the modes *golden* and *mountainous* in the same material substance.[54]

Like Descartes, the *Logic*'s authors appeal to false ideas to explain errors in science and morality.[55] The account is psychological. Children who regularly experience a sensation in which they apprehend at the same time modes of a material object and modes of the soul mistakenly believe that they are all instantiated in the same material substance. They then form an idea by combining the spiritual and material modes in a single comprehension. They habitually make the false judgement *S is P* in cases in which *S* is a spiritual and *P* is a material mode or vice versa. But they then go on to combine the comprehensions of *S* and *P* into a single comprehension and form a new idea, *an S that is P*. Because the modes are contrary, the idea fails to signify anything real.[56] The authors give *corporeal pain* as an example. Children develop the habit of falsely believing *fire causes pain* and subsequently form the false idea *corporeal pain*. The subject term *corporeal pain* fails to signify anything, and thus the proposition *corporeal pain is in my head* cannot be true. It is therefore false. Other false ideas cited are *heat caused by fire, gravity*, and *happiness caused by material wealth*.[57]

The relevance of false ideas to the interpretation of extension is that they are part of the *Logic*'s account of contingent truth, which presupposes accidents as inferior ideas. False ideas only entail falsity and error in the context of the truth-conditions of contingent propositions. As Chapter 6 explains, essential truths, on the one hand, are independent of what individuals actually exist. Their terms do not carry existential import. The terms of contingent propositions, on the other hand, do. The truth-conditions for a contingent universal affirmative read: *every S is P*

---

54 *LAP* I.2, *KM* V 136, *B* 32.
55 For Descartes' account of the role of false ideas in error see *Meditations* III.6, AT 7.37: a false idea "consist in this that I might judge that ideas, which are in me, are similar to things posited as external to me but without conforming [to them]":

> Praecipuus autem error et frequentissimus qui possit in illis reperiri, consistit in eo quòd ideas, quae in me sunt, iudicem rebus quibusdam extra me positis similes esse siue conformes.

56 *LAP* I.9, *KM* V 157–158, *B* 49–50.
57 For passages in which the formation of such ideas are described see *LAP Discour* I, *KM* V 110, *B* 9–10; *LAP* I.9, *KM* V 157–158, *B* 49–50; *LAP* I.11, *KM* V 168–170, *B* 58–60.

is true if, and only if, S signifies at least one thing and the extension of S is included in that of P.[58] Thus, the author's view that propositions with false ideas are false only makes sense as part of the theory of contingent truth, and this theory requires that accidental ideas occur as elements of the extensions of other ideas.

This chapter has set out the semantics of terms, both substantives and adjectives, and the special semantics of species. These are preliminaries to the theory of truth presented in Part II. This truth-theory is discussed here in Chapter 4. Before discussing the semantics of propositions, however, there is more to say about the semantics of the terms. In particular, there is more to say about the structure of ideas and what this structure entails about the semantic structure of things in the world. Of special interest is the degree to which this structure exhibits algebraic properties.

References

Aquinas, Thomas. 2006 [1970]. *De veritate (Textum Leoninum Romae)*, Fundación Tomás de Aquino OCLC nr. 49644264. Roberto Busa, S.J. and Enrique Alarcón (eds.).

Aristotle. 1989. *Prior Analytics*, Indianapolis, IN, Hackett. Smith, Robin (translator).

Ashworth, E. J. 1973. Existential Assumptions in Late Medieval Logic. *American Philosophical Quarterly*, 10, 141–147.

Auroux, Sylvain. 1992. Port-Royal et l'arbre de Porphyre. *Archives et documents de la Sociéte d'historie et d'épistémologie des sciences du langage*, 6, 109–122.

Auroux, Sylvain. 1993. *La Logique des Idées*, Montréal, Paris, Bellarmin, Vrin.

Buridan, John. 2001. *Summulae de dialectica*, New Haven, Yale University Press. Klima, Gyula (translator).

Caietanus, Thomas De Vio. 1936. *Commentaria in Porphyrii Isagogen, ad Praedicamenta Aristotelis Scripta Philosophica*, Roma, Insitutum Angelicum. Isnardus, P. and M. Marega (eds.).

Duns Scotus, John. 1999. *Questiones in librun Porohyrii Isagoge*, St. Bonaventure, NY, The Franciscan Institute. Etzkorn, Girard J., et al. (eds.).

Kneale, William and Martha Kneale. 1962. *The Development of Logic*, Oxford, Clarendon Press.

Martin, John N. 2013. Distributive Terms, Truth, and *the Port Royal Logic*. *History and Philosophy of Logic*, 133–154.

Martin, John N. 2016. A Note on "Distributive Terms, Truth, and the Port Royal Logic." *History and Philosophy of Logic*, 37:4, 391–392.

Morris, Charles W. 1939. Foundations of the Theory of Signs. In: Neurath, Otto, Rudolf Carnap, and Charles W. Morris (eds.) *International Encyclopedia of the Unified Sciences*, Chicago, University of Chicago Press.

Pariente, Jean-Claude. 1985. *L'Analyse du Language à Port-Royal*, Paris, C.N.R.S. Éditions de Minuit.

---

58 *Ashworth 1973*. Because particular affirmatives are subalterns to universal affirmatives, it follows that contingent particular affirmatives carry existential import as well.

Porphyry. 1995. *Isagoge. Translatio Boethii*, Leiden, E.J. Brill. Minio-Paluello, L. and B. G. Dod (eds.).

Stencil, Eric. 2016. Essence and Possibility in the Leibniz-Arnauld Correspondence. *Pacific Philosophical Quarterly*, 97, 2–26.

Thompson, Michael. 1995. The Representation of Life. In: Laurence, Gavin, Rosalind Hursthouse, and Warren Quinn (eds.) *Phillipa Foot and Moral Theory*, Oxford, Clarendon Press.

Toletus, Franciscus. 1985 [Köln 1615/16]. Cur de specie post genus & non de differentia egerit? In: Risse, Wilhelm (ed.) *Commentaria in universam Aristotlis logicam. Opera omina philsophica*, Hildesheim, Gerg Olms.

William of Ockham. 1995. *William of Ockham, from His Summa of Logic, Part I: Adam (of Wodeham's) Prologue, Ockham's 5 Prefatory Letter and Chs. 1–6, 8–13, 26–28, 30–31, 33, 63–66, 70, 72, with Summaries of Chs. 7, 29, 32*. ms. Spade, Paul Vincent (translator).

3 The Semantic of Terms. The Structure of Ideas[1]

The Issues

Chapter 2 laid out the *Logic*'s semantics in its own terms. From a modern perspective, however, the 17th-century vocabulary is suggestive of modern algebra. Ideas, intentional content-sets, significance ranges, and extensions are singled out as key explanatory groupings, and these exhibit identity conditions and ordering relations much like sets. Their respective ordering relations, moreover, are more or less parallel. These features are supplemented by mental operations: abstraction, restriction, and privative negation, which are suggestive of algebraic operations in a modern sense. Species, which are an important subclass of ideas, also have recognizable structure. They conform to a finite tree. This chapter considers these collections, orderings, and operations with more care. The focus is on several questions. How much of this structure is original to the *Logic* and how much was brought forward from earlier logic? How similar is the *Logic*'s structure to modern algebra, especially to the class logics of the 19th century?

The conclusion will be that important parts of the theory are directly adopted from medieval logic and are described in the same terms. New, however, is the explanation of ordering relations in terms of intentional content. Also new is the concept of extension. On the issue of anticipating 19th-century logic, Russell Wahl's observation proves correct. "It is a mistake," he writes, "to read into the *Logic* a prelude to set theory." Jean-Claude Pariente expresses a similar view:[2]

> L'originalité du livre ne réside pas, il est vrai dans ses innovations formelles. Arnauld et Nicole ne sont pas des inventeurs sur le plan du calcul logique. Rien n'est plus éloigné de leur style de réflexion que

---

1 Many of the ideas in this chapter are developed in *Martin 2016b* and *Martin 2016a*.
2 *Wahl 2008*, p. 673, and *Pariente 1995*, p. 246.

> les efforts diversifiés et inlassables d'un Leibniz pour mettre sur pied un formalisme efficace et rationnel.

The chapter begins by reprising in more rigorous terms the role of intentional content in defining the various ordering relations. At issue in particular is the degree to which it is fair to extract a modern interpretation from the *Logic*'s own language. The discussion addresses a technical issue that has divided commentators who have interpreted these orderings algebraically: whether ideas are "dual" to extensions in the algebraic sense of duality. The structural properties of species and their relation to privative negation are also discussed. Although the chapter concerns algebraic relations, when technical terms from algebra are introduced, they are explained informally and should be accessible to the general reader. Key formal definitions and reconstructions, however, are provided in the Appendix for those who are interested in or who would prefer a more rigorous account.

Ideas and Extensions as Partially Ordered Systems

As remarked in the previous chapter, ideas determine various ordering relations. If these were treated in modern logic, each would have a formal definition and a technical name. The *Logic*'s own presentation is more informal. It does not distinguish the orderings from one another precisely, nor does it employ a consistent terminology.[3] What is clear from the text is that the orderings proposed are based on two assumptions, one about ideas and the other about the world. The first assumption is that every idea, be it a substantive or an adjective, possesses an intentional content.

The second basic assumption governing structure is that intentional contents determine what ideas signify in the world. An idea signifies those entities that possess the modes in their intentional content. As in the last chapter, we will employ *significance range* as a name of convenience for

---

[3] Consider for example the informal term *includes*. A species "includes" its genus; an idea's comprehension "includes" a mode; and an idea's extension "includes" another idea.
  LAP I.5, *KM* V 143, *B* 38:

> Now in these abstractions it is clear that the lower degree includes the higher degree along with some particular determination, just as the I includes that which thinks, the equilateral triangle includes the triangle, and the triangle the straight-lined figure.

LAP I.7, *KM* V 149, *B* 42–43:

> So the entire difference between the idea of an animal and the idea of a brute is that the comprehension of the idea of an animal neither includes nor excludes thought—the idea even includes it in its extension because it applies to an animal that thinks—whereas the idea of a brute excludes thought from its comprehension and thus cannot apply to an animal that thinks.

the set of entities that an idea signifies, although the *Logic* itself has no terminology for this set. Because significance ranges are by definition sets, they are trivially ordered by set-inclusion. They form what is called a *partial ordering*: a binary relation ≤ on a set U is defined as a *partial ordering on U* if, and only if, ≤ is reflexive, transitive and antisymmetric.

Although the *Logic* does not use modern terms, from the properties explicitly attributed to intentional contents, ideas, significance ranges, and extensions in the *Logic*'s own words, it is clear too that each of these groups forms its own partially ordered structure. In the case of intentional contents, significance ranges, and extensions, this result follows because they are functionally sets, and thus the families of sets in question, namely the sets of all contents, all significance ranges, and all extensions, are ordered by the subset relation ⊆, which is trivially a partial ordering. These partial orderings are the first "algebraic" facts that it is fair to abstract from the text: intentional contents, significance ranges, and extensions are essentially partially ordered by set-inclusion.

In the case of ideas, the ordering is determined by the fact that they are defined by their intentional contents. Each idea is paired with one and only one intentional content, and conversely, each intentional content is paired with a unique idea. Thus, there is a one-to-one correspondence between ideas and intentional contents. The ordering relation on ideas is defined by reference to this correspondence. Idea A is contained in an idea B if, and only if, the intentional content of A is a subset of the content of B. The idea *animal* is contained in the idea *human being* because the set of modes definitive of *animal* is a subset of those definitive of *human being*. It follows that the mapping from contents to ideas is order-preserving: idea A is contained in an idea B if, and only if, the intentional content of A is a subset of B. In algebraic terms, the mapping from contents to ideas is an isotonic isomorphism, although the *Logic*'s authors would neither have thought to remark on this property explicitly nor to address it in formal language. Because of this tight correspondence, however, virtually any structural property true of ideas will also be true of their content-sets.

Next to consider is the mapping from ideas to significance ranges. An important fact is that two ideas may signify the same things. In modern terminology, the mapping from ideas to significance ranges is many-one. For example, a species and its difference both signify the same set and, on occasion, so do two accidents, e.g., the ideas *the boys in my class* and *the students sleeping in this room* are defined by modes that, as a matter of fact, may be true of the same substances. This coincidence of reference is due in part to the intentional contents of terms but also in part to the contingencies of nature that determine which entities the modes in these contents are true of. The mechanisms of nature cause it to be the case that the modes definitive of the one idea are true of the same things as the modes definitive of a second idea. The mapping from ideas to significance ranges also has the property that it reverses the order—it is antitonic. If idea A is contained in idea B, then B's content contains all the modes in A's content and generally more besides. These modes then are generally true of "fewer" things than those in A's content. It follows that the significance range of A is a subset of that of B or, in other words, that in general A is satisfied by "more" things than B. Thus, if A is contained in B, the significance range of B is a subset of that of A. The ordering between ideas and significance ranges is inverted, a fact that was remarked upon later by Leibniz.[4] In algebraic terms, the mapping from ideas to significance ranges is an antitonic homomorphism.

A subtler relation, yet one that underlies the *Logic*'s understanding of extensions, is the mapping from significance ranges to extensions. As remarked earlier, because significance ranges and extensions are functionally sets, they are ordered by the subset relation. Like the link between ideas and their contents, this relation between significance ranges and extensions is also tight, even though extensions contain ideas while significance ranges consists in the individuals that ideas signify in the world. The two structures are isomorphic.

> **Theorem.** There is a one-to-one order preserving mapping between significance ranges and idea-extensions.
>
> **Proof.** The proof of isomorphism follows from the definitions. It has three parts.

1. A significance range determines a unique extension. It does so because the content of an idea determines what it signifies, and hence it also determines the idea's inferiors, namely, those ideas that signify only things that the idea itself signifies. But the set of an idea's inferiors is another name for its extension.
2. The converse is also true: the extension of an idea uniquely determines its significance range. This is the case because an idea's significance range is the union of all the significance ranges of the ideas in its extension.

From parts 1 and 2 it follows that the mapping of significance ranges to extensions is one-to-one.

3. The mapping is order preserving. If the significance range of one idea A is included in that of another B, then the extension *of A* (i.e. the set of ideas that have significance ranges included in that of A) is a subset

---

4 On Leibniz see *Lenzen 2004*. Like modern logicians, Leibniz called significance ranges extensions.

of the extension of B (i.e. the set of all ideas that have significance ranges included in that of B).

QED.

Thus, in algebraic terms, the ordering of significance ranges is isomorphic to that of extensions. Due to this tight correspondence, any structural property true of significance ranges will be true of extension and conversely. In particular, if one significance range is a subset of another, or if one excludes another, or if two do not intersect, or if part of one is non-empty, these facts will likewise be true of the corresponding extensions. In Part II this correspondence is exploited by the *Logic*'s authors in defining the truth-conditions of categorical propositions. There truth is defined in terms of the properties of ideas. More precisely, truth is defined in terms of inclusion and exclusion relations on idea-extensions. Because these relations hold exactly when corresponding relations hold among ranges of significance, the conditions amount to a correspondence theory of truth. Whether propositions are true or false is a function of facts in the world, despite the fact that truth-conditions are stated in terms of relations on ideas. This Cartesian sleight of hand is one of the more interesting parts of the *Logic*'s truth theory and is discussed in detail in Chapter 4.

The theorem entails a technical corollary relevant to a dispute in the commentary literature. Extensions are not "dual" to ideas in the technical sense of duality employed in the algebra of partial orderings. The issue of duality has been raised by Marc Dominicy, who argues that ideas and their extensions are dual, and Sylvain Auroux, who holds that they are not.[5] Order-duality requires by definition that there be a one-to-one order-inverting mapping from one structure to the other. Because the issue is technical, a formal definition is in order:

> **Definition.** Let U be a set ordered by the relation $\leq$, let U' be a second set ordered by the relation $\leq'$, and let φ be a mapping from U into U'.
>
> φ is *dual* if, and only if, for any x and y in U, $x \leq y$ if, and only if, $\varphi(y) \leq' \varphi(x)$.

In the formal sense of duality, ideas are not dual to extensions. The reason is that the mapping between the two is not order preserving. The problem cases are those in which an idea is contained in the extension of another only contingently. Because the containment is accidental, the comprehension of the one is not a subset of the other. Suppose, for example, that it is a contingent fact that the proposition *Peter is prudent* is true. It is true

---

5 See *Dominicy 1984*, pp. 40–41, and *Auroux 1993*, pp. 80–85, 133–135.

because its truth-conditions are met: the extension of the idea *Peter* is a subset of the extension of the idea *prudent*. On the other hand, Peter is not necessarily prudent, and the proposition is not an essential truth. The comprehension of the idea *prudence* is not a subset of the comprehension of the idea *Peter*. Hence, the idea *prudence* is not contained in the idea *Peter*. Hence, although the proposition is true as a matter of fact, it is not a conceptual truth. The idea *prudent* is not part of Peter's essence.[6]

In concluding this section, it is appropriate to make a general remark on the fairness of using algebraic terminology to describe the *Logic*'s views. Using algebra to interpret the *Logic* is anachronistic inasmuch as it suggests that its authors held consequences entailed by a formal theory that they were unaware of. On the other hand, the observations that ideas, contents, significance ranges, and extensions have parallel structure is based on properties that the authors clearly declared. They assign to each idea an intentional content consisting of modes, and these contents determine orderings both on ideas and on what ideas signify. They define an idea's extension as the set of its inferiors and understand inferiors to be those ideas that signify only things the idea itself does. The formal summary is little more than a translation into modern terminology of the authors' own observations. The virtue of the more formal idiom, in this case, is that it provides to the modern reader a clear account of the way extension depends on content and signification. A more complete formal description of these various structures is provided in the Appendix.

Species provide another case in which concepts from algebra help clarify the *Logic*'s views on idea structure. As explained in Chapter 2, the hierarchy of species is headed by *being* and devolves in a finite number of pairwise divisions to terminate at individuals. This hierarchy is nicely described in modern terms as a finite, binary branching tree of nodes consisting of ideas, ordered by the containment relation. Describing the Cartesian "tree of Porphyry" as a tree in the algebraic sense makes it clearer to a modern logician. Moreover, it should not be thought that the authors themselves were muddled or unclear about the structure of species simply because they did not use algebraic terminology. Earlier logicians who viewed genera and species as forming a "tree" new perfectly well what they meant and had a clear understanding of the sort of structure they

---

6 Because neither Dominicy nor Auroux defines precisely what they mean by duality, they may well have had in mind a mapping between two different structures that are more complex than the partial ordered sets considered here. These are structures on ideas and extension that are not only ordered by the containment relations above but which also possess meet and join operations. These operations are formal versions of the *Logic*'s mental operations of restriction and abstraction. One such structure proposed by Auroux, which also possesses a proto-complementation operation, is discussed in the Appendix. It is argued below that the text does not support an attribution to the *Logic* of meet, join, or complementation operations in the modern sense.

intended. The *Logic*, for example, this structure is a direct consequence of its theory of real definition.

We turn next, however, to a case in which applications of algebra to the interpretation of the *Logic* is less successful. These are readings that suggest that the mental operations of restriction and abstraction are anticipations of algebraic meet and join operations of a modern sort, and that idea negation in the *Logic* is an incipient version of lattice complementation.

Abstraction

The *Logic* affirms Descartes' doctrine that ideas, which are conceived as spiritual modes, are caused in one of three ways: "some appear to me to be innate, others adventitious, and others to be made by myself."[7] Innate ideas are caused directly by God. Examples include *being, thought, extension, infinity, God, straight line, motion,* and *time*.[8] God also causes sensations directly. These occur on the occasion of simultaneous corporeal motions in the sensory organs and brain. Ideas are also caused directly by the agent, by either of two spiritual operations: abstraction or restriction, and also perhaps by privative negation. It is these that have been suggested to have some of the properties of modern algebraic meet, join and complementation operations. In this section we will investigate abstraction, and restriction and negation in the sections that follow.

Early in Part I, the authors distinguish three "kinds" of abstraction. Because it is one of the few texts in which abstraction is described in detail, it worth quoting in full:

> The remark we made in passing in chapter 2, that it is possible to consider a mode without reflecting distinctly on the substance of which it is a mode, provides an opportunity to explain what are called *abstractions of the mind*. Because of its small scope, the mind cannot perfectly understand things that are even slightly composite unless it considers them a part at a time, as if by the different faces they can assume. This is generally called knowing by abstraction.
>
> But there are different kinds of composition. Some things are composed of really distinct parts, called integral parts, such as the human body and different parts of a number. In this case it is quite easy to conceive how the mind can be applied so as to consider one part independently of another, because the parts are really distinct. This is not what we mean by "abstraction."

---

7 *Meditation* III.7, *AT* IXa 29. See also *Letter to Mersenne, AT* III 382–383. For a discussion of the causal origin of ideas in the *Logic* see *Nadler 1989*.
8 See *LAP* I.1, *KM* 132, *B* 29; and *VFI* Chapt. 27, *KM* 348–349, *G* 207–208.

Now in these same cases, it is so useful to consider the parts separately rather than the whole that without it we would have almost no distinct knowledge. How could we know the human body, for example, except by dividing it into all its similar and dissimilar parts and giving them different names? All arithmetic is also based on this. No skill is needed to calculate small numbers because the mind can grasp them in their entirety. The art consists entirely in calculating by parts what cannot be calculated as wholes. For example, it would be impossible, whatever the scope of one's mind, to multiply two numbers of eight or nine digits each, taken as wholes.

The second kind of knowledge by parts arises when we consider a mode without paying attention to its substance or two modes which [s6] are joined together in the same substance, taking each one separately. This is what geometers do who take the object of their science to be the body extended in length, width, and depth. In order to know it better they first consider it according to a single dimension, namely length, which they call a line. Next they consider it according to two dimensions, length and width, which they call a surface. And finally, considering all three dimensions together, length, width, and depth, they call it a solid or a body.

This shows how ridiculous is the argument of some skeptics who try to call into question the certainty of geometry, on the grounds that it presupposes lines and surfaces which are not found in nature. For geometers by no means assume that there are lines without width or surfaces without depth. They only think that it is possible to consider the length without paying attention to the width. This is indubitable, just as when, in measuring the distance from one city to another, we measure only the length of a path without bothering about its width.

Now the more we can separate the different modes of things, the more easily the mind can know them. It is obvious, for example, that no clear account of reflection and refraction was possible until the analysis of motion distinguished its determination in a particular direction from the motion itself, and even separated various aspects within this determination. Given these distinctions, the account follows easily, as is seen in chapter 2 of Descartes' *Dioptrics*.

The third way of conceiving things by abstraction takes place when, in the case of a single thing having different attributes, we think of one attribute without the other even though they differ only by a distinction of reason. Here is how this happens. Suppose, for example, I reflect that I am thinking, and in consequence, that I am the I who thinks. In my idea of the I who thinks, I can consider a thinking thing without noticing that it is I, although in me the I and the one who thinks are one and the same thing. The idea I thereby conceive of a person who thinks can represent not only me but all other thinking persons. By the same token, if I draw an equilateral triangle on a piece of paper, and if I concentrate on examining *it on this paper along with all the accidental circumstances determining it*, I shall have an idea of only a single triangle. But if I ignore all the particular circumstances and focus on the thought that the triangle is a figure bounded by three equal lines.... [I am] able to represent all equilateral triangles. Suppose I go further and, ignoring the equality of lines, I consider it only as a figure bounded by three straight lines. I will then form an idea that can represent all kinds of triangles. If, subsequently, I do not attend to the number of lines, and I consider it only as a flat surface bounded by straight lines, the idea I form can represent all straight-lined figures. Thus I can rise by degrees to extension itself. Now in these abstractions it is clear that the lower degree includes the higher degree along with some particular determination, just as the I includes that which thinks, the equilateral triangle includes the triangle, and the triangle the straight-lined figure. But since the higher degree is less determinate, it can represent more things.[9]

---

9 LAP I.5, KM V 143, B 37–38. The other complete description of abstraction is from *On True and False Ideas*:

> The philosopher Thales, having to pay twenty workers one drachma each, counted twenty drachmas and paid each worker. He would not have been able to do this unless there were at least two perceptions in his mind: one of twenty men and one of twenty drachmas. And I remind you for the last time that *idea* and *perception* are the same thing in my dictionary, and thus that, when I make use of the expression "idea" and "idea of an object," I understand by this the *perception of an object*.
>
> Having some spare time he began to reflect, and thinking about what the two *perceptions* or *ideas* have in common, namely that there is 20 in both, he abstracts from what is particular in them the abstract idea of the number 20, which can subsequently be applied to twenty horses, twenty houses, twenty stadiums. This is a third idea or perception.
>
> He then takes it into his head to reflect on this abstract idea of the number 20, i.e. he considers it with greater attention with a reflective vision, which is one of the most admirable faculties of the mind. And the first thing he discovers is that it can be divided into equal halves, for he easily sees that if he puts 10 on one side and 10 on the other this makes 20. And he sees at the same time that if he adds 1 to 20, the number 21 cannot be divided into two equal parts, because the closest one can get to an equal division is to put 10 on one side and 11 on the other. This leads him to judge that it is well to distinguish by different words the numbers that can and cannot be divided into two equal halves [*qu'il est bon de distinguer, par des mots particuliers, les nombres qui se peuvent ou ne se peuvent pas partager; en deux moitiés égales*], calling these *even* and *odd* respectively. Then, still considering what is contained in (*encore enfermé*) this idea or perception of the number 20, he asks what its factors are, i.e. what numbers taken together make exactly 20.
>
> He begins with *unity*, and sees immediately that unity must be one of the factors, since 1 taken twenty times makes 20. From this it is easy to derive [*aisé de faire*] the general rule that 1 is a factor of all numbers, since it is its own factor, 1 being 1, and all the other numbers are only definite multitudes of 1s.

There are three sorts of abstraction. The first is not abstraction in the strict sense, in that does not cause new ideas to be formed but consists simply in the realization that an integral whole is made up of integral parts, in the sense discussed earlier in which one mental act can be "part" of another. The second and third forms of abstraction described are mental operations that genuinely create new ideas. Both require the soul to "consider"—to be aware of—a perception or idea already instantiated in the soul. The mental operation consists in the act of separating or "cutting off" modes—"prescinding" them in Latinate terminology—from the content of this perception or idea. Of these two types of abstraction, the first consists of prescinding accidents, and the second consists of prescinding necessary properties definitive of a subject.

Since Boethius, abstraction had been a standard topic in logics. Earlier renditions of the abstraction operation were often formulated in terms of the Aristotelian mechanism by which modes of external objects are transmitted to the soul to form general or "abstract" concepts. Aquinas' account will serve as typical. In sensation the soul apprehends a "phantasm" by the faculty of intuition. The apprehension consists of an instantiation in the soul of "spiritual" versions of the modes instantiated in a particular material object outside the mind. This collection of sensible modes is called "the sensible species." The modes that make up the sensible species, on Aquinas' account, are normally sufficiently detailed to be true of only the unique particular thing that is being sensed. Given the intuitive understanding of a particular's modes, the soul's "active intellect" may then elect to separate out, or "abstract," a pared-down collection of the modes which are instantiated as a unit in the soul and are what Aquinas calls a "concept" or "intelligible species." A concept is

---

> Next he takes 2, and finds that 2 is a factor of 20, for in counting in 2s—2, 4, 6, etc.—he arrives at exactly 20. He takes 3 and discovers that this is not a factor of 20, for counting in 3s—3, 6, 9, 12, etc.—he finds that after having done this six times he arrives at 18, after which there is only 2 left before 20. He then takes 4 and finds that it is a factor of 20, because 4 taken five times is exactly 20. He finds the same for 5, for 5 taken four times is exactly 20. He next finds that neither 6, 7, 8, 9 can be factors of 20, for the same reason as he found 3 not to be. But 10 is a factor because 10 taken twice is 20. Neither 11, 12, 13, 14, 15, 16, 17, 18, nor 19 can make exactly 20, when taken any number of times, so they cannot be a factor of it. But 20 can be a factor because 20 taken once is 20. From this various reflections follow:
>
> First, because there can be numbers having no other factor than unity and themselves, it is a good idea to give them a name which distinguishes them from others and they can be called prime *numbers*.
>
> Second, all the even numbers, since they are divisible into two equal parts, have 2 as a factor.
>
> Third, 2 is the only even number which is *prime* because it alone of all the even numbers has only unity and itself as a factor.

VFI 6, KM I, 207–208, G 74–75 (translation adapted by the author).

abstract, general, common, and "confused"—these are all synonyms—to the degree that the modes in question are true of many things. In the first instance, according to Aquinas, the soul abstracts in the intelligible species only a few modes true of a wide number of things. Progressively larger and larger sets of modes are later abstracted, forming concepts that become less general or, in technical terms, more "determinate."

In essence, this model was still expounded by Descartes' Thomistic contemporaries. The Conimbricenses, for example, repeat Thomas' account in their *summa*, which was used as a textbook in the Jesuit colleges of the day.[10] In Eustachio de S. Paulo's textbook summary of philosophy, which Descartes knew and praised, Eustachio also propounds the same trifold division of abstraction found in the *Logic*:[11]

> ... for universals to be understood it is necessary that they be abstracted by the operation of the intellect from their inferiors. So that you might understand this, it should be noted that that abstraction, which is nothing other than one thing being separated from another, is of three kinds: real, by denial, and by precision. Real abstraction is that by which one thing is separated from another in reality as, for example, when a limb is severed from the body. Abstraction by denial is that in which one thing is denied of another within a proposition, for example, if you were to say *the raven is not white*. Lastly, abstraction by precision would be when two things are joined together, we apprehend one of them while leaving the other aside. Therefore, universals being abstracted from particulars by the

---

10 For Boethius' theory see *Boethius 1973, In Isagogen Porphyrii commenta*, lib. I, ca. 10–11, pp. 159–167. For Aquinas' account see *Summa theologiae* I.I, Q. 85. Compare also *John Buridan 1989*, III.8.2, pp. 650–652; and *Conimbricenses 1976 [reprint of 1607]*, Liber I, Q.V, A. I, p. 143. On abstraction as understood by Arnauld and Nicole see also *LAP* I.5, *KM* V 142–143, B 37–38; *LAP* I.11, *KM* V 168–170, B 58–59; *VFI* 6, *KM* II 207–210, G 74–76, and *KM* II 234–235, G 98–100.

11 *Eustachio de S. Paulo 1648, Philosophiae quadripartitia*, Pars Prima, Logica, Tractus 2, Question II, p. 27:

> Quarta conclusio; Ut universalia cognosci possint, necesse est ut per operationem intellectûs abstrahantur à suis inferioribus. Quod ut intelligas, nota abstractionem, quae nihil aliud est quam unius ab altero separatio, triplicem esse; nempe realem, negationis, praecisionis. Abstractio realis est, quâ aliquid ab alio realiter separatur; ut cùm membrum à corpore resecatur: Abstractio negationis, cùm unum de altero negatur in propositione; ut si dicas, Corvus non est albus: Abstractio praecisionis tum fit cùm è duobus conjunctis unum altero relicto apprehendimus; ut si praetermisso hominis corpore de solo ejus animo cogites. Cùm igitur universalia per operationem intellectûs abstrahuntur à particularibus, hoc non fit per abstractionem realem; cùm universalia non distinguantur realiter à particularibus: neque per abstractionem negationis; cùm universalia de suis inferioribus affirmari soleant; sed per abstractionem praecisionis; cùm videlicet relictis particularibus differentiis id solum quod commune est animo concipitur.

operation of the intellect would not be "real" abstraction because the universals are not distinguished in reality from particulars. Nor would it be abstraction by denial because universals are usually affirmed of their inferiors. Rather, since the differentiating particulars are left behind, what is conceived by the soul is only what is common.

Here, Eustachio's second type is the same as the *Logic*'s method of separating accidents because it is only accidents that, in Eustachio's words, can ever be "truly denied of a subject."

Like the earlier tradition, the *Logic* holds that abstraction begins with a conscious "consideration" (*considare* for Aquinas, *considere* in the *Logic*, *apprehendere* in the text from Eustachio) of an object. This object may be a perception or idea. The *Logic* is quite clear that the act of conception—of having an idea actively instantiated in the soul—is reflexive. The mind is both conscious of its content and of the fact that the act of apprehension is occurring at that moment:[12]

> every perception, which is essentially representative of something and therefore called an *idea*, cannot but be essentially reflective on itself, [and] that its immediate object can only be this idea; that is, *the objective reality* of the thing, which my soul is said to perceive.

In the medieval accounts that preceded the *Logic*, it was left unclear how the "cutting away" of abstraction was intended to work. On a standard account, a phantasm is made up of the modes of the perceived object that have traveled to the soul through sensation and intuition. It is a subset of these perceived modes which is then abstracted. The medieval accounts leave the mechanism by which this abstraction operation occurs largely unspecified. One issue that arises within the medieval version is that although the phantasm consists of only the perceived sensible properties of the object, the intellect nevertheless is able to abstract its essence or "species," which normally consists of non-sensible qualities. Another mystery in the medieval account is that concepts as modes of the soul appear to be ontologically simple entities. How can they both be simple entities yet differ in abstraction according to the number of modes they abstract? Abstraction, for example, seems to presuppose that a concept like *human* is decomposable into parts like *rational, self-moving, living, corporeal,* and *substantial*.

The *Logic* provides a straightforward explanation of these facts by attaching to an idea, which is a simple entity, a content which generally consists of multiple modes. In abstraction, there are two kinds of

---

12 *VFI* Chapt. 5, *KM* I, 199, *G* 66. See also *VFI* Chapt 6, *KM* I 204, *G* 71–72.

contentful mental acts: sensations and conceptions of abstract ideas. Consider first sensation. When the soul has a perception associated with sensation, the act is "about" an object outside the mind in the sense that the soul is aware of the relevant content of the perception. This content consists of a collection of modes. Some of these modes are true of the soul, and some are true of the object outside the mind. Together these make up the content of the perception. The perception is about the object outside the mind to the degree that the soul is aware of material modes that the object actually possesses.

In the act of abstraction, the soul conceives a new idea with a new intentional content that is a subset of the content of the perception. Ontologically, conception is a simple mental act: the instantiation of a mental mode. This simple act, however, is associated with a complex intentional content. The act of abstract conception—an abstract idea—consists of being aware of a reduced content. On the one hand, the perception associated with sensation and the abstract idea are both ontologically simple. They are simply mental acts, modes of the soul. The content of these acts, on the other hand, is complex because, in general, it consists of multiple modes. It is this complex set of modes that is open to simplification in abstraction.

It follows from this account that an abstract idea always has a simpler content than the perception or idea from which it is abstracted. As we shall see shortly, the operation of restriction, which is a second way the soul forms ideas, also creates an idea with a simpler content. One consequence of this fact is that the *Logic* seems to leave little room for imagination, which intuitively seems to combine the content of disparate ideas or perceptions. Moreover, in Section I.9 the authors ascribe an important role to imagination in mental life because they describe it as a major source of false and confused ideas. Imagination, it seems, often pulls together modes that are incompatible, as in the false ideas *subtle air* and *golden mountain*. Although the *Logic* mentions imagination, it does not explain its mechanism.[13] There is a sense, however, in which imagination is similar to sensation. A standard medieval view was that an "image"—the phenomenal experience associated with imagination—was like sensation in that it always detailed a collection of modes true of an individual thing. The content of the image, it was thought, consists of various modes collected from diverse sensations and memories. Moreover, these modes possess the specificity of a singular individual, even though in the case of imagination that individual might not exist. An imaginary idea, then, is an abstraction from a the detailed content of an image. For example, if the soul experiences an image of a particular golden mountain, it could abstract the general idea *golden mountain*. We

---

13 *LAP* I.1, *KM* 5.127, *B* 25 and *LAP* I.9, *KM* 5.162, *B* 52–54.

shall see that the idea *golden mountain* may also be formed by the operation of restriction.

Medieval authors, including Aquinas and Buridan, held that the intellect first abstracts very general ideas, and only later less general ones. As the quoted passages indicate, the *Logic*'s authors, in contrast, held that the soul first abstracts specific or "determinate" ideas, and only by degrees simplifies them by prescission to arrive later at more general or "confused" ideas.[14] The *Logic*'s account of abstraction fits well with its view of content. First, the soul apprehends the fully detailed content of the perception, from which it later abstracts and progressively simplifies. It should also be remarked that abstraction does not yield scientific knowledge easily. Part IV makes clear that it is not easy to arrive at knowledge of the real definitions of the species that make up the natural world or, in the language of abstraction, to abstract general ideas with contents that detail a species' essence.

One immediate consequence is that not all abstractions are species, a fact that has implications for the structure of ideas in general. In other words, there are varieties of abstract ideas that are not species. One type consists of accidents. Many accidents are abstracted from sensation. For example, if one were a witness to the scene of students sleeping in class, one might abstract from the content of the perception the idea *sleeping student*. The content of this idea consists of accidental modes inasmuch as no human is either necessarily a student or asleep—there is no species *sleeping student* in the tree of Porphyry.

A second case of non-species abstraction consists of abstractions from species themselves. An abstraction from a species is not itself a species. The species *man* has the comprehension {*rationality, animality, life, corporality, substantiality*}, but an idea that has as its comprehension a proper subset of this set is not a species. For example, *rational*, which is the difference of the species *man*, may be abstracted from the comprehension of *man*. It has the secondary signification {*rationality*}. Although the species and difference are coextensive, the difference is not a species because a species' comprehension must include all the differences of the species' higher genera. More precisely, because the comprehension of the species and the secondary signification of its difference are distinct sets,

---

14 See Aquinas, *Summa theologiae* I.1, Q 85, A 3. Buridan holds that in intuition one first apprehends a "vague individual," and the intellect then later abstracts a general concept. *John Buridan 1989*, pp. 510–515, 413–418, and 650–652:

> Speaking most strictly, the mode "this white," "this thing approaching," etc., has singular concepts corresponding to it because the demonstrative pronoun "this" is not correctly applied in the mode of signifying unless there is a cognition of the thing in the manner of something existing in the prospect of the person cognizing it.

the species and its difference are distinct ideas according to the criterion of idea identity.

Restriction

Like abstraction, restriction is conceived of as a mental operation by which the soul creates new ideas to serve as terms in mental language:

> Occasionally we join a term to various other terms, composing in the mind a complete idea, of which one can often affirm or deny what could not be affirmed or denied of each of these terms taken separately. For example, these are complex terms: "a prudent person," "a transparent body," "Alexander son of Philip."[15]

Restriction is a psychological operation on ideas, but it is also an operation in mental grammar. The ideas on which restriction operates are the causal preliminaries of the idea produced. In this sense, these prior ideas can be viewed as grammatical "parts" of the new idea formed by means of restriction. This relationship is represented in the grammar of spoken language by the complex series of words that signifies the newly formed idea. The spoken expression is formed by physically concatenating the spoken words that signify the two prior ideas. In the soul, the corresponding ideas are grammatical "parts" of the concatenated expression.

As an operation signifying mental language, restriction has a long history in medieval logic.[16] Descartes refers to it in *Meditation* III as an operation by which the soul "makes new ideas."[17] The mechanics of the operation in the *Logic* are clear. The soul operates on two prior ideas with fixed contents as "arguments" in the logical sense, or as "material causes" in Aristotelian terms, and forms from them a new idea with new content by combining the contents of the two prior ideas. The new idea signifies those things that satisfy the modes in content of both its "component" terms, and its extension is the intersection of extensions of the components.

What is novel in the *Logic*'s account of restriction is its explanation in terms of intentional content. The *Logic* distinguishes two types of restriction: determination and restriction. These differ according to whether the content of the new idea has an extension narrower than that of the term

---

15 *LAP* I.8, *KM* V 151–152, *B* 44–45.
16 For a description of restriction in medieval logic, see Buridan, *Treatise on Supposition* 4.1.46–47 and 4.4.63, and *Treatise on Consequence* 6.3.1 in *John Buridan 1985* and *John Buridan 2001*, Book III, pp. 286, 648, and 835. For an account more contemporaneous to the *Logic*, see *Fonseca 1964 [1575]*, Liber VIII, Caput 40, pp. 740–741.
17 *Meditation* III, *B* IXa, 29, and Letter to Mersenne, *AT* III 382–383.

restricted. Let *SP* represent the term formed by restricting the term *P* by the term *S*.

Explication is defined as restriction in which the new term has the same extension at the term restricted. This occurs if the intentional content of the complex *SP* contains modes true of all the same things as the modes in the content of *P*. The result is that *SP* signifies the same things as *P*, and therefore the extensions of *SP* and *P* are the same.

A rather trivial case of explication occurs when the restricted substantive and its restricting modifier have the same intentional content. For example, in the proposition *a human who is an animal endowed with reason made that watch on the beach*, the substantive *human* is not significantly restricted by the adjective *an animal endowed with reason* because the term and its modifier have the same intentional content:[18]

> Suppose I say, for example: "a human who is an animal endowed with reason," or "a human who naturally desires to be happy," or "a human who is mortal." These additions are only explications because they in no way change the idea of the term "human" or restrict it to signifying only some humans. They indicate merely what applies to all humans.

A more common case is that in which the term and its modifier have the same extension but different intensions. In the proposition *Alexander, the son of Philip, conquered the world*, the compound term *Alexander, the son of Philip*,[19] is "informative" in the sense that the two terms *Alexander* and *the son of Philip* have different content. On the other hand, restriction of *Alexander* by *the son of Philip* does not alter the signification of *Alexander* because the two terms have the same signification.[20] The account here is similar to Frege's when he explains that *the morning star* and *the evening star* have different senses but the same reference. Semantically, what is happening in cases of explication is a kind of conditional restriction. If the extension of the restricting term is a superset of the extension of the term it modifies, then the determination does not alter the extension of the term restricted. The intersection of a set with its superset is identical to the set itself: if $A \subseteq B$, then $A \cap B = A$.

In cases of explication, a spoken proposition represents a "longer" proposition in mental language. Consider the explication formulated in the spoken proposition *every SP is Q*. Here the substantive *P* is modified by the adjective or relative clause *S*. Let us suppose that the significance

---

18 *LAP* I.8, *KM* V 151, *B* 45.
19 *LAP* I.8, *KM* V 151, *B* 44.
20 For a statement of the distinction as drawn in earlier logic see *John Buridan 2001*, p. 286.

range of S is a subset of the ranges of both P and Q. In this case the spoken proposition is equivalent to, and may be as "expounded" in mental language as, the mental conjunction *every P is Q and every S is P*. In the first conjunct *every P is Q*, the predicate Q is affirmed of the subject P without a restricting modifier. This conjunct is true because the significance range of P, and hence its extension, is included in that of Q. The second conjunct *every S is P*, which the *Logic* refers to as a "subordinate proposition," provides new information if the intentional contents of S and P differ. This conjunct is true also because the significance range of S, and hence its extension, is a superset of that of P, and hence of that of Q. For example, the *Logic* cites the proposition *Alexander, who was the son of Philip, defeated the Persians*. This spoken proposition is short for a conjunction consisting of the primary proposition *Alexander defeated the Persians* and the subordinate proposition *Alexander was the son of Philip*.[21] In like manner, *some SP are Q* is equivalent to *some P are Q and every S is P*; and *some SP are not Q* is equivalent to *some P are not Q and every S is P*.

The second type of restriction described in the *Logic* is called determination. In determination, the extension of the restricted term *SP* is narrower than that of the restricted term *P*. The narrower extension results from the fact that modes in the intentional content of *SP* are not true of everything that the modes in the content of *P* are true of. The significance range of *SP* is, in general, a proper subset of that of *P*, and thus the extension of *SP* is, in general, a proper subset of the extension of *P*.

One example is the term *equilateral triangle*, which signifies those things that are signified both by the substantive *triangle* and the adjective *equilateral*. The two ideas *equilateral triangle* and *triangle* are distinct. They possess different contents—the set of modes definitive of *triangle* is a proper subset of the modes definitive of *equilateral triangle*. It follows that, in general, there exist figures signified by *equilateral* that are not signified by *triangle*—for example, equilateral rectangles. The *Logic* explains these relations as follows:

> by joining another distinct or determinate idea to it [the head noun], as when I join the idea of having a right angle to the general idea of a triangle. Then I narrow this to the single species of a triangle, namely to right triangle.[22]
>
> ... *determination* occurs when the addition to a general word restricts its signification and causes it no longer to be taken through its entire extension, but only for a part of it, as when I say, "transparent bodies," "knowledgeable people," "a rational animal." These

---

21 *LAP* II.7, *KM* V 209–209, *B* 92.
22 *LAP* I.7, *KM* V 147, *B* 40.

additions are not simple explications but determinations, because they restrict the extension of the first term, causing the word "body" to signify no more than some bodies, the word "people" only some people, and the word "animal" only some animals.[23]

An important application of determination in the *Logic*'s metatheory occurs in the truth-conditions of categorical propositions in Part II. Determination is employed there to describe a subject term's restricted extension in two different ways (*se peut faire en deux manières*), which are appropriate, respectively, to the universal and particular affirmative categorical propositions:

> Now the extension of a general idea can be restricted or narrowed in two ways.
> The first is by joining another distinct or determinate idea to it, as when I join the idea of having a right angle to the general idea of a triangle. Then I narrow this idea to a single species of a triangle, namely the right triangle.
> The other is by joining to it merely an indistinct and indeterminate idea of a part, as when I say "some triangle." In that case the common term is said to become particular because it now extends only to a part of the subjects to which it formerly extended, without, however, the part to which it is narrowed being determined.[24]

The universal affirmative *every S is P* asserts that the extension of the subject terms *S* is identical to that of the compound term consisting of the subject restricted by the predicate. In set theoretic terms, *every S is P* asserts that the extension of *SP* is identical to that of *S*. The view is similar to the equivalence in set theory: $A \subseteq B$ iff $A \cap B = A$:[25]

> The extension of the attribute is restricted by that of the subject, such that it signifies no more than the part of its extension which applies to the subject.

Here determination functions roughly as modern set intersection, although as we shall see later in this chapter, the correspondence here is imperfect, and a number of qualifications will be required.

In a second application of determination to truth-conditions, determination again acts as a kind of set intersection, although this time it is applied as part of an existential quantification over ideas in the

23 *LAP* I.8, *KM* V 151–152, *B* 44–45.
24 *LAP* II.6, *KM* V 145, *B* 40.
25 *LAP* II.17, *KM* V 249, *B* 130.

metalanguage. This application occurs in the statement of the truth-conditions of the particular affirmative:[26]

> When the common term is taken only through an indeterminate part of its extension, because it is restricted by the indeterminate word "some," the proposition is called particular, whether it affirms, as in "some cruel people are cowardly," or whether it denies, as in "some poor people are not unhappy."

In the words of the text, in a particular affirmative *some S is P*, the subject term is understood as restricted by what it calls an "indistinct and indeterminate idea" or "an indeterminate part." The use of "some" and "indeterminate" here indicates an metalinguistic existential quantification over ideas. The proposition is true if, and only if, there is some idea such that the extension of the compound term formed by restricting the subject by that idea is identical to that formed by restricting the predicate by that idea. More formally, *some S is P* is true if, and only if, there is some idea, call it Q, such that the extension of QS is identical to that of QP.[27] Similarly, the negative particular *some S is not P* is true if, and only if, for some Q, the extension of QS and intersect of P is empty.[28]

The technique here consists of reformulating a particular proposition by an equivalent proposition. This equivalent describes a "part" of the subject's extension by means of a new term. In the case of the particular affirmative, this term has as its extension a subset of the extensions of the subject and predicate. In the *Logic*'s terminology, this partial extension is the extension of the restriction of the subject and predicate by the new term—it is the intersection of the extensions of the three terms. In the case of the particular negative, this term has as its extension a

---

26 *LAP* II.3, *KM* V 199, *B* 83.
27 *LAP* I.7, *KM* V 147–148, *B* 41–42; *LAP* I.7, *KM* V 150, *B* 44; *LAP* II.3, *KM* V 199, *B* 83.
28 *Pariente 1985*, pp. 247–238 and *Auroux 1993*, p. 74 have interpreted the sense of restriction referred to in the truth-conditions of particular categorical propositions as a mental operation distinct from determination in the normal sense. This type of determination is supposed to operate on a special type of idea called "indefinite ideas," which differ from regular ideas in that they are not defined by a fixed intentional content. The postulation of this special category of ideas, with *ad hoc* notions of comprehension and determination, is unnecessary. The only place where the expression "indefinite ideas" occurs in the *Logic* is in the texts quoted above. In particular, there is are no texts that justify a reading positing the existence of a special category of "indefinite ideas," which would have as their only role their use in this *ad hoc* variety of restriction, occurring nowhere other than in the truth-conditions for particular propositions. Rather, as the interpretation above shows, the expression "indefinite idea" is to be understood as a way of indicating a metalinguistic existential quantification over ideas understood in the standard sense with fixed contents. These are employed in the truth-condition using a single, univocal sense of determination.

subset of the relative complement of extension of predicates extension relative to that of the subjects. The method goes back to Aristotle. It is similar a proof technique used in the *Prior Analytics* called "setting out" (*ekthesis*).[29] There a new term, one not mentioned in the syllogism, is introduced to signify the relevant part of what the subject signifies. Like Aristotle, the *Logic*'s authors do not specify how this new term is to be found; it may be fixed by previous knowledge or by the speech context. As Aristotle remarks, there may not even be a spoken word for it.[30]

The distinction between what the *Logic* calls determination and explication was well-known in medieval logic. Buridan, for example, draws the distinction between two senses of restriction: one in which the subject term is "an aggregate" of "a determinable and a determination," and a second sense in which the proposition is equivalent to an "explication," which is essentially the conjunction described above.[31] What is novel in the *Logic*'s account is the semantic differentiation of the two uses. In determination, the modes in intentional content of the unrestricted term are jointly true of some entities that the modes in the union of the contents of that term and its modifier are not. Thus, the extension of the complex term is a proper subset of the extension of the unrestricted term. In explication, the modes in the intentional content of the unrestricted term are true of the same entities as the modes in the union of the contents of that term and its modifier. Thus, the extension of the complex term is identical to the extension of the unrestricted term.

There is a third mental operation by which the soul forms new ideas. This is the *Logic*'s version of "term negation." Distinct from algebraic complementation, which obeys elegant rules like double negation and distribution, the *Logic*'s term negation operation is privative negation, a traditional notion dating back to Aristotle that obeys rules quite unlike modern complementation.

Privative Negation

Negation is the final contributor to the idea structure under consideration. What the *Logic* has to say about negation has been the subject of some controversy. More than one scholar has denounced the *Logic*'s account of negation as incoherent. These criticisms rest on the failures of the *Logic*'s negation to conform to the rules of a complementation operator in modern lattice theory or Boolean algebra. These interpretations belong to the same program that reads into the *Logic*'s mental operations

---

29 See, for example 28a23–26, *Martin 2004* and *Smith 1982*.
30 Terence Parsons has suggested this to me in correspondence. See *Prior Analytics*, 48a30.
31 For a statement of the distinction as drawn in earlier logic see *John Buridan 2001*, p. 286.

of abstraction and restriction the properties of modern meet and join operations in the modern algebra.[32] We shall see, however, that these critiques miss their mark because the *Logic*'s negation was never intended to approximate modern complementation. It is rather an adaptation of the traditional notion of privative negation to the context of the *Logic*'s metatheory. This sense of negation had been a standard feature of logic since Aristotle, and although it is unlike modern complementation, it has its own well-defined formal structure.

Idea-negation in the *Logic* occurs in the context of species definition. It is used to divide a genus into two species, one defined by a difference in the normal way and the other defined by the privation of that difference. The second species can be thought of as containing in its comprehension a "negative mode," the privation of the difference of its collateral species. This privation is true of all those things within the genus that do not instantiate the difference of the collateral species. More formally, relative to a genus G and a species S of G defined by a difference D, *the privative negation of S is the species*—call it *non-S*—that has its difference the privation of D within G. Placed in its historical context, this use by the *Logic* of this negation was consonant with its broader policy of carrying over standard parts of traditional logic that fitted its purposes. To counter the suggestions that negation in the *Logic* is ill-conceived, it will be necessary to review some of the history of privative negation and its formal properties.

The history of "privation" in logic begins with Aristotle. His account was profoundly influential, so much so that various of his observations became standard and are preserved in the *Logic*'s own account many centuries later. Aristotle introduces privation (*sterēsis*) in *Categories* X as a variety of "opposition" (*antikeimenos*). A privation, he says, is an ontological state in which something lacks a dispositional property (*hexis*)[33] that would naturally hold of the members of a genus but that fails to be instantiated in one of its species:[34]

> "privatives" (*sterēsis*) and "positives" (*hexis*) have reference to the same subject. Thus, sight and blindness have reference to the eye. It is a universal rule that each of a pair of opposites of this type has reference to that to which the particular "positive" is natural (*pephuke*). We say that that is capable of some particular faculty or possession has suffered privation when the faculty or possession in question is in no way present in that in which, and at the time at which, it should

---

32 These interpretations are found in *Auroux 1993* and *Dominicy 1984* and are discussed in detail below.
33 A privation is contrasted with a *hexis*, translated here as a dispositional property. See the discussion of *hexis* in *Joachim 1951*, esp. p. 88.
34 *Categories* 12a27–34, E. M. Edghill trans.

naturally be present. We do not call that toothless which has not teeth, or that blind which has not sight, but rather that which has not teeth or sight at the time when by nature it should. For there are some creatures which from birth are without sight, or without teeth, but these are not called toothless or blind.

In the grammar of classical Greek, privations are referred to by negative adjectives, which are often "marked" in their grammar by a negative affix, frequently by the so-called alpha-privative. There are also many fully lexicalized privative adjectives, which signify a privation even though they lack a negative affix. Aristotle provides examples:[35]

> Indeed there are just as many kinds of privations as there are words with negative prefixes (*aphairesis*); for a thing is called unequal because it has not equality though it would naturally (*pephukos*) have it, and invisible either because it has no colour at all or because it has a poor colour, and apodous either because it has no feet at all or because it has imperfect feet. Again, a privative term may be used because the thing has little of the attribute (and this means having it in a sense imperfectly), e.g. "kernel-less"; or because it has it not easily or not well (e.g. we call a thing uncuttable not only if it cannot be cut but also if it cannot be cut easily or well); or because it has not the attribute at all; for it is not the one-eyed man but he who is sightless in both eyes that is called blind. This is why not every man is "good" or "bad," "just" or "unjust," but there is also an intermediate state.

Here examples of privative predicates include *unequal (anisos)*, *footless (apodous)*, *colorless or invisible (aoratos)*, *seedless (apurēnon)*, *uncut (atmētos)*, and *unjust (adikos)*, which are all marked by alpha-privatives, as well as *blind (typhlos)* and *bald (phalakros)*, which are lexicalized.

The cases that interested later logicians were privations that consisted in the failure of members of a genus or accidental group to possess a property they would naturally be expected to have as a consequence of their genus membership. This failure might affect all the members of the class or just some, and may fail to obtain all the time or only occasionally:[36]

> We speak of "privation" (1) if something has not one of the attributes which a thing might naturally (*ti tōn pephukotōn*) have, even if this thing itself would not naturally (*pephukos*) have it; e.g. a plant is said to be "deprived" of eyes.—(2) If, though either the thing itself or its genus would naturally have an attribute, it has it not; e.g. a blind man

---

35 *Metaphysics* 1022b33–1023a8, W. D. Ross trans.
36 *Metaphysics* 1022b22–1022b33, 1046a29–37, W. D. Ross trans.

and a mole are in different senses "deprived" of sight; the latter in contrast with its genus, the former in contrast with his own normal nature.—(3) If, though it would naturally have the attribute, and when it would naturally have it, it has it not; for blindness is a privation, but one is not "blind" at any and every age, but only if one has not sight at the age at which one would naturally have it. Similarly a thing is called blind if it has not sight in the medium in which, and in respect of the organ in respect of which, and with reference to the object with reference to which, and in the circumstances in which, it would naturally have it.—(4) The violent taking away of anything is called privation.
. . .

Privation has several senses; for it means (1) that which has not a certain quality and (2) that which might naturally (*pephukos*) have it but has not it, either (a) in general or (b) when it might naturally have it, and either (a) in some particular way, e.g. when it has not it completely, or (b) when it has not it at all. And in certain cases if things which naturally have a quality lose it by violence, we say they have suffered privation.

Aristotle also allows that privations may come in degrees:

In the case of "positives" and "privatives," however, change in both directions is impossible. There may be a change from possession to privation, but not from privation to possession. The man who has become blind does not regain his sight; the man who has become bald does not regain his hair; the man who has lost his teeth does not grow a new set.[37]

Of the properties attributed by Aristotle to privatives, the most influential was likely their role in species definitions. As the preceding texts show, he contrasted a privation with "what is natural." A privation in this sense is a state in which something fails to possess a property it would naturally have. He employs this failure in his account of species definition. The nature or essence of an entity is laid out in its species' definition. He observed that, in some cases, it is appropriate to define one species under a genus as failing to have the natural property definitive of another species under that genus. In these cases, the differentia of one species is the privation of the differentia of the other:[38]

Another rule [of definition] is to examine all cases where a predicate has been either asserted or denied universally to belong to something.

---

37 *Categories* 13a33–37, E. M. Edghill trans.
38 *Topics* 109b13–109b25, *Aristotle 1994–2000*.

Look at them species by species, and not in their infinite multitude: for then the inquiry will proceed more directly and in fewer steps. You should look and begin with the most primary groups, and then proceed in order down to those that are not further divisible: e.g. if a man has said that the knowledge of opposites is the same, you should look and see whether it be so of relative opposites and of contraries and of terms signifying the privation or presence of certain states, and of contradictory terms. Then, if no clear result be reached so far in these cases, you should again divide these until you come to those that are not further divisible, and see (e.g.) whether it be so of just deeds and unjust, or of the double and the half, or of blindness and sight, or of being and not-being: for if in any case it be shown that the knowledge of them is not the same we shall have demolished the problem.

The notion of privative negation was significantly enriched by the Neoplatonists, who used it as a conceptual tool to explain their metaphysical hierarchy. Some of the properties added by the Neoplatonists resurface in the *Logic*'s version of privative negation a thousand years later. The followers of Plotinus contribute three important properties: privative negation determines an order, this order ranks elements according to their value, and the operation obeys a set of distinctive logical laws.[39]

The Neoplatonist who most fully developed the logic of privative negation was Proclus. Typical of many of the Neoplatonists, he lectured on Aristotle's logic and geometry. In his commentary on Euclid, for example, he contrived a proof that claimed to show that the parallel postulate followed as a theorem. Although mistaken, the proof was accepted for a millennium.

Proclus' logic of privative negation is grounded in what we would today call the logic of gradable adjectives. Modern theory tells us that natural languages possess families of terms linked in systematic ways to a mass noun like *heat* or *happiness*. Because a "mass" can manifest itself to varying degrees, is it is frequently associated in language with a comparative adjective that compares two things according to how much they "possess" the mass quantity. For example, *heat* is a mass noun, and *is-hotter-than* is an associated comparative adjective. Another example is *happiness*, which has the associated comparative *is-happier-than*. Often, there is a set of gradable adjectives associated with a characteristic mass noun. These adjectives discriminate among entities according to the degree to which they possess the associated mass quantity. Associated with heat is the set of gradable adjectives {*boiling, hot tepid, cool, cold, freezing*}. Associated with *happiness* is the set {*ecstatic, happy, content, sad, miserable*}. Importantly, adjectival affixes act as intensifiers relative to the mass quantity associated with the conjoined mass noun. Some

---

39 Some of the ideas in this section are developed in *Martin 1995* and *Martin 2001*.

affixes convert a gradable adjective into one that is true of things that have more of the mass quantity, and some convert an adjective to refer to things that have less of the mass. For example, one way to talk about something being hotter—as having "more heat"—is to use the negation *non* or the affix *super*: *it's not hot, it's boiling; it's superhot*. Positive intensifiers in English include *super* and *hyper*. One way to express that something has a lower degree of happiness is to use a lexicalized adjective lower in the scale, or else to use a negative affix like *un* applied to an adjective higher in the scale: *he is sad; he is unhappy*. Here *unhappy* is a privative negation—it describes the possession of a diminished quantity of the "mass" happiness. Other privative affixes in English include *sub* and *less*, as in *substandard* and *clueless*.

While Plotinus frequently used negative forms to characterize levels of his ontic hierarchy, Proclus systematized this use. He recognized that the ontic ordering constituting the Neoplatonic hierarchy could be described by comparative adjectives and privative negation. In Proclus' case, the mass is Being. As part of the Platonic tradition, degrees of Being were believed at the same time to be degrees of perfection, power, causation, moral goodness, beauty, generality, and so forth, each with its associated comparative adjectives:

> the higher cause (*aitioterōn*), being the more efficacious (*drastikōteron*), operates sooner upon the participant (for where the same thing is affected by two causes it is affected first by the more powerful (*dunatōteron*); and in the activity of the secondary the higher is co-operative, because all the effects of the secondary are concomitantly generated by the more determinative cause (*aitiōteron*).... All those characters which in the originative causes have higher (*huperteran*) and more universal (*holikōteron*) rank become in the resultant beings, through the irradiations which proceed from them, a kind of substratum for the gifts of the more specific principles (*merikōteron*).[40]

As we shall see in the account of analysis and synthesis presented in Part IV, the *Logic* preserves the Neoplatonic doctrine that the order of causal generation coincides with both the order from the more general to the less general, and the order from the more perfect to the less perfect. What is relevant here is the logical role Proclus gives to intensifiers, especially privative negation:

> Being, after all, is the classic case of assertion whereas Not-Being is of negation.... So then in every class of Being, assertion in general

---

40 Propositions 70 and 71 in *Proclus 1963*.

is superior to negation. But since not-Being has a number of senses, one superior to Being, another which is of the same rank as Being, and yet another which is the privation of Being, it is clear, surely that we can postulate also three types of negation, one superior to assertion, another inferior to assertion, and another in some way equally balanced by assertion.[41]

In truth my view is that negations come in three sorts, one sort is for beings of a form more fundamental than affirmations. These are generative and perfective of those things generated in affirmation. Another type is placed at the same level as affirmations, and here affirmation is not in any way more worthy than negation. Finally, there are those with a nature inferior to affirmations, namely privations of affirmations.[42]

Proclus sometimes uses *hypernegation* to refer to the intensifier that moves a term up the hierarchy. It is clear that in his view, the affix that moves a term down the hierarchy is a version of Aristotle's privative negation.

Proclus' logical theory becomes more interesting when it is combined with the doctrine that lesser degrees of Being "emanate" in layers or "hypotheses" from the One. The details in Plotinus are vague at best, but in Proclus they are clearer. The structure of emanation is a ranked or layered tree with the One as its root. Each node gives rise to a generation of immediate descendants, which Proclus calls a *taxon*. Frequently he describes the immediate descendants as forming a triad—his famous triad "thesis," "antithesis," and "synthesis." According to Proclus, the descending branches of the tree are infinite. There is no least degree of Being. Branches descend forever into lesser and lesser degrees of goodness and perfection, fading off into "evil." The whole picture is an adaptation of Aristotle's hierarchy of genera and species into Neoplatonic metaphysics. It becomes interesting algebraically when it is combined with another Neoplatonic doctrine: the nodes that form the tree also determine a single linear ordering in which all nodes are all ranked relative to one another by degrees of perfection. This line is Lovejoy's "Great Chain of Being."[43] The linear ordering depends on the additional assumption that the nodes at each generation immediately beneath a node are ordered among themselves. The order within a rank is determined by privative negation. Each node at a given rank, save for one that is more perfect than all the others, is the privative negation of a sibling at that rank. A rank of the tree in

---

41 *Proclus 1987*, p. 426.
42 *Proclus 1968–1997*, vol. II:5, 38:18–25, author's translation.
43 *Lovejoy 1936*.

effect forms as a line of nodes ordered from left to right with each node having its privative negation on its left. The negation indicates a privation of Being. A privative negation is a less perfect node than the node negated. A linear ordering of perfection of all the nodes in the tree is then recoverable by reference to the two prior orderings: that every rank is more perfect than its descendants, and that each node at a rank is more perfect than its privative negation. The technique is formally the same as the transformation that turns the family tree of the British royal family into the line of royal succession. Each generation take precedence over its descendants, and anybody in one generation takes precedence over his or her younger siblings. The Appendix provides a formal reconstruction of Proclus' transformation.

The formal properties of the Neoplatonic tree were reinterpreted in the Middle Ages to describe species definition within the tree of Porphyry. Medieval logicians retained the Neoplatonic doctrine that the nodes of the tree can be ranked in a line, that divisions under a genus can be ranked by privative negation, and that the ranking was evaluative—that privations are states of diminished perfection. These doctrines resurface in the *Logic*'s own use of privative negation.

Before turning to the transition in medieval logic, however, it is important to make some formal points about the logic of privative negation. These are most clearly seen in Proclus' account. Privative negation obeys a set of well-defined logical laws, although these are different from those of complementation in Boolean algebra. Let ≤ represents the linear "ontic" ordering defined in part by privative negation. Let $x \leq y$ be read *x is more perfect than y*. Let 0 represent the tree's first or "root" element, which is for Proclus is the One. In the *Logic* the "root" node is the genus *being*. Let ~ be privative negation and ¬ its inverse, hypernegation. The ordering and operations obey these laws:

$$\neg\neg x \dashv x \leq x \leq\sim x \leq\sim\sim x$$
$$x \leq y \rightarrow\sim x \leq\sim y$$
$$\neg x \leq \neg y \rightarrow x \leq y \rightarrow\sim x \leq\sim y$$

The laws hold generally in the logic of gradable adjectives in which ≤ represents the order on the relevant mass quantity and the operations represent intensifiers, including privative negation.[44] In these logics, privative negation is well-defined but differs formally from complementation in modern algebra. For example, neither ¬ nor ~ is idempotent or

---

44 For a fuller account of Proclus' logic of privative negation and gradable adjectives see Martin 2001.

98 The Structure of Ideas

antitonic, which are elementary properties of complementation in complemented lattices and Boolean algebras.[45]

This review of Proclus' conception of privative negation is relevant to the *Port Royal Logic* for two reasons, one historical, the other theoretical. First, early logic is the source of several of the *Logic*'s views on privative negation. Formally, the operation of privative negation is well-defined in the formal semantics of gradable adjectives.[46]

That it is formally sound and a recognizable part of natural language logic bears on the charge that the *Logic*'s negation, which is a version of privative negation, is incoherent or equivocal. Sylvain Auroux has argued that the *Logic*'s negation is an incoherent variety of proto-lattice complementation. Marc Dominicy has argued that its negation equivocates between a Boolean and non-Boolean negation. Neither recognizes that negation in the *Logic* is a variety of privative negation nor correctly describes its formal properties.[47] See the Appendix for a review of Auroux' formal reconstruction. The issue of equivocation is addressed below.

Privative negation in the *Logic* is a straightforward importation of the standard medieval operation. Medieval logicians melded the Neoplatonic tree with Aristotle's hierarchy of genera and species with the result that some Neoplatonic doctrines were associated with the tree of Porphyry. It was recognized that one way to divide a genus into two subspecies was to define one species in the usual way by an essential differentia and to define the second species by the privation of the difference of the first species—the very technique referred to by Aristotle in the *Topics*.[48]

---

45 $\sim$ is not idempotent because $\sim\sim x \neq x$. Nor is it antitonic because $x \leq y \rightarrow \sim x \leq \sim y$.

46 See the Appendix for a formal statement of the theory within the context of the *Logic*'s account of species. See Horn 1989 for the properties of comparatives, associated gradable adjectives, and intensifiers.

47 *Auroux 1982*, p. 89, proposes as a reconstruction of the *Logic*'s negation with in a kind of proto-matrix in which idea containment has some of the properties of an ordering, and abstraction, restriction and negation have some of the properties of the matrix operations of join, meet, and complementation. He also posits maximal and minimal elements. See the Appendix for a review of this reconstruction. In a later work (*Auroux 1993*, p. 94) he suggests that ideas ordered by containment and structured by abstraction and restrictions are isomorphic to a structure of comprehension-sets. He rejects the *Logic*'s idea-negation as incoherent. *Dominicy 1984*, p. 43, suggest a reconstruction of the *Logic*'s structure of ideas as a Boolean algebra of Carnapian intensions (functions from possible worlds to predicate extensions within those worlds). On pp. 44–45 he rejects the *Logic*'s account of idea-negation as equivoc. Neither commentator recognizes the *Logic*'s idea negation as privative negation.

48 Modern linguistics retains the terminology *privative negation* for a variety of this traditional distinction. The term is there used to refer to the marked name of subset of a broader set in cases in which the unmarked term refers ambiguously to both the broader set and the relative complement of the marked subset within the broader set. One example is *man*, which refers ambiguously to the broad class human being and the subset males, while *woman* is a privative negation. It is the same term only marked and

The negated species, moreover, was regarded as the less perfect, as in Neoplatonism.

Ockham in the *Summa Logica* gives a representative account of the medieval understanding of privation:[49]

> affirmative propositions that contain privative terms not equivalent to infinite terms have more than two exponents. Hence, the proposition "He is blind" has these exponents: "He is something," "By nature he should have sight," "He will never be able to see naturally." But it is not possible to give firm rules for such propositions, for because of the variety of such terms the propositions in which they occur have to be expounded in different ways. Hence, "Socrates is blind" has the exponents that have been mentioned. But the proposition "Socrates is foolish" has these exponents: "Socrates is something" and "Socrates does not have the wisdom which he ought to have." Still, this is consistent with its being the case that he is able to have wisdom ... even though a privative term occurs in each.

In this text Ockham makes use of the technical term *infinite negation*. Infinite negation is what we today call Boolean complementation: relative to a domain D of existing things, the infinite negation of A in D is the set of all things that are in D but not in A. He mentions infinite negation here in order to distinguish it from privative negation. Privative negation is a kind of relative complementation within a genus. Roughly, the privative negation of a species S of a genus G is the set of all things in G that are not in S. Being medieval logic, however, the distinction is subtler. The negated term is often "lexicalized" in the sense that it is not marked by a negative affix. Moreover, the spoken proposition that affirms a privatively negated predicate of its subject signifies (is "expounded to") a conjunction in mental language. This conjunction has three parts. First, it affirms that the species falls in its genus. Second, it denies that the difference definitive of the collateral species holds of the subject. Lastly, the conjunction specifies that the negated property holds naturally of the genus. This last conjunct carries forward the doctrine held by both Aristotle and the Neoplatonists that a privation is a lack of something "natural." More precisely, the spoken proposition *S is not P* in which *not* is a privative negation "expounds" in mental language to the complex proposition: *S falls in genus G, members of G would naturally possess*

---

refers to the relative complement of males within the class humans. See *Jespersen 1924*, p. 326.

49 *Summa Logicae* Part II, 12–13, *William of Ockham 1980*, pp. 119–122. See also Part I, 36, *William of Ockham 1974 [ca. 1323]*, p. 117. For privative negation in Ockham see Martin 2003.

property P, and S does not possess P. For example, *blind* and *foolish* are lexicalized privative terms. *Socrates is blind* expounds to *Socrates is a human, humans naturally see, and Socrates does not see*. *Socrates is foolish* expounds to *Socrates is a human, humans are naturally wise, and Socrates is not wise*. Thus in Ockham's view, privative negation is a negative operation that when applied to a term signifying a property that is naturally true of members of that genus generates a concept that signifies the relative complement of that term within the genus.

John Buridan in the *Summulae* is clearer about the role of privative negation in species division:[50]

> For if a term that is dividing and a finite term that is divided are related to each other by univocal predication, then one of them will be a genus and the other its species or difference, or one will be a species and the other its individual. The infinite term, however, will be taken for the other single species or the other several species, for the other difference or differences, or for the other individual or individuals.
>
> This happens sometimes because some species or difference does not have a positive name imposed on it, as when we say that of sounds some are utterances and others are non-utterances. And that a name is not imposed sometimes occurs on account of our not knowing the species or difference. It is because of this mode of division that sometimes a species is defined by means of its genus and the negations of another species, or several other species, or their differences, as when Porphyry says that an accident is a predicable that is neither a genus, nor a species, nor a difference, nor a property, or if we said that brute is a non-rational animal. Oftentimes in such divisions we use a privative in place of an infinite term as when we say, "of substances some are corporeal, others incorporeal" and "of corporeal substances some are animate, others inanimate."

Buridan remarks that in a "division" made by applying the privative negative operator *non* to a species or its difference, the negation is not infinite (Boolean) negation but rather signifies a subset of the genus. In the later terminology of the *Port Royal Logic*, the negated term signifies a subset of the significance range of the genus, namely those things that are not in the significance range of the collateral species or difference. The explicit negative prefix *non* is used, he remarks, when the language lacks an appropriate lexicalized term for that species or its difference.

Buridan goes on to illustrate division by privation by the very example that Arnauld and Nicole use later in the *Logic*. The marked privative

---

50 *John Buridan* 2001, *Summulae* 8.1.8, p. 628.

adjective *non-rational* distinguishes the species *brute* from its collateral species *man* within the genus *animal*. He draws special attention to privative affixes. In the passage, Buridan notes that a marked privative signifies members of the species directly. For example, *incorporeal* is distinguished from the *corporeal* relative to the genus *substance*, and *inanimate* from *animate* relative to the genus *corporeal substance*.

Elsewhere Buridan further makes clear that he subscribes to the Neoplatonic view, which we shall also see in the *Logic*, that division by privative negation is evaluative. "We say," he says, "that [a man] is a more perfect, or more noble, animal than a horse."[51] This echoes the Neoplatonic view that the species to which the negation is applied is more "perfect" or "noble" than the species signified by the marked privative term.

Medieval logic bequeathed this standard view to the *Logic*.[52] Species definition, it remarks, sometimes divides a genus into two immediate subspecies, one of which is defined by a difference and the other by the privative negation of that difference. Moreover, this differentia holds of the one species naturally, and the privation signified by the negated difference renders the collateral species less perfect.

The *Logic* refers to idea-negation in three texts. These are quoted below. A fourth text from Arnauld's correspondence is also relevant:

Text 1:

Finally, some [modes] can be called negative because they represent the substance with a negation of some real or substantial mode.[53]

Text 2:

Finally, we should note that it is not always necessary for the two differences dividing a genus both to be positive, but it is enough if one is, just as two people are distinguished from each other if one has a burden the other lacks, although the one who does not have the burden has nothing the other one does not have. This is how humans are distinguished from brutes in general, since a human is an animal with a mind, *animal mente praeditum*, and a brute is a pure animal, *animal merum*. For the idea of a brute in general includes nothing [63] positive which is not in a human, but is joined only to the negation of what is in a human, namely the mind. So the entire

---

51 *John Buridan* 2001, *Summulae* 3.2.8, p. 161.
52 Acceptance of privative negation for species definition was standard among the *Logic*'s contemporaries. See *Eustachio de S. Paulo* 1648, *Logica*, Part I, *De categoriis* Tract II, *Postpredicamenta*, paragraph XI, p. 87; *Raconis* 1651, Physics, section II, pp. 44–45; and *Fonseca* 1964 [1575], Bk II, Chapt. 17, p. 128.
53 *LAP* I.2, KM V 136, B 32.

difference between the idea of an animal and the idea of a brute is that the comprehension of the idea of an animal neither includes nor excludes thought—the idea even includes it in its extension because it applies to an animal that thinks—whereas the idea of a brute excludes thought from its comprehension and thus cannot apply to an animal that thinks.[54]

Text 3:

The second rule: which is a consequence of the first, is that members of the of the first classification, such as even and odd; rational and irrational. But we should recall what we already said in Part I, that it is not necessary for all the differences which make these members opposites to be positive, but it is enough if one of them is and if the other is only the genus with the negation of the other difference. This is how to make sure that the members are really opposites. Thus the difference between a beast and a human is only the privation of reason, which is nothing positive. Oddness is only the negation of divisibility into two equal parts. A prime number has nothing that a compound number lacks; since both [163] have the number one for a divisor, what is called a prime differs from a compound number only in having no other divisor than the number one. Nevertheless, we must admit that it is better to express opposing differences by positive terms whenever possible, because it helps us understand better the nature of the members of the classification. This is why the classification of substances into those that think and those that are extended is much better than the usual classification into material and immaterial, or corporeal and incorporeal substances, because the words "immaterial" and "incorporeal" give us only a very imperfect and confused idea of what can be made clearer by the words "thinking substance."[55]

Text 4:

[T]he two members are such that the more noble contains all that is in the less noble, and such that they differ only in that the more noble has something that the other does not. It is in this way that man and beast differ. For a beast is not purely only *animal*, which man is also. But man in addition has a rational soul which a beast does not. This is why I can say when comparing a beast to a man that a beast eats, nourishes itself, walks and acts by the impression of its

---

54 *LAP* I.5, *KM* V 148–149, *B* 42–43.
55 *LAP* II.15, *KM* V 242, *B* 124–125.

senses, but that a man acts by reason. And it would be an absurdity to reply to this comparison by objecting as does M. Mallet that one does not say of a beast anything [positive, non-privative] that does not [also] apply to a man, which is true. But it suffices in these sorts of comparisons, [to point out] that what one says of the more noble member [*qua* what makes it more noble] is not found in the other.[56]

These texts repeat the view standard at the time illustrated by the earlier texts of Buridan. The genus *animal* divides into two species *human* and *brute; human* is defined by the differentia *rational*, and *animal* by its privative negation. They also suggest how the standard account of privation is to be explained within the *Logic*'s wider ontology and metatheory.

The first text refers to negative modes. It suggests that the *Logic*'s ontology of ideas should be understood as recognizing the existence of both positive and negative modes. On this interpretation an idea defined in terms of negative modes is a "negative idea." A negative idea, whether a substantive or adjective, would be one such that its intentional content contains a negative mode. In more traditional terms, a negative mode is a privation. A negative idea is sometimes signified in spoken language by a word marked by a negative affix. This affix would be a privative negation in the grammar of spoken language. But the texts suggest that privative negation is also a well-defined operation in mental language. It is an operation by which negative ideas, which are a species of mental mode, are caused to be instantiated in the soul. This operation renders a new idea with new intentional content by replacing the positive mode in one idea's content with the corresponding privative mode.

The second text makes clear that it is possible to distinguish a species by a privation. Such a species is distinguished by the privation of a positive mode. For example, the idea *beasts* is defined by the property

---

[56] Arnauld 1776, Livre 5, Chapt. 1, pp. 351–352:

> Mais est-ce que M. Mallet ne fait pas qu'il se fait beaucoup de comparaisons, *inter excedens & excessum*, comme on parle dans l'École; c'est-à-dire, dont les deux membres sont tels, que le plus noble comprend tout ce qui est dans le moins noble, de sorte qu'ils ne diffèrent qu'en ce que le plus noble a quelque chose que n'a pas l'autre. C'est en cette manière que l'homme & la bête sont différents. Car la bête n'est purement qu'*animal*, ce qu'est aussi l'homme. Mais l'homme de plus a une âme raisonnable, ce que n'a pas la bête. C'est pourquoi je puis bien dire, en comparant la bête avec l'homme, qu'une bête mange, se nourrit, marche & agit par l'impression de ses sens, mais que l'homme agit par raison. Et ce seroit une absurdité de trouver à redire à cette comparaison, en objectant, comme fait M. Mallet, qu'on ne dit rien [positif] de la bête qui ne convienne à l'homme, ce qui est vrai. Mais il suffit, dans ces sortes de comparaisons, que ce qu'on dit du membre le plus noble [qua noble] ne se trouve pas dans l'autre.

Dominicy 1984, p. 45 comments on portion of this text.

of failing to instantiate the mode *having a mind*. A negative mode, then, seems to be true of an individual relative to a genus if, and only if it fails to instantiate the corresponding positive mode. Moreover, the text explains negative modes or "privations" by appeal to the *Logic*'s technical terms *comprehension* and *extension*. It explains that the comprehension of the idea *animal* does not contain the mode *having a mind* and that, on the other hand, the idea defined by *having a mind* is contained in the extension of *animal*. The idea *not having a mind* or *brute* is also contained in its extension of *animal* because anything that the idea signifies is also signified by the idea *animal*. Moreover, the comprehension of *brute* excludes the mode *thought*. Because a comprehension consists of modes, this exclusion is effected by including a negative mode in the comprehension of the negative idea. The example the authors give of a privative mode is the mode *unthinking* or *irrational*.

In this second text the authors employ the *Logic*'s technical vocabulary of comprehension and extension to describe privative negation. The fact that they do so indicates that privative negation, negative modes, and negative ideas are not merely unintentional vestiges of medieval theory. Rather, these negative concepts were intentionally included by the *Logic*'s authors as tools to fill out their general account of ideas, in which intentional content figures prominently. A privative substantive is one whose comprehension contains a negative mode, and a privative adjective is one that signifies a privative mode secondarily.

The third text provides further evidence that certain modes are negative in describing classification of one idea by the negated differentia of a second idea. The differentiae and their negations referred to here are clearly understood to be modes, for they are spoken of as being in an idea's comprehension, which by definition consists of modes. For example, the differentia of *beast* is the negative mode that is satisfied by a privation of the mode *rational*, and the differentia of *oddness* is the negative mode signified by the privation of the mode *divisible by two*. The text also makes the point that privative ideas—those defined by a differentia that is satisfied by the privation of a positive mode—are "imperfect" and "confused" relative to ideas defined in terms of positive modes. The authors here are probably using *confused* in the then contemporary sense (i.e. as the converse of determinate). While a positive idea specifies in its content a definite mode or set of modes that must be true of the things it signifies, a privative idea does not. A privative idea is regarded as "confused," in that any number of unspecified positive modes may be true of these things, and any number of ideas may signify them. The use of *confused* here is similar to the unspecified quantification over ideas that is contained in the truth-conditions of particular categorical propositions. A particular affirmative is true if the extension of some unspecified idea is included in the extensions of the subject and predicate. There are potentially many such ideas—their specification is "confused" in this sense.

Presumably, for any privative idea, there are some positive ideas, all of which would be included in the privative idea's extension, and these ideas signify only those things that the privative idea itself signifies.

In the third text, examples of privation are discussed in the context of species definition. The authors do not address the possibility that privative negation might also appear in the intentional content of non-species. These would be non-species because they would be "defined" in terms of the privation of accidental modes. Elsewhere the authors make a point of allowing classification by accidents. It would seem to follow that if one idea is defined by an accident—if it has a comprehension that includes an accidental mode—then a collateral idea could be defined in terms of the privation of this accident. The *Logic* does not discuss this sort of use of privative negation, which would fall outside the context of species definition. One historical factor speaks against imputing privative accidental ideas to the *Logic*. This is the fact that privations were traditionally understood in relation to the separation between what is and what is not "natural." Nature traditionally was explicated in terms of essential definitions, which are limited to species, and these are not defined by accidents. It is for this reason that privative negation was usually understood to negate a natural property of a species within a covering genus. The authors simply do not address whether their theory should be understood as accommodating negative ideas defined by the privation of accidents.

The fourth text is quoted here because it makes explicit that the authors accepted the view traceable to the Neoplatonists that privation is evaluative. A positive mode, it says, is more perfect and nobler than its privation. Thus, a positive idea is more perfect and nobler than one defined by privative negation.

Although privative negation in the *Logic* is only distantly related to Proclus' formal logic of intensifiers, the texts make clear that the *Logic*'s negation exhibits several formal properties traceable to its non-Boolean antecedents. Genera and species are arranged in a version of the tree of Porphyry, which has *being* as its maximal element. The structure of the genera and species, moreover, entails formal properties typical of privative negation, but which fail for modern complementation. These can be expressed in terms of the *is-more-noble-than* relation $\leq$. Let A, B, and C range over ideas; let $Sig(A)$ be the significance range of an idea A; let $\sim$ be privative negation understood as an operation on ideas; and let $\subseteq$ be the subset relation on significance ranges. Let B be a species defined by a positive mode that is immediate descendant of genus A. The various non-Boolean "laws" characteristic of gradable adjectives that were mentioned earlier with regard to Proclus' logic would continue to hold within the *Logic*'s tree structure. Among the laws that the authors themselves would have recognized, rendered into modern notation, are these:

$$A \leq B \leq \sim B; \; Sig(B) \cup Sig(\sim B) = Sig(A); \; and \; Sig(B) \cap Sig(\sim B) = \emptyset.$$

From the perspective of interpreting the *Logic*, what is important is that the *Logic*'s account of negation, although inconsistent with modern Boolean algebra, is well-defined and coherent.

Overview of Idea Structure

The general picture that emerges is that the structure of ideas in the *Logic* is that it shares features with the structure of concepts and species in medieval logic: ideas are formed by abstraction and restriction, species are organized in a tree hierarchy, and species are sometimes defined by privative negation. On the other hand, the *Logic*'s account differs from medieval logic in its repeated appeal to intentional content. Content-sets identify ideas and determine the containment relation on ideas. Content also determines an idea's significance range defined as the set of things it signifies. An idea's significance range in turn determines its extension. Sets of significance ranges and extensions are ordered by set-inclusion. Perhaps more clearly than in any earlier account, it follows that there is a many-one order-inverting mapping (an antitonic homomorphism) from ideas and content-sets to significance ranges and extensions.

The preceding principles define a good deal of structure. It must be stressed, however, that what structure there is differs from Boolean algebra and lattice theory. The *Logic*'s vocabulary comes from ontology and psychology, not mathematics. The "operations" it posits are understood as mechanisms of mental causation. In these operations the soul creates new ideas by manipulating intentional content. The theory is not mathematical. The authors make no use of letters or symbols. There are no formal definitions, equations, axioms, proofs, or laws defining the formal properties of orderings or operations typical of algebra. It is true that the orderings on content-sets, ideas, significance ranges, and extensions are essentially partial orderings, and that ideas and contents are homomorphic to significance ranges and extensions. The authors, however, do not remark on these facts because they did not develop the background theory or vocabulary to do so, and doing so was not their concern. Restriction and abstraction were not conceived, even by implication, as lattice operations. Abstraction is not a dyadic operation because it "operates" on a single idea only. Nor are ideas "closed" under either operation. Ideas are not mathematical abstractions, the existence of which is assured by principles like the axiom of comprehension in set theory. Their existence depends, rather, on various *ad hoc* acts of God and the soul. Although there is a highest genus, no texts suggest that the authors believed that among ideas, which include non-species, the soul or God has caused either a maximal or minimal idea. The authors never considered whether abstraction is distributive over restriction or vice versa. Finally, as the earlier discussion shows, the only notion of idea-negation the *Logic* envisages is privative negation, which, while possessing structural properties, these are not those of lattice complementation. The *Logic* is not a treatise on algebra. A more accurate interpretation is that it is an effort to explain the semantic foundations of language and logic in manner consistent with Descartes' dualism.

The next chapter directs attention up from the logic of terms to that of propositions, to the semantics of truth and validity, and to what medieval logicians called the theory of consequences.

References

Aristotle. 1994–2000. *Topics*, Web Atomics. Stevenson, Daniel C. (ed.), M.I.T., Boston.

Arnauld, Antoine. 1776. Nouvelle Défense du Nouveau Testament imprimée à Mons contre le Livre de M. Mallet. In: *Œuvres de Messire Antoine Arnauld Docteur de la Maison et Société de Sorbonne*, Paris, Sigismond d'Arnay.

Auroux, Sylvain. 1982. *L'Illuminismo Francese e la Tradizione Logica di Port-Royal*, Bologna, CLUEB.

Auroux, Sylvain. 1993. *La Logique des Idées*, Montréal, Paris, Bellarmin, Vrin.

Boethius. 1973. *Boethius: The Philosophical Tractates and the Consolation of Philosophy*, Cambridge, MA, Harvard University Press.

Buridan, John. 1985. *Jean Buridan's Logic: The Treatise on Supposition, the Treatise on Consequence*, Dordrecht, Reidel.

Buridan, John. 1989. Question on Aristotle's De Anima. In: Zupko, John Alexander (ed.) *John Buridan's Philosophy of Mind: An Edition and Translation of Book III of His "Questions on Aristotle's De Anima (Third Redaction)," with Commentary and Critical and Interpretative Essays*, Ph.D. Dissertation, Ann Arbor, MI, Cornell University. University Microfilm.

Buridan, John. 2001. *Summulae de dialectica*, New Haven, Yale University Press. Klima, Gyula (translator).

Conimbricenses. 1976 [reprint of 1607]. *Commentarii collegii conimbricensis e societate jesu in universam dialecticam aristotelis*, Hildesheim, Georg Olms Verlag.

Dominicy, Marc. 1984. *La Naissance de la Grammaire moderne*, Bruxelles, Pierre Mardaga.

Eustachio de S. Paulo. 1648. *Summa philosophiae quadripartita, de rebus dialecticis, ethicis, physicis et metaphysicis*, Cantabrigia [Cambridge], Rogerus Danielis.

Fonseca, Pedro da. 1964 [1575]. *Instituciões Dialécticas [Institutionum dialecticarum libri octo]*, Coimbra, Universidade de Coimbra.

Horn, Laurence R. 1989. *A Natural History of Negation*, Chicago, University of Chicago Press.

Jespersen, Otto. 1924. *The Philosophy of Grammar*, London, Allen and Unwin.

Joachim, H. H. (ed.). 1951. *Aristotle, the Nicomachean Ethics*, Oxford: Clarendon Press.

Lenzen, Wolfgang. 2004. Leibniz's Logic. In: Gabby, D. M. and John Woods (eds.) *Handbook of the History of Logic*, Amsterdam, Elsevier-North Holland.

Lovejoy, Arthur Onchen. 1936. *The Great Chain of Being: A Study in the History of Ideas*, Cambridge, Harvard University Press.

Martin, John N. 1995. Existence, Negation, and Abstraction in the Neoplatonic Hierarchy. *History and Philosophy of Logic*, 16, 169–196.

Martin, John N. 2001. Proclus and the Neoplatonic Syllogistic. *Journal of Philosophical Logic*, 30, 187–240.

Martin, John N. 2003. All Brutes Are Subhuman: Aristotle and Ockham on Privative Negation. *Synthese*, 134, 429–461.

Martin, John N. 2004. Ecthesis and Existence in the Syllogistic. In: *Themes in Neoplatonic and Aristotelian Logic*, Aldershot, Ashgate.

Martin, John N. 2016a. Privative Negation in *the Port Royal Logic. Review of Symbolic Logic*, 9, 23.

Martin, John N. 2016b. The Structure of Ideas in the Port Royal Logic. *The Journal of Applied Logic*, 19, 1–19.

Nadler, Steven M. 1989. *Arnauld and the Cartesian Philosophy of Ideas*, Manchester, Manchester University Press.

Pariente, Jean-Claude. 1985. *L'Analyse du Language à Port-Royal*, Paris, C.N.R.S. Éditions de Minuit.

Pariente, Jean-Claude. 1995. Les Termes singuliers dans la *Logique* de Port-Royal. In: Pariente, Jean-Claude (ed.) *Antoine Arnauld (1612–1694): Philosophe, Écrivain, Théologien*, Paris, Bibliothèque Mazarine.

Proclus. 1963. *The Elements of Theology*, Oxford, Clarendon Press. Dodds, E. R. (translator).

Proclus. 1968–1997. *Théologie Platonicienne*, Paris, Les Belles Lettres. Saffrey, H. D. and L. G. Westerink (translators).

Proclus. 1987. *Proclus' Commentary on Plato's Parmenides*, Princeton, NJ, Princeton University of Press. Morrow, Glenn R. and John M. Dillon (translators).

Raconis, C. F. d'Abra de. 1651. *Tertia pars philosophiae seu physicae, quarta pars philosophiae seu metaphysicae. Totius philosophiae, hoc est logicae, moralis, physicae et metaphysicae, brevis et accurata, facilique et clara methodo disposita tractatio*, Lugdunum [Lyon], Irenaeus Barlet.

Smith, Robin. 1982. What Is Aristotelian Ecthesis? *History and Philosophy of Logic*, 3, 113–127.

Wahl, Russell. 2008. Port Royal: The Stirrings of Modernity. In: Gabbay, Dov M. and John Woods (eds.) *Handbook of the History of Logic: Mediaeval and Renaissance Logic*, Amsterdam, Elsevier—North Holland.

William of Ockham. 1974 [ca. 1323]. *Ockham's Theory of Terms: Part I of the Summa Logicae*, Notre Dame, IN, University of Notre Dame.

William of Ockham. 1980. *Ockham's Theory of Propositions (Part II of Summa Logicae)*, Notre Dame, IN, Notre Dame University Press.

4 The Semantics of Propositions. Truth and Consequences

Overview

The early portions of the *Logic*, Parts I and II, address the "logic of terms," setting forth its account of the ontology, psychology, and semantics of the terms in mental language. The final portion in Part IV concerns method, or what today we would call the "semantics of discourse" or pragmatics. The middle portions, which include the final sections of Part II and the entirety of Part III, concern the "logic of propositions." It is here that the authors set out their account of the truth-conditions for categorical propositions as well as the theory of inference for syllogistic arguments and some of its elementary extensions. This chapter will accordingly assume that the reader is familiar with the basics of the traditional theory of the syllogism and with the notation of standard first-order logic.[1] The *Logic* devotes the last sections of Part III to informal fallacies and to various misuses of intentional content. Both the technical discussion of the syllogistic and the informal logic associated with fallacies are largely unoriginal and, from the perspective of modern logic, trivial. An exception is the characterization of the syllogistic's valid moods, first by a set of six rules and later by what it calls "the containment principle." Although the sections on fallacies make many sensible points about the use of language, they fall into what today would be called informal logic and are of little theoretical interest. In the present study they will be touched on only in passing.

---

1 The discussion in this and later chapters assumes a familiarity with the elementary vocabulary and results of the syllogistic. Because this book is intended to be accessible to historians of philosophy and modern logicians who, by and large, manage to avoid instruction in the technicalities of the syllogism, the Appendix, in the section on Chapter 4, contains a short primer on the relevant parts of syllogistic theory. A syllogism and its parts are defined there and the valid moods explained. Also sketched is the medieval technique of reducing the valid moods to the fundamental syllogisms called *Barbara* and *Celarent*.

Perhaps the most significant treatment of the book from both a historical and theoretical stance is the section at the end of Part II on the truth-conditions for categorical propositions. Its historical interest lies in the fact that it is an abstracted version of medieval supposition theory applied to the analysis of truth. Truth is there defined in terms of what the *Logic* calls a "universal term," a concept abstracted from the medieval distributive supposition. The section's theoretical interest lies in the fact that the concept of universal term, called in later logic a distributive term, is defined directly in terms of the referential properties of terms. This analysis makes it possible to define truth in terms of distribution in a non-circular way. Formally, the resulting truth-conditions are recursively sound.

The characterization of the valid moods by the so-called containment principle is of interest because, in effect, it makes appeal, in effect, to the modern distinction between conservative and non-conservative quantifiers from general quantification theory.

Part II contains a short discussion of the alethic modalities, which are explained very briefly in terms of the grammatical position of modal adverbs and several basic inference rules.

It will be appropriate to summarize briefly here the topics of the *Logic*'s central sections that will not be discussed further in this study. These are concentrated in the sections of Part II on "parts of speech" and in the final sections of Part III on fallacies and usage. The early sections of Part II contain a rather unsystematic discussion of syntax and semantics of various simple parts of speech. Examples of term types are drawn from both ordinary speech and from the stylized syntax of the syllogistic and its extensions. The types of expression discussed include nouns, pronouns, and verbs (II.1); the four categorical propositions (II.3); gappings (II.4–5); false ideas (II.7); "exclusives" (propositions formulated in terms of *only*, II.10.1); "exceptives" (propositions formulated in terms of *except*, II.10.2); the alethic modalities (II.8); comparative adjectives (II.10.3); various compound sentences (II.9); and nominal definitions (II.16). The first sections of Part III concern argument types that can be stated in the syllogistic and its extensions. These include categorical syllogisms (III.1–10); complex and compound syllogisms (III.11–13, 15–16); and some simple argument forms sentential logic including conjunction introduction and elimination, disjunctive syllogism, *modus ponens, modus tollens*, and proof by cases (III.12, 13, 16). The remainder of Part III treats a series of traditional topics: enthymemes (III.14); "topics" (methods for extending an incomplete syllogism to prove a desired conclusion, III.17–18); sophisms; and fallacies including begging the question, equivocation, and errors of composition and division (III.19–20).

Truth-Conditions[2]

In the final sections of Part II, Arnauld and Nicole advance a definition of truth for categorical propositions, offering the first historical instance of truth defined in non-circular manner in terms of distributive term. The distributive properties of categorical propositions had been studied in logic since they were first broached by Aristotle. Aristotle, for example, knew that a true universal affirmative has a distributive subject and non-distributive predicate, and it was a standard doctrine in medieval logic that the subject of a universal affirmative has distributive supposition while its predicate has "merely confused" supposition. Although such rules of thumb provide necessary and sufficient conditions for a proposition's truth, these equivalences were not understood as statements of non-circular truth-conditions. Either distribution was not understood as a semantic concept at all, or if it was, it was explained in terms of entailments, which were in turn explained in terms of truth. A circle then results if truth is defined in terms of distribution. If distribution were defined in terms of valid entailments and valid entailment in terms of truth, a definition of truth in terms of distribution would be circular. What is novel in the *Logic* is that it abstracts to a definition of distribution independent of entailment and truth. The result is that distribution can be used in a statement of non-circular truth-conditions.

The issues that arise in the definition of truth in terms of distribution are partly historical and partly technical. There are two components to the relevant historical considerations. In the Middle Ages there was a proto-syntactic sense of distribution distinct from what we would recognize as a semantic concept. This syntactic sense was employed in "tests" for the validity of syllogistic moods. A version of this syntactic technique is described in the *Logic* and discussed below. Distributive term in a semantic sense, however, also has roots in the medieval logic, in the notion of distributive supposition. In medieval theory, distributive supposition, in the semantic sense, was usually explained by reference to so-called entailments of "ascent" and "descent." What is relevant to this discussion is that these entailments depended conceptually on the concept of truth. A valid entailment is one that preserves truth. Hence, distributive supposition explained in terms of entailment is conceptually dependent on the concept of truth. In other words, if distribution were defined in terms of valid entailments, and valid entailments in terms of truth, distribution could not be defined in terms of truth without circularity. What the

---

[2] The sections below on the truth-conditions of categorical propositions are based on *Martin 2013* and *Martin 2016*.

authors of the *Logic* gleaned was that it is possible to abstract from medieval formulation to a *definiens* of distributive term that referred directly to the referential properties of terms without an appeal to the notion of truth. It is then possible to state truth-conditions for categorical proposition in terms of distribution.[3]

The Syntactic Sense of Distribution and Syntactic Rules for the Syllogistic

In modern logic, a clear distinction is drawn between syntax on the one hand and semantics on the other. In Morris' definition, syntax is the study of the relation of signs to signs, and semantics the study of the relation of signs to both signs and the world.[4] In modern logic, a "syntactic" set is defined either by a finite list of syntactic entities or by an inductive definition that closes previously defined syntactic sets under syntactic rules. Syntactic sets in this sense include sets of expressions in formal grammar defined in terms of formation rules and sets of theorem and deductions in proof theory defined in terms of inference rules. Syntactic sets in grammar, moreover, are generally decidable, and are frequently so in proof theory. Modern semantics, on the other hand, often assumes the full resources of set theory and more. It postulates the existence of sets constructed from other sets, and sometimes the existence of sets that contain primitive non-set theoretic entities. Sometimes sets in semantics are defined by appeal to the principle of comprehension (a set exists if it can be defined by an open sentence) rather than by induction, and sets of this sort are often undecidable. Much of this theory is irrelevant to the *Logic*.

In pre-19th-century logic, the distinction between syntax and semantics was muddled at best. This confusion affects the concept of distribution, which was historically ambiguous between a syntactic and semantic sense. The ambiguity dates to its first technical use by Aristotle. The semantic sense is found in the *De Interpretatione*, where Aristotle distinguishes a term that "stands for many," which he calls *universal*, from a term that "stands for a particular"—in later logic the terms *distributive* and *universal* were used interchangeably. This distinction here would

---

3 Jean-Claude Pariente has argued that the *Logic*'s theory of truth was in fact a rejection of medieval supposition theory. Although he is correct that the Cartesian notion of distributive terms is not the same as that of medieval distributive supposition, he does not remark on the fact that it is nevertheless an abstraction from it and that this abstraction has the theoretical motivation of obviating any circularity in a definition of truth in terms of distributive term. See *Pariente 1985*, pp. 41–42.
4 Prior 1962.

today be regarded as semantic because it concerns the relation of a sign to its referent:[5]

> I call universal [*catholou*] that which is by its nature predicated of a number of things, and particular that which is not; man, for instance, is a universal, Callias a particular.

In this passage a universal term appears to be what later logicians referred to as a general term or common noun, and the *Logic* later retains this usage in its account of grammar where it classifies some ideas as general or universal.[6]

In the same paragraph, however, Aristotle goes on to use universal in what we would regard as a syntactic sense. He characterizes a universal proposition as one that states "universally of a universal" (*catholou epi tou catholou*). In other words, a term is called universal because of its place in the syntax of the proposition in which it occurs:[7]

> what I mean by "stating universally of a universal" are "every man is white" and "no man is white."

A term is universal due to its position within a categorical proposition: it is universal if it occurs as the proposition's subject term and is modified by *every* or *no*. Indeed, in the Middle Ages and for centuries afterward, students learning syllogisms memorized a rule defining distributive term by its position within its containing proposition: the subject of a universal proposition is distributed but not of a particular; the predicate of a negative proposition is distributed but not of an affirmative.

In the *Logic*, Arnauld and Nicole retain this syntactic sense of distributive or, as they prefer to call it, universal term. Formulations of this syntactic understanding occur at various points throughout the text: the subject of a universal affirmative is general, while that of a particular is a particular;[8] the subject of an affirmative is universal;[9] the predicate of an affirmative proposition is not universal;[10] the predicate of a negative proposition is universal;[11] and the subject of a particular negative is not universal.[12] These descriptions are syntactic because the defining distinctions, namely affirmative and negative, and universal and particular

---

5 17a40, *Aristotle 1963*, Ackrill trans.
6 *LAP* I.6, *KM* V 145, *B* 39.
7 17b5, *Aristotle 1963*, Ackrill trans.
8 *LAP* II.3, *KM* V 198–199, *B* 83.
9 *LAP* II.7, *KM* V 248, *B* 130, Axiom 1.
10 *LAP* II.7, *KM* V 249, *B* 130, Axiom 4.
11 *LAP* II.8, *KM* V 251–252, *B* 133, Axiom 5, remark, and Axiom 6.
12 *LAP* II.8, *KM* V 252, *B* 133, Axiom 6, remark.

propositions themselves have syntactic definitions in terms of the syntactic positions of terms, quantifiers, the copula, and negative markers. It should be noted that the concept of universal term in this syntactic sense is not simply that of a common noun, as it appears to be in the preceding text from *De Interpretatione*, because a common noun can grammatically occupy both the subject and predicate position of any categorical proposition.

The authors of the *Logic* complicate the situation by defining a semantic distinction between universal and particular propositions by appeal to a semantic sense of universal terms:[13]

> The universality or particularity of a proposition depends on whether the subject is taken universally or particularly.
>
> Since the attribute of an affirmative proposition never has a larger extension than the subject, it is always regarded as taken particularly, because it is only accidental if it is sometimes taken generally.
>
> The attribute of a negative proposition is always taken generally.

In this passage a universal term is one that is "taken universally," and a particular term is one that is "taken particularly." Exactly what is meant by these expressions, and why a term taken universally is not the same as a common noun is a large topic, one which is addressed in the following discussion. In general, however, it is unsurprising that the same concept might have both a syntactic and semantic analysis. In modern metatheory, for example, entailment and consistency each have coextensive syntactic and semantic definitions. We shall see that a similar correspondence holds between the syntactic sense of distributive term and one of its semantic definitions. First, however, it is necessary to distinguish more carefully and set to one side the syntactic sense of distribution as it occurs in the *Logic*.

The *Logic* has a special use for a syntactic sense of distributive term. It is employed as part of what is essentially a syntactic characterization of the valid syllogistic moods. The characterization consists of a set of syntactic rules that identify the valid moods. The notion of distributive term occurs in two of these six rules. Prior to the statement of the rules, the *Logic* introduces a series of syntactic distinctions in a definitional order. The terms include, in order, *universal* and *particular proposition; affirmative* and *negative proposition; syllogism; major premise, minor premise*, and *conclusion*; and *major, middle*, and *minor term*. The precise definitions need not be repeated here.[14] It is sufficient to observe that they are syntactic because they are defined in terms of word order and

---

13 *LAP* III.3, *KM* V 258, *B* 139.
14 Readers are referred to the Appendix for details.

position. A syntactic sense of *distributive term* is defined later in this series: a distributive term is the subject of universal propositions or the predicate of negative propositions; all other terms are non-distributive.

The *Logic*'s six "general" rules for the valid syllogistic moods became well-known and have been repeated in Aristotelian logic texts since. To modern readers who are sensitive to the difference between syntax and semantics, and to students who have employed them in exercises, the rules are understood syntactically:[15]

> Rule 1. *The middle term cannot be taken particularly twice, but must be taken universally once.*
> Rule 2. *The terms of the conclusion cannot be taken more universally in the conclusion than in the premises.*
> Rule 3. *No conclusion can be drawn from two negative propositions.*
> Rule 4. *A negative conclusion cannot be proved from two affirmative propositions.*
> Rule 5. *The conclusion always follows the weaker part. That is, if one of the two propositions is negative, the conclusion must be negative; if one of them is particular, it must be particular.*
> Rule 6. *Nothing follows from two particular propositions.*

The first two rules employ the notion of distributive (universal) term, which is identified syntactically by its position as subject or predicate in the various categorical propositions.

Understood syntactically, the rule set provides a syntactic characterization of the valid syllogisms in the following sense: a mood is valid if, and only if, it does not violate any rule in the set. Moreover, applying the test is straightforward—there is a straightforward effective process that consists of inspecting a syllogism's syntactic form to determine whether it violates any of the six rules. The rule set, in short, provides a decision procedure for determining whether a mood is valid.

The authors clearly believe that the rules characterize the valid moods because they argue for a kind of completeness. They present the rules one by one in Book III, and for each they argue that a syllogism that violates the rule is invalid. Thus, if a syllogism is valid, it does not violate a rule. The rules capture all the valid moods. The converse (soundness)—that every syllogism that does not violate a rule is valid—also holds, although the authors do not argue for it. In principle, however, it is possible review each of the 256 possible moods and show that any one that is invalid violates a rule, say by Venn diagrams or examples. Unfortunately, from the perspective of modern logic, the *Logic*'s own efforts to show that a syllogism is invalid if it violates a rule is circular because it identifies an

---

15 *LAP* III.3, *KM* V 258–263, *B* 138–142.

argument as invalid by the syntactic fact that it violates a rule. It offers no semantic account of a syllogism's validity independent of its syntax.

The authors identify the valid moods one by one in Part III. The approach is to review in order the various moods as they occur in the four figures. They list, for each figure, the moods that are valid, and they then rule out others as invalid. The justifications offered, however, are entirely syntactic. The justification consists of the applications of rules to a candidate mood. The rules employed are the six general rules and various specific rules that follow in that figure from the six general rules. They do not attempt to first identity the valid moods semantically and then show that every mood that violates a rule is semantically invalid or, equivalently, that every semantically valid mood does not violate any of the six rules. The authors simply declare that a set of moods is valid in that figure, presumably because it is easy to check that the arguments do not violate any of the six general syntactic rules. They then rule out other moods as invalid because they violate a rule. In general, the authors do not exhibit an appreciation of the modern concern that syntactic accounts of validity should be supported by an independent semantic account.

It should also be remarked that the explicit list of valid moods the authors provide is incomplete. Their process is to divide the possible moods in the first, third, and fourth figures according to whether the mood's premises are all positive, and those in the second figure according to whether its premises are all universal. These divisions, however, are not exhaustive. They omit some cases. As a result, the authors fail to list several valid moods: EAO and AAI in the first figure, AEO and EAO in the second, and AEO in the third. A possible reason for their not listing these particular moods is that they are what are called "indirect." An indirect mood is one that is "reducible" to another valid mood in the same figure by the application of conversion rules to the syllogism's conclusion. The method of reduction is described in the Appendix.

It should also be pointed out that the set of six general rules is not new to the *Port Royal Logic*. Rules of this sort were a part of a long tradition for identifying the valid moods, a tradition that includes the various well-known mnemonic tests found in medieval logic textbooks.[16] Rules 3–6 and similar rules had been cited in treatises since ancient times. Rules 1 and 2, which mention distribution, were called "process rules" in later Aristotelian logic. The distinct group of the *Logic*'s six rules for capturing the valid moods is found in earlier 16th-century logic texts.[17]

---

16 See, for example, *William of Sherwood 1966, Introduction to Logic*, p. 66; Peter of Spain, *Peter of Spain 2014, Tractatus* IV.13, p. 190, and *de Rijk 1962–1967*, p. 52; *John Buridan 2001, Summulae* 5.2.2, p. 320.
17 For example, for Rules 3–7, *William of Sherwood 1966, Introduction to Logic*, III.ix, p. 67; *Peter of Spain 2014, Tractatus*, IV.4, p. 174, and *de Rijk 1962–1967*, p. 45; *John Buridan 2001, Summulae* 5.1.8, pp. 312–313; *Fonseca 1964 [1575], Institytionum*

Too much, however, can be made of these syntactic points. In premodern logic there simply did not exist a clear notion of the difference between syntax and semantics, or of the modern notion of decision procedure as a calculable characteristic function of a set. Though earlier logicians rightly regarded the rules as a simple test for the valid syllogisms, it would be an anachronism to think that the authors understood their rules to define an effective syntactic decision procedure for the chain of valid categorical arguments conforming to the twenty-four valid moods.[18] Nevertheless, as an elegant presentation of the syllogistic, the rules clearly contributed to the *Logic*'s historical influence. They are, no doubt, partly responsible for the *Logic*'s reputation as step in the direction of formal logic. Kneale and Kneale, for example, appraise the rules in this way:[19]

> Their quasi-mathematical treatment of these subjects may indeed be the first of its kind, as it is certainly the course from which later writers of logical manuals derive the details of their formal theory, e.g. the determination of the valid moods of the syllogism and their proofs of the special rules of the various figures . . . the general conception of logic which they expounded in this book was widely accepted and continued to dominate the treatment of logic by most philosophers of the next 200 years.

Taking the *Logic*'s proto-syntactic formulation one step further, Leibniz reformulated the six rules symbolically and proved that they characterize the valid moods in a way suggestive of modern formal methods.[20] It is

---

dialecticarum, Liber VI, Caput 18, p. 382. For Rules 1 and 2 see *Toletus 1580, In Lib I posteriorum analyticorum*, Cap XIX, p. 202; and *Fonseca 1964 [1575], Institytionum dialecticarum* VI, Caput 20, p. 386. All six rules are presented as a group in Eustachio de San Paulo's summary of scholastic philosophy, which was read by Descartes and praised for its clarity. *Eustachio de S. Paulo 1648, Summa philosophiae quadripartita, Logia*, III.2.I, p. 117.

18 A generalized sense of *syntactic derivability within the syllogistic* may be defined as follows: $P_1, \ldots, P_n \vdash Q$ iff there are $R_1, \ldots, R_m$ such that $R_m = Q$ and for each $i \leq m$, either $R_i \in \{P_1, \ldots, P_n\}$ or there is a valid syllogism $R_j R_k \vdash R_i$ such that $j, k < i$.
19 *Kneale and Kneale 1962*, p. 320.
20 Leibniz' list contains the same rules but divides the *Logic*'s fifth rule into two. See *Lenzen 1990*, pp. 29–59. It should be remarked that though Leibniz presents the rule set as an "axiomatization," neither his account nor that of the *Logic* is, strictly speaking, an axiomatization of the valid moods in the modern sense. An axiom system characterizes the set of theorems as an inductive set, i.e. as a set defined as the closure of a set of basic elements (construction rules) under a set of construction rules (rules of inference). The *Logic*'s rules provide a decision procedure, not an axiomatization. The student's traditional mnemonic poems, on the other hand, in which they memorize the "names" and forms of the valid moods are, theoretically, equally as effective in identifying the 24 valid moods, and in a way are more interesting because, as explained in the Appendix,

fair to conclude that in places the *Logic* made use of *distributive term* in a syntactic sense, in which it has a role in what was in effect a decision procedure for the valid moods. Although the *Logic* does not attempt to do so, it is well-known that the syntactic characterization of the valid moods is sound and complete for a standard interpretation of the syllogistic, in which terms in categorical propositions assert inclusion and exclusion relations on elements of a Boolean algebra.[21]

Distributive Supposition in Medieval Semantics

The *Logic*'s semantic sense of distribution derives from medieval supposition theory. Supposition became a standard part of the "logic of terms" in the 13th century. Although logicians of the period differed on details, the elements that influence the *Logic* were widely taught. The theory turns on two semantic concepts: signification and supposition. Signification, which was introduced in Chapter 1, corresponds to the modern concept of reference. Although the explanation of signification was disputed, there was agreement on several points. Most concurred that a term could signify entities that were possible but not actual.[22] Most also agreed that the mechanism that fixes signification for mental terms—whether causation, abstraction, or objective being—is a natural process, one not subject to convention. They also held that signification is a precondition for various contextually dependent features of ordinary speech, most notably supposition.

Supposition is contextually dependent reference. The standard view was that though a term has a fixed signification, exactly which of its *significata* it stands or "supposits" for on a given occasion of use varies according to features of the speech context. The contextual parameters affecting reference include the term's grammatical role, the time and place of the speech act, the participants, and the participants' intentions. The theoretical role of supposition theory was to catalogue the various ways in which context limits or alters what is signified. A list of these various ways that context determines reference became more or less standard. The concept of distributive term in later logic arises from one of the supposition types found in this catalog.

---

their "names" encode how to "reduce" the valid moods to *Barbara* and *Celarent* via four "inference" rules. This sort of "reduction" is easily converted into a proof in the modern sense.
21 See *Smiley 1973*, *Corcoran 1972*, and *Martin 1997*.
22 See the discussion of the alethic modalities below. Arnauld himself denied the existence of possible objects. See *Arnauld 2003*, "Arnauld to Leibniz," May 13, 1686, VI, pp. 31–32.

The classificatory tree of supposition first divides into the subtypes personal and material supposition. A term in personal supposition stands for entities outside the mind, but a term in material supposition stands for the term itself understood as a mental act. Personal supposition is divided into discrete and common supposition. A term having discrete supposition "stands for" a single individual; a term in common supposition "stands for" many things.

These varieties of supposition are determined by contextual features. For example, in *that man is an animal* the grammatical marker *that*, which modifies *man*, determines that *man* has discrete supposition, but in *every man is an animal* the marker *every* determines that *man* has common supposition. In *a man is an animal* the predicate determines that *man* has personal supposition, but in *man is a species* that it has material supposition.

The particular variety of supposition relevant to the *Logic*'s truth theory is a subspecies of common supposition distinguished by a term's "quantity." A term's quantity is marked by the modifiers *every* and *some*, which today we call quantifiers. A term modified by *every* was said to have distributive common supposition, and one modified by *some* was said to have non-distributive common supposition.

Quantification is, of course, tricky to explain. The explanation employed by medieval logicians appealed to entailment. A proposition containing a term modified by *every* was thought to entail—or, in the jargon of the day, "descend to"—all singular instances of that proposition for that term. For example, a singular instance of *every man is mortal*, in which the subject man has common supposition, is *Socrates is a mortal*, in which the general subject *man* is replaced by the proper name *Socrates*. They also said that the universal affirmative descends to the long conjunction of conjuncts consisting of singular instances (singular propositions) naming each man individually. If *Socrates, Plato, ...* were the list of proper names of all individual men, *every man is mortal* would descend to *Socrates is mortal and Plato is mortal and....* Conversely, this long conjunction was said to entail or "ascend to" the proposition itself. With some important qualifications to be explained shortly, a proposition containing a term modified by *some* was held to entail or descend to at least one singular instance of that proposition for that term or, equivalently in their view, to the long disjunction made up of all its singular instances. It does so because the disjunction says, in effect, that at least one of these instances is true. Conversely, this disjunction was held to entail or ascend to the proposition itself.

A valid entailment was universally acknowledged to be defined in terms of truth because a valid consequence is one that preserves truth. If distributive supposition is defined in terms of descent and ascent, ascent and descent in terms of validity, and validity in terms of truth, distributive supposition would ultimately be defined in terms of truth. A definition of truth in terms of distributive supposition would then be circular.

The distinction between distributive and non-distributive supposition was also held to apply to the predicates of categorical propositions because they too support valid descents and ascents to conjunctions and disjunctions of instances. The details of the theory, however, quickly become technical because the inferences themselves are complex. Nevertheless, it is from these entailments that the Cartesians abstracted their notion of distributive term.

For the moment it is sufficient to restrict attention to the four primary categorical forms. Let S represent a proposition's subject term and P its predicate. Let two terms that occur in the same proposition be called *collateral*. The entailments in question presuppose that the actual referents (*supposita*) of any term in a true proposition are named individually. That is, it is assumed that for any subject term S, there is an associated series of singular terms (proper names) $s_1, \ldots, s_n$, usually assumed to be finite in number. These terms stand for all of the entities that S supposits for. Likewise it is assumed that for any predicate P there is an associated series of singular terms $p_1, \ldots, p_m$ that name all the objects that P supposits for. Let i be a variable for subscripts that ranges over $\{1, \ldots, n\}$, where n is the number of a subject term's instances, and j a variable that ranges over $\{1, \ldots, m\}$, where m is the number of a predicate term's instances. An instance of a proposition for a term is then defined in terms of these associated names. In the following definitions, an instance of a proposition for a term is a singular proposition in which an associated singular term is the subject and in which the term in question is the predicate.

Definitions

Relative to a subject term S and predicate term P,
a *positive instance of S for P* is any proposition s_i *is P*;
a *negative instance of S for P* is any proposition s_i *is not P*;
a *positive instance of P for S* is any proposition *S is* p_j;
a *negative instance of P for S* is any proposition *S is not* p_j.
A *conjunctive instance of a term* is the conjunction of that term's instances for its collateral term, and a *disjunctive instantiation* is the disjunction of these instances.

A term may then be said to have distributive supposition if it entails its conjunctive instances. John Buridan's explanation is typical:[23]

> Distributive supposition is that in accordance with which from a common term any of its supposita can be inferred separately, or even

---

23 *John Buridan 2001, Summulae* 4.3.6, p. 264.

all of them at once conjunctively, in terms of a conjunctive proposition. For example, from "Every man runs" it follows that therefore "Socrates runs," . . . therefore "Socrates runs and Plato runs . . ." and so on for the rest.
. . .
distributive supposition differs from the other suppositions, for in its case a common term implies any of its singulars separately, while the other suppositions do not. Therefore, if the proposition is true, it has to be true for any suppositum, which is not required in the other cases of supposition.

If a term is used in distributive supposition the proposition entails ("descends to") all the term's immediate instances. Equivalently, it entails their conjunction. Let *iff* abbreviate *if and only if*.

> **Definition.** Relative to a categorical proposition, a term is used in *distributive* supposition iff the proposition entails all of the term's instances for its collateral term or, equivalently, iff it entails their conjunction.

By this criterion the four terms that count as distributive are the subject of the universal affirmative, the subject and predicate of the universal negative, and the predicate of the particular negative. For the purpose of later comparison, it is helpful to display here the relevant conjunctive entailments. Let $\models$ represent syllogistic entailment. That is, $P \models Q$ means the argument from P to Q is valid; $\dashv$ is the converse relation:[24]

---

24 The syllogistic model theory in which $\models$ is defined is stated formally below. For present purposes, a singular term is to be understood as a special case of a general term or common noun (see *LAP* II.3, *KM* V 199, *B* 84): a singular term is a general term that happens to supposit for a unique actual object. Thus, a singular term is understood below as a term that stands for a unit set. A universal affirmative with a singular term as subject is then understood as a special case of a universal affirmative, one in which the quantifier *every* is not explicitly expressed—such is the way it is understood in the *Logic*. It will follow from the semantics that a universal affirmative with a singular term as subject and a common noun as predicate is true iff the unique object in the set that is the referent of the subject is an element of the set that is the referent of the predicate. Further, a proposition with either a singular term or a common noun as subject and a singular term as predicate is true iff the sets referred to by both terms contain one and the same individual. For perspicuity when the two terms are both singular, we shall use = to represent the copula. The connectives ∧ and ∨ here should be understood as representing conjunction and disjunction and as conforming to the truth-conditions described by the standard truth-tables, which also describe the common medieval understanding of conjunction and disjunction.

Theorem

every S is P	⊣ ⊢	s_1 is P $\wedge$ ... $\wedge$ s_n is P
no S is P	⊣ ⊢	s_1 is not P $\wedge$ ... $\wedge$ s_n is not P
no S is P	⊣ ⊢	no S is not p_1 $\wedge$ ... $\wedge$ no S is not p_m
some S is not P	⊢	some S is not p_1 $\wedge$ ... $\wedge$ some S is not p_m

Note that the converse of the last entailment fails:

some S is not p_1 $\wedge$ ... $\wedge$ some S is not p_m ⊭ some S is not P

If it were not for the failure of this last entailment, a distributive term could have been explained as one in which its proposition is analytically equivalent to the conjunction of instances derived by instantiating that term.

The case of non-distributive supposition is similar. It can almost but not quite be explained by saying that its proposition is equivalent to the disjunction of instances derived by instantiating that term. To capture this idea at least in part, non-distributive supposition is traditionally divided into two subtypes: determinate and "merely confused." A term has determinate supposition if the proposition entails at least one of the term's instances. The criterion is also formulated in terms of disjunction. A term has determinate supposition if the proposition entails the disjunction of all the term's instances. The entailments also hold in the converse direction. Buridan formulates the distinction as follows:[25]

> I should say that in determinate supposition the proposition need not be true for one suppositum only, indeed, sometimes it is true for any suppositum. But it is necessary and sufficient that it should be true for one. So we have to note immediately that there are two conditions for the determinate supposition of some common term. The first is that from any suppositum of that term it is possible to infer the common term, the other parts of the proposition remaining unchanged. For example, since, in "A man runs," the term "man" supposits determinately, it follows that "Socrates runs; therefore, a man runs," "Plato runs; therefore, a man runs," and so on for any singular contained under the term "man." The second condition is that from a common term suppositing in this manner all singulars can be inferred disjunctively, by a disjunctive proposition. For

---

25 *John Buridan* 2001, *Summulae* 4.3.5, pp. 262–263.

example, "A man runs; therefore, Socrates runs, or Plato runs or John runs . . ." and so on for the rest.

Definition. A term is used in *determinate* supposition iff the proposition entails and is entailed by at least one of the term's instances for its collateral term or, equivalently, iff it entails and is entailed by the disjunction of those instances.

By this criterion the three terms that count as distributive are the subject and predicate of the particular affirmative and the subject of a negative particular. Again it is helpful to display the relevant entailments.

Theorem

some S is P ⊣⊢ s_1 is P ∨ ... ∨ s_n is P
some S is P ⊣⊢ some S is p_1 ∨ ... ∨ some S is p_m
some S is not P ⊣⊢ s_1 is not P ∨ ... ∨ s_n is not P

The second variety of non-distributive supposition is called *confused non-distributive supposition* or, briefly, *merely confused* (*confusus tantum*) *supposition*. As Buridan explains, its logical relation to its instances is more complicated than either distributive or determinate supposition:[26]

> But merely confused supposition is that in accordance with which none of the singulars follows separately while retaining the other parts of the proposition, and neither do the singulars follow disjunctively, in terms of a disjunctive proposition, although perhaps they do follow by a proposition with a disjunct term.
> . . . in the case of confused supposition the singulars cannot be inferred from the common term by means of a disjunctive proposition, whereas this can correctly be done with determinate supposition. For example, in the proposition "Every man is an animal" the term "animal" has merely confused supposition and the inference "Every man is an animal; therefore every man is this animal or every man is that animal . . ." (and so on for the rest) is not valid, for the antecedent is true and all the consequents are false.

Because there are only eight term positions in the four categorical propositions and seven have already been determined to have either distributive or determinate supposition, there is only one term that is neither. It

---

26 *John Buridan* 2001, *Summulae* 4.3.6, p. 264.

124   *The Semantics of Propositions*

is the predicate of the universal affirmative. Only this could be merely confused, and the category could simply be defined by negation:

> **Definition.** A term has *merely confused* supposition iff it has neither distributive nor determinate supposition.

The tradition, however, holds that merely confused supposition is also definable by characteristic descent and ascent entailments. The relevant entailment is to an instance that has what Buridan calls a "disjunctive predicate." Consider the universal affirmative *every man is an animal*. Let the names of the various individual animals be, as medieval logicians would say, *this animal, that animal*.... It is clear that *every man is an animal* does not entail *every man is this animal and every man is that animal*, and so forth. Thus, *animal* does not have distributive supposition. Nor does it have determinate supposition because the proposition does not entail the disjunction of its instances: *every man is an animal* does not entail *every man is this animal, or every man is that animal*, and so forth. What does follow is that what Buridan calls a "disjunctive predicate" is true of the actual individuals that the subject supposits for.

To construct this predicate, observe that the proposition *every man is an animal* may be reformulated in a logically equivalent way as *every man is such that he is some animal*. The anaphoric syntax of the reformulation is similar to that of the bound variable syntax of the translation into first-order logic of a universal affirmative:[27]

$$\forall x (Sx \rightarrow Px)$$

Here, although *S*, which translates *man*, is rightly rendered as syntactically simple, the predicate *P* represents the complex expression *some animal*. It is this complex that is translated by Buridan's disjunctive predicate. The relevant semantic intuition is that the open sentence *x is some animal* is satisfied iff *animal* is true of at least one individual that it actually supposits for. That is, *x is some animal* is equivalent to the disjunction *x is a_1* $\vee \ldots \vee$ *x is a_n*, where $a_1, \ldots, a_n$ name all the actual animals. Since *x* ranges over individuals, the relevant sense of the copula is identity. More generally, if $p_1, \ldots, p_n$ name the individuals in the (model

---

27 As explained in Chapter 6, in the special case of contingent propositions the truth-conditions of an affirmative proposition should also contain a clause that requires the subject term to be "non-empty," i.e., that it refer to something existing in the domain of quantification. In that case the first-order representations of their truth-conditions should contain the additional conjunct $\exists x Sx$. The issues raised by contingency and existential presupposition are discussed in detail in Chapter 6.

theoretic) extension of P, then the universal affirmative $\forall x(Sx \to Px)$ is equivalent to the first-order formula:

$$\forall x\big(Sx \to (x = p_1 \vee \ldots x = p_m)\big)$$

Using naïve set theory, it is even possible to recast this in a syntax more like that of Buridan:

$$\forall x(Sx \to x \in \{y \mid y = p_1 \vee \ldots y = p_m\})$$

Here $\{y|y = p_1 \vee \ldots y = p_m\}$ is the set of all things that is either p_1 or ... or p_m. It represents *some P*, and $\in$ represents the copula.

In practice, medieval logicians considered that the logical grammar available to them was much broader than the four categorical propositions. We have seen this already in the use of singular terms and connectives. It is this latitude that enables Buridan to wave his hands at the notion of a complex predicate without pausing to define it carefully. In principle, however, by appeal to singular terms and disjunction, it is not difficult to define "disjunctive predicate" precisely. For the discussion here, however, it is not necessary to do so. It will be sufficient to identify confused supposition negatively as that which is neither distributive nor determinate.

The suppositional properties of the eight propositional term occurrences as standardly defined may then be summarized in a table:

	Subject	*Predicate*
A	Common Distributive	Merely Confused
E	Common Distributive	Common Distributive
I	Determinate	Determinate
O	Determinate	Common Distributive

In later logic, including the *Port Royal Logic*, it was common to collapse the two non-distributive types:

	Subject	*Predicate*
A	Distributive	Non-distributive
E	Distributive	Distributive
I	Non-distributive	Non-distributive
O	Non-distributive	Distributive

Terms in the *Logic* continue to conform to this pattern, although Arnauld and Nicole use the terminology *universal* for *distributive* and *particular* for *non-distributive*.[28]

---

28 For a discussion of similar issues in medieval logic see *Priest and Read 1980*.

Qualifications

The attempt to provide a semantic analysis of the distinction between distributive and non-distributive term that would validate the six syllogistic rules—an attempt to provide a semantic analysis coextensive to the syntactic concept—is only partly successful. The distinction succeeds extensionally. All and only the four term occurrences that count as distributive in the syntactic sense count as distributive semantically. The others are non-distributive.

The definitions do less well, however, at achieving an analytic goal. The suppositional distinction cannot be drawn in terms of the equivalence of a categorical proposition to a characteristic conjunction or disjunction of term instances.

In the case of distributive supposition, the analysis is vitiated by the predicate of the particular negative. The problem is that converse entailment ("the ascent") fails from the disjunction of instances.

A more egregious failure occurs in one case of non-distributive supposition. This is the case of the predicate of the universal affirmative. Its categorical form neither entails nor is entailed by the disjunction of the predicate instances. It is for this reason that the term is assigned to its own *ad hoc* class of merely confused supposition.

These failures, however, do not mean that the attempt to capture a proposition's meaning by equivalent conjunctions and disjunctions of instances is ill-conceived but only that it has been imperfectly implemented. The non-conforming cases too are open to the analyses if quantifier scope is properly observed. If scope is observed, a categorical proposition is fully equivalent to a complex formed by conjunction and disjunction from its term instances, and there is no need to distinguish the *ad hoc* subclass of merely confused supposition.

A unified account turns on the recognition that to obtain a combination of instances fully equivalent to a categorical proposition, the proposition must be instantiated both for the subject and the predicate. It must express both the instances of the subject relative to the predicate and those of the predicate relative to the subject. Moreover, since the subject determines what the predicate is true of—since, in modern terminology, the subject has wider scope—there is an order in which the terms should be instantiated. The intuitions underlying the correct process will be described first informally—if somewhat tediously—and then more succinctly in a formal manner. Let an *assertion* be either an affirmation (an affirmative assertion) or a denial (a negative assertion).

Informally, a proposition's proper quantifier scope is captured by the rule that a categorical descends first from the subject. That is, in the first instance, the proposition asserts that, and entails, a second proposition in which the predicate P is (either affirmatively or negatively) asserted to be true of the relevant "quantity" of subject constants $s_1, \ldots, s_n$. The quantity in this instance is determined by the proposition's quantifier marker, *every* or *some*. If the mark is universal, the categorical descends to a proposition in which P is asserted of every subject constant s_i conjunctively. If it is particular, it descends to a proposition in which P is asserted of them disjunctively.

Further, each occurrence of the common noun P in this entailed proposition must in turn be instantiated. That is, within the entailed proposition each assertion that the predicate P holds of a subject constant s_i is replaced by a complex proposition. The predicate's quantity in this second instance is again marked by the syntax of the original proposition, in this case either by the quantifier alone or by a combination of the quantifier and the negative marker *not*. For any subject constant s_i, both *every* and *no* mark that every p_j is asserted of s_i; *some* without *not* indicates that some p_j is asserted of s_i; and *some* with *not* that every p_j is denied of s_i.

Whether these component assertions are affirmations or denials—whether they are affirmative or negative—is determined also by markers, by the presence or absence in the categorical of the negative markers *no* or *not*. If the categorical lacks a negative marker, the proposition entails (i.e. descends further to) the proposition in which each of the proposition's component assertions that p_j is true of s_i is replaced by an identity proposition $s_i = p_j$. If the marker is negative, it descends to one in which each assertion that p_j is not true of s_i is replaced by $s_i \neq p_j$.[29]

Describing these descents formally is straightforward. Again the assumption is made that $s_1, \ldots, s_n$ name all the actual supposita of S, and that $p_1, \ldots, p_m$ name those of P. Let the notions of positive and negative instances of *S for P* and of *P for S* be as defined earlier. Because descent proceeds to an additional step, let what was called earlier a *conjunctive instance of a term* be renamed. It will now be called a *mediate conjunctive instance*, and let what was called a *disjunctive instance* be now called its *mediate disjunctive instance*. What must be defined is a relevant instantiation of a mediate instance. For this purpose it is necessary to first define the instantiation of a proposition for a term when its collateral term is a singular term. It is propositions of this sort that make up the conjuncts and disjuncts of mediate instantiations.

Definitions

Relative to a subject term s_i and predicate term P a *positive instance* of *P for s_i* is any $s_i = p_j$, and a *negative* instance is any $s_i \neq p_j$.

---

29 As explained above, strictly speaking, in a representation of the *Logic*'s syllogistic syntax in which singular terms are a special case of common nouns, $s_i = p_j$ should be read as the universal affirmative *every s_i is p_j*, and $s_i \neq p_j$ as its contradictory, which would be read as the particular negative *some s_i is not p_j*.

Relative to a subject term S and predicate term s_i a *positive instance* of
S for p_j is any $s_i = p_j$, and a *negative instance* is $s_i \neq p_j$.
A *conjunctive instance of a term relative to a singular term* is the conjunction of that term's instances for that term, and a *disjunctive instantiation* is the disjunction of these instances.

It remains to define the final step in the descent, which is the proposition arrived at by substituting complexes of their instances for the constituents of a proposition's mediate instance. Much like the way a normal form in sentential logic details the possibilities that hold, the final entailment in descent details which facts about identity actually hold. For this reason it is a kind of "state description" as Carnap uses that term.[30]

Definition. A categorical proposition's *state description* is any proposition that results from a mediate instance of the proposition's subject for its predicate or of its predicate for its subject either by the replacement of each of its atomic parts by its conjunctive instance or by the replacement of each of its atomic parts by its disjunctive instance.

It follows directly from the standard truth-conditions for categorical propositions that each of the four forms is logically equivalent to a state description.

Theorem

every S is P ⊣ ⊢ s_1 is $P \wedge ... \wedge s_n$ is P ⊣ ⊢ $(s_1 = p_1 \vee ... \vee s_1 = p_m) \wedge ... \wedge (s_n = p_1 \vee ... \vee s_n = p_m)$

no S is P ⊣ ⊢ s_1 is not $P \wedge ... \wedge s_n$ is not P ⊣ ⊢ $(s_1 \neq p_1 \wedge ... \wedge s_1 \neq p_m) \wedge ... \wedge (s_n \neq p_1 \wedge ... \wedge s_n \neq p_m)$

some S is P ⊣ ⊢ s_1 is $P \vee ... \vee s_n$ is P ⊣ ⊢ $(s_1 = p_1 \vee ... \vee s_1 = p_m) \vee ... \vee (s_1 = p_1 \vee ... \vee s_n = p_m)$

some S is not P ⊣ ⊢ s_1 is not $P \vee ... \vee s_n$ is not P ⊣ ⊢ $(s_1 \neq p_1 \wedge ... \wedge s_1 \neq p_m) \vee ... \vee (s_n \neq p_1) \wedge ... \wedge s_n \neq p_m)$

Definition. By the *preferred instantiation* of a categorical proposition is meant the state description equivalent to it in the preceding theorem.

It is now possible to simplify supposition theory by defining a term's distributive and non-distributive suppositional properties by appeal to the proposition's preferred instance.

Definitions (Revised)

Relative to a categorical proposition,
a subject has *distributive* supposition relative to the predicate if the proposition is equivalent to the conjunction of the subject's instances for the predicate;

---

[30] Carnap 1947.

a subject has *determinate* supposition relative to the predicate if the proposition is equivalent to the disjunction of the subject's instances for the predicate;

a predicate has *distributive* supposition relative to the subject if the proposition's preferred instantiation is a conjunction;

a predicate has *determinate* supposition relative to the subject if the proposition's preferred instantiation is a disjunction.

These revisions correct the analytical flaws of the standard theory. The new semantic notion of distribution remains coextensive with the syntactic concept discussed earlier. Now, moreover, in both distributive and determinate uses the containing proposition is equivalent to a conjunction or disjunction of instances that may be fairly said to capture the meaning of the original proposition. Moreover, all four cases of non-distributive supposition now share a single defining property, obviating the need for the special subcategory of merely confused supposition.

Abstraction to a Definition of Truth

The importance of supposition theory is that it points the way to the *Logic*'s new analysis of truth. The terms of a true categorical proposition have characteristic suppositional properties that could serve as parts of a statement of the proposition's truth-conditions if these properties could be defined independently of truth itself. Though, as shown earlier, by means of characteristic conjunctions and disjunctions of instances the relevant suppositional properties can be defined in terms of logical equivalents of the proposition as a whole. These entailments, however, cannot be used directly in an analysis of truth because to do so would be circular. Entailment cannot be used to define truth because, in the meta-semantics of the object language, entailment itself is defined in terms of truth.

It should be said that although truth is conceptually prior to both distributive and non-distributive supposition, this dependency does not constitute a flaw in the medieval theory because historically it was not the purpose of supposition theory to define truth-conditions. The distinction between distributive and non-distributive supposition, in particular, was part of a broader classification of the way terms stand for things relative to context of use, and this explanation presupposes an understanding of truth-conditions.

The repurposing by the Port Royal logicians of the notion of distributive term for truth-theory was novel. In doing so, they had to avoid circularity. Their device was to characterize distributive and non-distributive uses not in terms of a proposition's entailments to conjunctions and disjunctions of instances but rather to abstract from the conjunctions and disjunctions themselves to the conditions that hold among the referents of the terms that make these conjunctions and disjunctions true. Since term reference is defined prior to truth in the object language's metatheory, a

130 The Semantics of Propositions

concept of distributive term defined in terms of term reference could be used to define truth without circularity. Such is the approach of Arnauld and Nicole.

The abstraction will be demonstrated here formally because it is much simpler, and more elegant, to do so in logic than in English. The first step is to state the standard reconstruction in set theory of the syntax and semantics for the version of the syllogistic that the authors took as their model. The next is to define the metatheoretic concepts that Arnauld and Nicole require for their abstraction. Last is the metatheorem affirming that the new truth-conditions are equivalent to the old.

The Standard Theory

Syntax

By a *syllogistic syntax* is meant a set of basic expressions called *terms*, the four *quantifiers* A, E, I, and O, and the set of *propositions* (or *sentences*) that result from concatenating any two distinct terms to the right of a quantifier, i.e., any A*SP*, E*SP*, I*SP*, or O*SP* for any term *S* (called the *subject*) and *P* (called the *predicate*). We shall let Q range over {A, E, I, O}.

Semantics

To define the notion of interpretation in a way that accommodates the *Logic*'s abstraction, it will be convenient to use the framework of general quantification theory. In this framework relative to a domain D, an interpretation $\Im$ assigns to the terms *S* and *P* subsets of a domain D, and to the quantifier Q a binary relation $\Im(Q)$ on the set of subsets of D (its power set). Thus, $\Im(Q)$ is a relation on subsets of D. To aid in exposition, it is helpful to employ the notation of restricted quantification, which is defined by eliminative definition:

$$\forall_A v F =_{def} \forall v (Av \to F)$$
$$\forall_{AB} v F =_{def} \forall v (Av \land Bv \to F)$$
$$\exists_A v F =_{def} \exists v (Av \land F)$$
$$\exists_{AB} v F =_{def} \exists v (Av \land Bv \land F)$$

To distinguish clearly between object and metalanguage usage, let ∀ and ∃ represent the quantifiers in a first-order object language, and $\forall$ and $\exists$ the quantifiers that occur the semantic theory of the metalanguage. The semantics of the syllogistic are then easily stated:

> **Definition.** A *syllogistic structure* is defined to be any power set algebra <P(D), ∪, ∩, −, ∅> i.e. Boolean algebra in which P(D), the power

The Semantics of Propositions 131

set of D, is the family of subsets of D. A *(syllogistic) interpretation relative to a syllogistic structure* is any function $\Im$ such that:

1. $\Im$ assigns to each term T a non-empty subset $\Im(T)$ of D, called the extension of T.[31]
2. $\Im$ assigns a two-place relation on D to the quantifiers as follows:

$\Im(A) = \{<A,B>|A \subseteq B\} = \{<A,B>|\forall_A d \exists_{BA} d'(d=d')\}$

$\Im(E) = \{<A,B>|A \cap B = \emptyset\} = \{<A,B>|\forall_A d \, \forall_B d'(d \neq d')\}$

$\Im(I) = \{<A,B>|A \cap B \neq \emptyset\} = \{<A,B>|\exists_{AB} d \exists_{BA} d'(d=d')\}$

$\Im(O) = \{<A,B>|A \cap B \neq \emptyset\} = \{<A,B>|\exists_A d \forall_{AB} d'(d \neq d')\}$

3. I assigns truth-values to propositions as follows:

$\Im(QSP) = T$ iff $<\Im(S), \Im(P)> \in \Im(Q)$.

Definition. An argument from X to F is *syllogistically valid* (briefly $X \vDash_{syl} F$) relative to a family of structures iff for any syllogistic interpretation $\Im$ for a structure in that family, if for all $G \in X$, $\Im(G) = T$, then $\Im(F) = T$.

Theorem. The logical relations of immediate inference (those of the Square of Opposition) hold, and the traditional 24 valid moods are exactly the valid syllogisms.

The standard theory is completed by two further results, which need only be mentioned here. First, it is possible to reformulate the traditional reduction of the valid moods to Barbara and Celarent as an axiom or natural deduction system.[32] Such a reformulation would be sound and complete for not only the valid moods but also for the set of categorical arguments that link finite chains of syllogisms. Second, the *Logic*'s six rules from the early part of the chapter constitute a decision procedure not only for the valid moods but also for any finite argument composed of syllogisms.[33]

The Cartesian Theory. To state the *Logic*'s version of categorical truth-conditions, it is necessary to make use of some terminology that singles out the various parts of a quantifier's definition.

---

31 Note that here *extension* is being used in its modern sense, as the set of entities in the world that the term stands for. Its coincidence with the *Logic*'s sense of extension as a set of ideas is discussed later in the chapter.
32 These are described in the *Logic*'s first edition. See *Arnauld 1993*, p. 203, and B 156.
33 For a more precise statement of the proof theoretic system in both axiomatic or natural deduction form and the completeness theorem see *Martin 1997*.

Definitions

1. Relative to a syllogistic syntax and structure $<P(D), \cup, \cap, -, \emptyset>$, let us call Q a *Cartesian quantifier* iff $\Im(Q) = \{<A,B>|Q_{iC}dQ_{jC'}d'(F[d, d'])\}$, where Q_i, Q_j range over $\{\forall,\exists\}$; Q_{iC}, $Q_{jC'}$ are quantifiers restricted to the subsets C and C' of D respectively; and $F[d,d']$ is either the formula $d = d'$ or $d \neq d'$.
2. If Q is a Cartesian quantifier, let us call $F[\Im(S), \Im(P)]$ *the truth-conditions* of QSP, Q_i the proposition's *subject quantifier (in the metalanguage)*, Q_j the proposition's *predicate quantifier (in the metalanguage)*; and C and C' *the relevant extensions* of the subject and predicate, respectively.

According to these definitions, the traditional four syllogistic quantifiers all count as Cartesian.

Cartesian quantifiers have the nice property that it is possible to read off from a proposition's truth-conditions three important bits of information: a quantifier's relevant extension; a term's quantifier's status as universal or existential; and a proposition's status as affirmative or negative. Moreover, the term's quantificational status determines whether the term is distributive. It was the insight of the authors of the *Logic* that these properties alone determine a proposition's truth-conditions. These properties must now be defined within the current semantics.

Term Extension: Monotonic Up and Down Quantified Terms

As defined in general quantification theory, a quantifier's term is monotonic if the quantifier ranges systematically over the subsets or supersets of its extension. There are two types of monotonic quantifiers. A quantifier is *up monotonic* for a term if it ranges over the term's supersets and is *down monotonic* if it ranges over its subsets. In Arnauld's terminology, a term's *relevant extension* is its entire extension if the term is down monotonic, and is it the intersection of its extension with that of its correlative term if the term is up monotonic.[34]

Definitions. Relative to an interpretation $\Im$ over a domain D,

Q is *subject up monotonic* iff,

$\forall A,B,C \subseteq D, <A,B> \in \Im(Q) \ \& \ A \subseteq C . \rightarrow <C,B> \in \Im(Q)$;

---

34 See *Doyle 1995*.

Q is *subject down monotonic* iff,

$\forall A,B,C \subseteq D, \langle A,B\rangle \in \Im(Q) \ \& \ C \subseteq A \ . \rightarrow \langle C,B\rangle \in \Im(Q);$

Q is *predicate up monotonic* iff,

$\forall A,B,C \subseteq D, \langle A,B\rangle \in \Im(Q) \ \& \ B \subseteq C \ . \rightarrow \langle A,C\rangle \in \Im(Q);$

Q is *predicate down monotonic* iff,

$\forall A,B,C \subseteq D, \langle A,B\rangle \in \Im(Q) \ \& \ C \subseteq B \ . \rightarrow \langle A,C\rangle \in \Im(Q).$

The monotonic properties of the four syllogistic quantifiers relative to a proposition's terms may be summarized in a table:

Subject	Predicate
Down monotonic	Up monotonic
Down monotonic	Down monotonic
Up monotonic	Up monotonic
Down monotonic	Up monotonic

Distributive and Non-distributive Terms

It is possible to read a term's distributive status from the term quantifiers in a proposition's truth-conditions. If the quantifier over a term's relevant extension is universal, the term is distributive. If it is existential, it is non-distributive.

> **Definition.** A syllogistic term is *distributive* or, in the *Logic*'s usage, *universal* in a proposition iff in the proposition's truth-conditions its term quantifier is universal, and is *non-distributive* or *particular* iff its term quantifier is existential.
>
> **Theorem.** A term is distributive iff its term quantifier quantifies universally over its relevant extension. The table listing the distributive status of terms under the suppositional definition of distribution equally describes their distributive status under the new definition.
>
> **A Proposition's Quality.** Syntactically, a proposition's quality is determined by negative markers. However, it is a semantic notion of quality that is relevant to fixing truth-conditions. A categorical is affirmative in a semantic sense if it asserts that identities obtain and negative if it denies them.
>
> **Definition.** A categorical proposition is (*semantically*) *affirmative* iff its truth-conditions assert that values in the relevant extension of the subject are identical to those in the relevant extension of the predicate, and is (*semantically*) *negative* iff its truth-conditions assert that they are non-identical.

Truth-Conditions

It is now possible to state the truth-conditions for categorical propositions in the manner of Arnauld and Nicole. As expressed in the following theorem, the clauses characterizing a proposition's truth-conditions appeal only to the concepts of distributive term, conservative quantifier, and affirmative and negative proposition. To capture more closely the *Logic*'s wording in the theorem, a distributive term is called *universal* and a non-distributive term *particular*.[35] In the following theorem the truth-conditions for each propositional type are stated twice. The first statement is expressed in terms of the deeper distributive and non-distributive properties of terms and is essentially a reformulation of the formal truth-conditions above. It makes no reference to truth. The second is expressed in terms of the quality, quantity, and monotonicity of the quantifiers and in terms of whether the proposition's terms are distributive. As the earlier formal definitions indicate, the metalinguistic properties essentially summarize features of the first formulation. Together the formulations are very close to the vocabulary used by the authors in their statement of truth-conditions in II.17–20.

Theorem. Relative to a syllogistic syntax and structure $<P(D), \subseteq, \cap, \emptyset>$, the set of syllogistic interpretations is identical to the set of all function $\Im$ that assigns to each term T a non-empty subset of D and a truth-value to each proposition as follows:

$\Im(ASP) = T$ iff A is a Cartesian quantifier, the relevant extension of S is its entire extension, the relevant extension of P is the restriction of its extension of P by that of S, and every element of the relevant extension of the subject is identical to some element of the relevant extension of P;

iff A is a Cartesian quantifier, the proposition is affirmative, the quantifier A is subject down monotonic but predicate up monotonic, and S is universal but P is particular.

$\Im(ESP) = T$ iff E is a Cartesian quantifier, the relevant extension of S is its entire extension, the relevant extension of P is its extension, and every element of the relevant extension of the subject is non-identical to every element of the relevant extension of P;

---

[35] Keenan 1984.

| | iff | E is a Cartesian quantifier, the proposition is negative, the quantifier N is subject and predicate down monotonic, and both S and P are universal. |

$\Im(ISP) = T$ iff I is a Cartesian quantifier, the relevant extension of S is the restriction of its extension by that of P, the relevant extension of P is the restriction of its extension by that of S, and some element of the relevant extension of S is identical to some element in the relevant extension of P;

iff I is a Cartesian quantifier, the proposition is affirmative, the quantifier E is both subject and predicate up monotonic, and both S and P are particular.

$\Im(OSP) = T$ iff O is a Cartesian quantifier, the relevant extension of S is its entire extension, the relative extension of P is its extension restricted by that of S, and there is some element in the relevant extension of S that is not identical to any element in the extension of P;

iff O is a Cartesian quantifier, the proposition is negative, the quantifier O is subject down monotonic and up predicate monotonic, and P is universal but S is particular.

Because the first formulations are essentially restatements of the usual formal truth-conditions for the syllogistic, this theorem shows that the second formulation in Cartesian vocabulary are equivalent to their correlates on the standard account. Accordingly, all the metalogical properties of the syllogistic continue to hold under the Cartesian analysis of truth, including the theory of immediate inference, the soundness and completeness of the standard reduction of the valid moods to Barbara and Celarent, and the effectiveness of the *Logic*'s six-rule decision procedure for the valid moods and for valid categorical arguments generally. A more detailed first-order abstraction of the *Logic*'s truth-conditions is set out in the Appendix.

Although the wording used in the *Logic* to state the truth-conditions of categorical propositions (in Axioms 1–7 and accompanying explanations in II.17–20) is very similar to that in the preceding theorem, there are several points of divergence worthy of note. Some are relatively trivial. For example, instead of formulating a single notion of monotonic quantifier to cover all cases, the authors explain case by case when a term's relevant extension is restricted by that of its collateral term.

A more consequential difference is due to the authors' more global Cartesian project. One purpose of the *Logic* is to formulate a theory of truth in terms of relations among ideas rather than among corporeal individuals outside the mind. Accordingly, as explained in Chapter 2, Arnauld and Nicole define the extension as sets of ideas and not as objects in the world. As explained in Chapter 3, however, there is a one-to-one correspondence between a term's Cartesian extension and its extension in the modern sense—its significance range. There is a sense, then, in which the *Logic*'s truth theory is doubly abstract: it first abstracts from medieval supposition theory to truth-conditions in terms of distribution, and then to ideas corresponding to objects outside the mind. The theory of truth above, stated in terms of significance ranges, incorporates this first-level abstraction. The second level of abstraction is from things to ideas, from significance ranges to Cartesian extensions. Due to the one-to-one correspondence between the two domains, the preceding theorem remains true when read in either sense of extension.

Modality

The *Logic* devotes only a brief discussion (in II.8) to the alethic modalities—*possible, contingent, impossible* and *necessary*. They are distinguished only by their syntax, which is set forth by displaying propositions with the relevant modal adverbs. There is no attempt to provide a semantic analysis or to state truth-conditions.

By means of mnemonic names, the authors describe some simple modal inferential properties. By means of four "squares of opposition," one for each of the modalities, various relations of immediate inference are laid out. The authors do not argue for the validity of the inferences displayed or provide any theoretical framework in terms of which they might be evaluated.

It is worth noticing that in doing so, the *Logic*'s authors conflate *contingent* with *possible*, a deviant usage in the history of logic traceable to Aristotle, who conflated the two at various places, for example in *De Interpretatione* 12 and 13. Medieval logicians and most of the *Logic*'s contemporaries generally understood *it is contingent that P* to be equivalent to the conjunction *it is possible that P and it is possible that not-P*, the so-called double-sided sense of contingency. They rejected the reading of *it is contingent that P* as *it is possible that P*, the so-called single-sided sense of contingency. An identical conflation of contingency with possibility and the same mnemonic names had appeared shortly before the *Logic* in the logical treatise of Eustache de St.-Paul, which Arnauld and Nicole may have copied.[36] At roughly the

---

36 Eustachio de S. Paulo 1648, Logica, D2, Q. III.

same time, when commenting on the views of Aristotle, Fonseca repeats in his treatise Aristotle's conflation of the contingent with the single-sided possible, but he goes on to remark that contrary to Aristotle the then current usage of *contingent* in the 17th century was consistent with the double-sided sense.[37] It is relevant to note that the authors themselves do not conflate contingency with possibility—they do not use the single-sided sense of contingency described in II.8—in their own writing. When they have occasion to use the term *contingent* in the discussion within the *Logic*, they follow the prevailing practice of using it in the double-sided sense.[38]

Perhaps one reason that the authors do not attempt to make explicit the truth-conditions of the modalities is that the standard semantic accounts in earlier logic typically held that terms in alethic modal contexts signify *possiblia*. Arnauld makes clear in several places that he rejected the existence of possible entities.[39]

---

37 *Fonseca 1964 [1575], Logica*, LII, C10.
38 There are four cases:

> *LAP* II.13, *KM* V 234, *B* 118. The authors treat contingency as an alternative to necessity. Since they also hold that necessity entails possibility, if necessity also entailed contingency, contingency would not be an alternative to necessity.
>
> *LAP* III.18, *KM* V 307, *B* 187. Here contingency is described as free. Freedom entails the possibility not to do something.
>
> *LAP* IV.13, *KM* V 398, *B* 263. Here the double-sided sense is used explicitly. The example given, which is the conversion of the king of China to Christianity, is clearly understood to be possibly false because it was in fact false at the time.
>
> *LAP* V.16, *KM* V 408, *B* 273. Future accidents are referred to as contingent. Future accidents are possibly false because they are currently false.

39 For example, "Arnauld to Leibniz," May 13, 1686, *KM* VI, pp. 31–32:

> I acknowledge in good faith that I have no idea of substances purely possible, that is to say, which God will never create. I am inclined to think that these are chimeras which we construct and that whatever we call possible substances, pure possibilities are nothing else than the omnipotence of God who, being a pure act, does not allow of there being a possibility in him. Possibilities, however, may be conceived of in the natures which he has created, for, not being of the same essence throughout, they are necessarily composites of power and action. I can therefore think of them as possibilities. I can also do the same with an infinity of modifications which are within the power of these created natures, such as are the thoughts of intelligent beings, and the forms of extended substance. But I am very much mistaken if there is any one who will venture to say that he has an idea of a possible substance as pure possibility. As for myself, I am convinced that, although there is so much talk of these substances which are pure possibilities, they are, nevertheless, always conceived of only under the idea of some one of those which God has actually created. We seem to me, therefore, able to say that outside of the things which God has created, or must create, there is no mere negative possibility but only an active and infinite power.

> Likewise, because Arnauld rejects possible beings, there is no discussion of modal ampliation in the *Logic*. For further examples see *Stencil 2016*.

The Containment Principle

In Part III.10 and 11, the authors advance what they call a "containment principle" as a general rule for evaluating syllogistic validity. If successful, it short-circuits the *Logic*'s own six-rule decision procedure described earlier. Because it is formulated in terms of containment, it also appears to be an example of the *Logic*'s general effort to account for as much as it can through "containment." In this case the containment in question is extensional. The principle is succinct:[40]

> *That one of the two propositions must contain the conclusion, and the other must show that it contains it.*

The authors also provide a more complete explanation:[41]

> Whenever we want to prove a proposition whose truth is not obvious, it seems that all we have to do is to find a better known proposition confirming it, which for this reason can be called the *containing* proposition. But because this proposition cannot contain the first one explicitly and in the same terms—since if it did it would not differ from it in any way and so would not help make it clearer—there must be yet another proposition that shows that what we call the *containing* proposition actually does contain the one we wish to prove. This proposition can be called *applicative*.

From the explanation and examples given, what seems to be intended is that a universal affirmative premise, called the *applicative proposition*, states that a term that is contained within the syllogism's other premise, called the *containing proposition*, "contains" a term that occurs in the conclusion. The rule requires interpretation because the authors themselves do not spell out the sense of containment intended.[42] A key to its

---

40 *LAP* III.11, *KM* V 284, *B* 165.
41 *LAP* III.10, *KM* V 282, *B* 163.
42 John Corcoran and Jacuzzo in *Corcoran 2014* have argued that the claims made for the containment principle in the *Logic* are mistaken. Their argument turns on the fact that the principle does not cover argument forms like *modus tollens* because these lack statements of containment. Their example is

> If Abe is Ben, Ben is Abe
> Ben isn't Abe
> Abe isn't Ben

This objection, however, is misdirected. The text makes clear that the authors did not intend for the principle to apply to all argument forms but only to simple and complex syllogisms—those that contain simple or complex terms. They did not intend it to apply to arbitrary valid arguments in sentential or first-order logic. That being said, its meaning is provided in the similarity the principle bears to the rule referred to in earlier logic as *dici de omni et nullo*. According to some historians of logic, this rule is found in the opening chapter of the *Prior Analytics*. There Aristotle says:

> For one thing to be in another as a whole is the same as for one thing to be predicated of every one of another.[43]

Versions are of the rule are found in William of Sherwood, Peter of Spain, Alfred the Great, Aquinas, Ockham, and Buridan, among many others. Buridan provides the formulation: "*Dici de omni* applies when nothing is taken under the subject of which the predicate is not predicated."[44]

Dean Buckner points out that there is dispute about whether the principle was intended by Aristotle to serve, as some think, as the basis for all of the valid syllogisms. Giles of Rome and much later J. N. Keynes held that it was. Ockham regularly appealed to *dici de omni* to validate syllogisms.[45] Lukasiewicz, however, has argued that the principle is not to be found in Aristotle.[46] The *Logic*'s authors fall somewhere in the former camp.[47]

Technically, there is a sense of containment in which the authors are correct. It is possible to lay out the properties of distributive and non-distributive terms in such a way that they can be used to determine the validity of term-substitution within simple syllogisms. Valid substitution turns on whether, in the syntactic context, the relevant ordering or "containment" on interpretations is preserved (monotonic) or reversed (antitonic).

What is lacking in the authors' formulation of the containment principle is an explicit acknowledgment that the direction of containment is a function of the distributive and non-distributive properties of the propositions' terms. Accordingly, to state the principle properly a prior account of distribution must be presupposed. The *Logic*'s own definition of distributive term, as explained earlier in this chapter, is sufficient but rather elaborate. The analysis there was abstracted from medieval supposition theory and used by Arnauld and Nicole to state the truth-conditions for categorical propositions. For the sake of brevity here, however, it will be convenient simply to appeal to the shorter but coextensional definition

---

algebraic formulation below is abstract and applies to logics with an expressive power richer than the syllogistic's.
43 24ᵇ26–30, *Aristotle 1928*.
44 In *John Buridan 2001, Summulae* 5.1.2, p. 306.
45 See *Bocheński 1961*, 33.20, 33.23, and 34.02.
46 See *Lukasiewicz 1957*, pp. 46–47.
47 For details of this history see *Buckner 2015*.

of distributive term on the understanding that the shorter version may be taken as a stand-in for the authors' deeper analysis. It is also the case that the success of the principle is independent of the *Logic*'s special interpretation of extensions as sets of ideas. The containment principle holds for any Boolean interpretation of the syllogistic that assigns values to terms in a Boolean algebra. The *Logic*'s own semantics which interprets terms within a Boolean algebra of idea-extensions is a special case.

The containment principle, stated more precisely, establishes that, relative to dispositional properties of terms, the substitutability of one term for another *salve veritate* varies with the containment of term extensions. The relevant containment relation in the background is the partial-ordering relation within the Boolean algebra over which the terms are interpreted.

To apply these notions to the syllogistic, it is necessary first to specify the background syntax and semantics for the syllogistic. Because the examples of syllogisms the *Logic* discusses in III.9–11 include ones that have so-called complex terms, the categorical syntax of the syllogistic must be augmented here to include propositions with complex terms. Complex terms are one formed from simpler terms—a substantive and a modifier—by the operation of restriction. Syllogisms that contain a complex term are called *complex*.

Syntax

Let *SimpTerms* be a set of primitive (undefined) expressions, called *simple terms*, and let *Terms* be the set that contains all simple terms and any concatenation ("restriction") of one simple term by another. Let P(*Terms*) be the set of all subsets of *Term*, i.e., its power set. By a *proposition* is meant any of the four categorical forms defined as the result of concatenating one of the quantifiers A, E, I, or O with two elements of *Terms*. Relative to a proposition, the term to the left is the proposition's *subject*, and the one to the right is its *predicate*. Let *Prop* be the set of all propositions and P(*Prop*) its power set. By a *complex syllogistic syntax* is meant any structure <*Prop, SimpTerms, Terms*>.

Semantics

A simplified and more abstract version of the semantics stated earlier in the chapter will suffice here. An interpretation is a function that assigns sets to simple terms, the intersection of the extensions of its components to a complex term, and truth-values to categorical propositions according to their standard truth-conditions. An interpretation is defined relative to a domain consisting of sets. Technically, this domain is part of a Boolean algebra <P(U), ∪, ∩, −, ∅> that has as its domain P(U), the set of all subsets (the power set) of some universe U of entities. By an *interpretation of a complex syllogistic syntax* <*Prop, SimpTerms, Terms*> relative to the power set algebra of sets, <P(U), ∪, ∩, −, ∅> (i.e. a Boolean algebra in which power P(U) is the family of subsets of U) is meant a function ℑ on *Terms* and *Prop* such that

1. If t is in SimpTerms, $\Im(t) \subseteq U$, and if tt' is in *Terms−SimpTerms* then $\Im(tt') = \Im(t) \cap \Im(t')$;
2. ℑ maps *Prop* into {T, F} as follows:

   $\Im(ASP) = T$ iff $\Im(S) \subseteq \Im(P)$;

   $\Im(ESP) = T$ iff $\Im(S) \cap \Im(P) = \emptyset$;

   $\Im(ISP) = T$ iff $\Im(S) \cap \Im(P) \neq \emptyset$;

   $\Im(OSP) = T$ iff $\Im(S) - \Im(P) \neq \emptyset$.

The Boolean algebra in question is often understood in Aristotelian logic to be one of sets. As explained earlier in this chapter, the *Logic* understands these to be sets of ideas.[48] For algebraic reasons, which will be clear below, let the truth-values be identified with sets. Let T = U and F = ∅.

The relevant containment relation ≤ℑ is an ordering relation on sets, and these sets form the range of the interpretation function ℑ:

Definition. For any expressions e and e', $e \leq \Im e'$ iff $\Im(e) \subseteq \Im(e')$

Clearly, because ℑ is defined on both terms and proposition, ≤ℑ is likewise well-defined for both terms and propositions. In both cases it is reflexive, transitive and antisymmetric, and therefore <*Terms*, ≤ℑ> and <*Prop*, ≤ℑ> meet the formal conditions for being partially ordered structures. The ordering ≤ℑ on *Terms* counts as one of "extensional" containment. In contrast, ≤ℑ on *Prop* is an ordering of truth-values. The motivation for identifying T with U and F with ∅ is that ≤ℑ on truth-values then conforms to the truth-table for the material conditional. Suppose that the syntax were expanded to contain the material conditional → defined on propositions with the usual truth-table relative to an interpretation ℑ. Because T = U and F = ∅, it would follow that for any propositions p and q, and any interpretation ℑ, $p \leq \Im q$ holds if, and only if, the material conditional $p \to q$ is true relative to ℑ.

Substitution. To describe the inferences covered by the containment principle, it is helpful to have a device that allows reference to the

---

[48] The syllogistic continues to be valid when interpreted over yet more abstract matrices. For a more complete statement of the relevant model theory for the syllogistic see *Martin 1997, Andrade-Lotero 2008,* and *Andrade-Lotero 2012.*

result of substituting one occurrence of a term for another without otherwise changing the form of the proposition. This goal is achieved by defining a substitution operation as a function Φ that maps term occurrences to propositions such that when Φ(t) is proposition, Φ(t') is also a proposition but contains an occurrence of t' where Φ(t) contains one of t. For example, for the occurrences of *man* and *cow*, if Φ(*man*) is *every man is mortal*, then Φ(*cow*) is *every cow is mortal*.

Definition. By a *substitution function* is meant a function Φ that pairs a term t with a unique proposition Φ(t) that contains t as a subject or predicate term, but not both, and is such that, for any term t', Φ (t') is like Φ(t) except for containing t' as subject wherever Φ(t) contains t as subject or that contains t' as predicate wherever Φ(t) contains t as predicate.

The conditions under which the extensional containment of one term by another determines valid term substitution *salve veritate* can be described in terms of the ordering ≤ℑ. What is required is that the condition specifies whether the substitution function Φ mirrors or reverses ≤ℑ. The property of a mapping "mirroring" or "reversing" the order of a structure is a familiar one in algebra and has a special technical vocabulary. Let be <U, ≤ > and <U', ≤' > be partially ordered sets. If a mapping f from the first structure to the second mirrors the order of the first in the second, then f said to be monotonic. If it reverse the order, it is said to be antitonic:

Definitions. A mapping f from one partially ordered set <U, ≤ > to another <U', ≤' > is *monotonic* iff for any x and y in U, $x \leq y$ iff $f(x) \leq f(y)$, and *antitonic* (*monotonic downwards*) iff, for any x and y in U, $x \leq y$ iff $f(y) \leq f(x)$.

The substitution function Φ is a mapping from *Terms* in <Terms, ≤ℑ> to *Prop* in the structure <Prop, ≤ℑ>. Whether it mirrors or reverses the order of terms in the order of propositions depends on the distributive properties of the terms.

Distribution

The *Logic*'s definition of distributive term is set out at some length earlier in this chapter where it was defined in terms of the referential properties of terms. For the purposes here it will be sufficient to employ a more succinct definition, one that is coextensional with the *Logic*'s earlier definition. The definition below of distributive term is semantic and ensures that the correct terms are distributive, namely, the subject of an A and E proposition, and predicate of an E and O proposition.[49]

> **Definition.** A subject or predicate term t of a proposition is *distributive* iff, $\Im(\Phi(t)) = T$ iff, for any t', if $\Im(t') \subseteq \Im(t)$ then $\Im(\Phi(t')) = T$, and *non-distributive* otherwise.

Order

It is a property of a non-distributive term that its extension can be inflated without altering truth-value or, in algebraic terms, that the interpretation function is monotonic with respect to the ordering $\leq\Im$:

> **Theorem.** For any non-distributive term t of a proposition, Φ is monotonic (upwards) with respect to $<Terms, \leq\Im>$ and $<Prop, \leq\Im>$, i.e. for any t and t' in *terms*, $t \leq \Im\ t'$ iff $\Phi(t) \leq \Im\ \Phi(t')$.

In the general quantifier literature, this result is usually expressed in a manner that obscures the link to the algebraic concept of monotonicity: for any t and t' in *terms*, $\Im(t) \subseteq \Im(t')$ only if $\Im(\Phi(t)) = \Im(\Phi(t'))$.

Correspondingly, it is a property of a distributive term that its extensions can be constricted without altering truth or, in algebraic terms, their interpretation function is antitonic with respect to the ordering $\leq\Im$:

> **Theorem.** For any distributive term t of a proposition, Φ is antitonic with respect to $<Terms, \leq\Im>$, $<Prop, \leq\Im>$, i.e. for any t and t' in *Terms*, $t' \leq \Im\ t$ iff $\Phi(t) \leq \Im\ \Phi(t')$. Hence, $\Im(t') \subseteq \Im(t)$ only if $\Im(\Phi(t)) = \Im(\Phi(t'))$.

Proofs of the two theorems follow directly from a review of each case of a distributive or non-distributive term in a simple categorical proposition.

Dici de Omni *and the Containment Principle*

That the theorems above are suggestive of *dici de omni* is shown by the following two corollaries, which are in effect versions of the containment principle. The first says that if one term is non-distributive and its extension is contained in that of a second term, then replacing the first by the second preserves truth. The second says that if one term is distributive and its extension contains that of a second term, then replacing the first by the second preserves truth.

---

[49] The author is indebted to Stephen Read for the observation that distributive term for the purposes of the containment principle must be defined relative to the term's occurrence.

Corollaries

(**Dici de Omni**.) If t is a non-distributive term of a proposition, then for any t', if $\Im(t) \subseteq \Im(t')$ and $\Im(\Phi(t)) = T$, then $\Im(\Phi(t')) = T$.
If t is distributive term of a proposition, then for any t', if $\Im(t') \subseteq \Im(t)$ and $\Im(\Phi(t)) = T$, then $\Im(\Phi(t')) = T$.

A review of the examples discussed by the *Logic* in the sections on the containment principle shows how closely these formal versions capture the *Logic*'s intention.[50] In the first example in III.10 the relevant distributive term t' is *slave of the passions*.[51]

Every slave of the passions is unhappy.	$\Phi(t')$
<u>Every evil person is a slave of the passions.</u>	$t \leq \Im(t')$
Thus every evil person is unhappy.	$\Phi(t)$

As the authors remark, because the above syllogism is a case of *Barbara*, the major premise could also have served as the containment statement. In the next example in III.10 the non-distributive t' is *content*:[52]

Every happy person is content.	$t \leq \Im(t')$
<u>No miser is content.</u>	$\Phi(t')$
Therefore, no miser is happy.	$\Phi(t)$

Again, as the authors' remark,[53] because the negative syntax of the minor premise does not assert containment, the task falls to the major premise.

The last two examples in III.11 are of complex syllogisms. In the first the distributive term t' is *those who commit criminal acts*:

The duty of a Christian is not to praise those who commit criminal acts.	$\Phi(t')$
<u>Now those who fight duels commit criminal acts.</u>	$t' \leq \Im(t)$
Thus the duty of a Christian is not to praise those who fight duels.	$\Phi(t)$

---

50 *LAP* III.10, *KM* V 281, *B* 162 and *LAP* III.11, *KM* V 284, *B* 165.
51 *LAP* III.10, *KM* V 281–282, *B* 163.
52 *LAP* III.10, *KM* V 281, *B* 163.
53 They continue:

> For negative syllogisms, since there is only one negative proposition and since negation is properly contained only in a negative proposition, it seems that the negative proposition should always be taken as the containing proposition, and the affirmative proposition alone as the applicative proposition.

In the last example distributive term t' is *against God's law*:

Christianity requires servants to serve their masters only in matters that are not against God's law.	$\Phi(t')$
<u>*Now improper commerce is against God's law.*</u>	$t \leq \Im(t')$
Christianity does not require servants to serve their masters in improper commerce.	$\Phi(t)$

The containment principle as it stands, however, is not complete in the technical sense. There are some valid moods like *Ferio* that do not contain a premise affirming that one term is "contained" in another (the so-called applicative proposition). To accommodate these cases, the rationale could be invoked that is sometimes used to argue that *de omni et nullo* underlies all the valid moods even though its discussion in the *Prior Analytics*, if at all, is in relation to the so-called perfect syllogisms, *Barbara* and **Celarent**. The principle, it might be argued, underlies all twenty-four valid moods because all the valid moods may be "reduced" by well-known rules suggested in the *Prior Analytics* to *Barbara* and *Celarent*, which do contain explicit containment premises.[54]

Apart from its intrinsic interest as a rule characterizing validity, the principle is another example of the authors' attaching explanatory power to the semantics of containment, in this case, extensional containment. Conceptual containment is, however, included because every case of conceptual containment entails extensional containment. If one idea is contained in a second because it is part of its intentional content, the extension of the second is a subset of that of the first. The authors, in fact, remark of one example, "Now everything contained in the comprehension of an idea can be affirmed universally of it."[55] The sense of containment relevant to the principle, however, is not conceptual because many valid syllogistic inferences turn on the contingent containments of one extension in another. Moreover, when introducing the containment principle in III.11, the authors refer to both comprehension-inclusion and extensional containment. Extensional containment, however, is the more general.

It is clear that the sense of inference validated by the principle is semantic rather than syntactic. It refers not to syntactic form but to whether the extensions of the terms stand to each other in a containment relation. The notions of distributive and non-distributive term are also semantic. Moreover, the *Logic*'s own definition of distributive term outlined earlier in the chapter does not appeal to the notion of truth. In sum,

---

54 The *Logic*'s 1662 edition, however, explains these reductions but refers to them as "useless." For the text see *Arnauld 1993*, p. 203, and *B* 156.

55 *LAP* III.10, *KM* V 283, *B* 164.

the containment principle goes some way towards characterizing valid syllogistic inference. When the notion of distributive term is understood according to the *Logic*'s own definition, the containment principle provides a non-circular characterization of syllogistic validity for those syllogisms with a "containing proposition." Moreover, by the application of the procedure of reducing first complex to simple syllogisms, and then all the simple syllogisms to *Barbara* and *Celarent*, the principle may, with some plausibility, be said to underlie all syllogistic validity, much as some have thought the principle *de omni et nullo* did.

Chapters 1 through 3, on the semantics of terms, explored how content—in the intentional sense—determines the structure of ideas and extensions. This chapter on the semantics of propositions has investigated how content in the sense of extensional inclusion is used in the definition of truth-conditions and as a marker for syllogistic entailments. The next chapter considers the semantics of larger linguistic units, the discourse that makes up scientific explanation. This consists of the language in which scientific discovery takes place and is then presented to the world. The study of the invention and dissemination of scientific knowledge was called "method."

References

Andrade-Lotero, Edgar and Catarina Dutilh Novaes. 2012. Validity, the Squeezing Arguments and Alternative Semantics Systems: The Case of Aristotelian Syllogistic. *Journal of Philosophical Logic*, 41, 387–418.

Andrade-Lotero, Edgar and Edward Samuel Becerra. 2008. Establish Connections Between Aristotle's Natural Deduction and First-Order Logic. *History and Philosophy of Logic*, 29, 309–325.

Aristotle. 1928. *Analytica Priora*, Oxford, Oxford University Press. Ross, Sir David (ed.), Jenkinson, A. J. (translator).

Aristotle. 1963. *Categories and De Interpretatione*, Oxford. Ackrill, J. L. (translator).

Arnauld, Antoine. 2003. *Œuvres philosophiques d'Arnauld*, Bristol, Theommes Press. Kremer, Elmar and Denis Moreau (eds.).

Arnauld, Antoine and Pierre Nicole. 1993. *La Logique ou d'Art de Penser*, Paris, Librairie Philosophique J. Vrin. Clair, Pierre and François Girbal (eds.).

Bocheński, I. M. 1961. *A History of Formal Logic*, New York, Chelsea.

Buckner, Edward [Dean]. 2015. *Dici de omni*. www.logicmuseum.com/wiki/Dici_de_omni.

Buridan, John. 2001. *Summulae de dialectica*, New Haven, Yale University Press. Klima, Gyula (translator).

Carnap, Rudolf. 1947. *Meaning and Necessity*, Chicago, University of Chicago Press.

Corcoran, John. 1972. Completeness of an Ancient Logic. *Journal of Symbolic Logic*, 37, 696–702.

Corcoran, John and Leonard Jacuzzo. 2014. Port-Royal Containment Principle. *Bulletin of Symbolic Logic*, 20, 131–132.

de Rijk, Lambertus Marie. 1962–1967. *Logica Modernorum, a Contribution to the History of Early Termist Logic*, Assen, Van Gorcum.

Doyle, John P. 1995. Another God, Chimerae, Goat-Stags, and Man-Lions: A Seventeenth-Century Debate About Impossible Objects. *The Review of Metaphysics*, 48, 771–808.

Eustachio de S. Paulo. 1648. *Summa philosophiae quadripartita, de rebus dialecticis, ethicis, physicis et metaphysicis*, Cantabrigia [Cambridge], Rogerus Danielis.

Fonseca, Pedro da. 1964 [1575]. *Instituciões dialéctica [Institutionum dialecticarum libri octo]*, Coimbra, Universidade de Coimbra.

Keenan, Edward and L. Moss. 1984. Generalized Quantifiers and the Expressive Power of Natural Language. In: van Benthem, J. and A. ter Meulen (eds.) *Generalized Quantifiers in Natural Language*, Foris, Reidel.

Kneale, William and Marth Kneale. 1962. *The Development of Logic*, Oxford, Clarendon Press.

Lenzen, Wolfgang. 1990. On Leibniz's Essay *Mathesis rationis*. *Topoi*, 9, 29–59.

Lukasiewicz, Jan. 1957. *Aristotle's Syllogistic*, Oxford, Clarendon Press.

Martin, John N. 1997. Aristotle's Natural Deduction Reconsidered. *History and Philosophy of Logic*, 18, 1–15.

Martin, John N. 2013. Distributive Terms, Truth, and *the Port Royal Logic*. *History and Philosophy of Logic*, 133–154.

Martin, John N. 2016. A Note on "Distributive Terms, Truth, and the Port Royal Logic." *History and Philosophy of Logic*, 37:4, 391–392.

Pariente, Jean-Claude. 1985. *L'Analyse du Language à Port-Royal*, Paris, C.N.R.S. Éditions de Minuit.

Peter of Spain. 2014. *Tractatus*, Oxford, Oxford University Press. Copenhaver, Brian P., Calvin Normore, and Terence Parsons (eds. and translators).

Priest, Graham and Stephen Read. 1980. Merely Confused Supposition. *Franciscan Studies*, 40, 265–297.

Prior, Arthur. 1962. *Formal Logic*, Oxford, Oxford University Press.

Smiley, Timothy. 1973. What is a Syllogism? *Journal of Philosophical Logic*, 2, 136–154.

Stencil, Eric. 2016. Essence and Possibility in the Leibniz-Arnauld Correspondence. *Pacific Philosophical Quarterly*, 97, 2–26.

Toletus, Franciscus. 1580. *Commentaria, una cum questionibus, in universam aristotelis logicam*, Venice, Juntas.

William of Sherwood. 1966. *Introduction to Logic*, Minneapolis, University of Minnesota.

5 The Semantics of Discourse. Method

Introduction

Parts I–III of the *Logic* deal with traditional topics from medieval logic, each of which builds on the one before: the logic of terms, propositions, and arguments. Part IV concerns method, a new topic of concern in Renaissance and 16th-century logic. The study of method assumes a fourth level of complexity beyond terms, propositions, and arguments. It concerns the chains of arguments characteristic of two aspects of science: discovery and teaching. Viewed as speech behavior, discovery and teaching would be classified by linguists today as part of pragmatics or discourse analysis. In the 15th and 16th centuries, however, they were discussed in abstraction from behavior. Method was described in terms of the logical form of the arguments used in science, akin to the way modern philosophers describe scientific explanation in terms of the logical structure of scientific theories and inferential patterns such as induction and statistical inference.

The present chapter describes the way Arnauld and Nicole explicate method in terms of logical form. The relevant form of scientific logic is deduction. Deduction in this case consists of syllogisms, which the *Logic*'s authors believe do not require much explanation because, as they frequently observe, syllogisms are not very complicated. In any case, they have described syllogistic logic in Part III. They devote discussion in Part IV more to the content and arrangement of syllogisms. The central sections of Part IV concern the care to be taken in the choice of words and definitions and in meeting the special epistemic requirements demanded of scientific axioms. In a style typical of the period, the authors summarize their advice in methodological rules. The rules they advance expand on formulations found in Descartes and Pascal, mainly in adding various cautions of their own. The new advice largely concerns the precision required in dealing with the meaning of terms. They are voluble on various abuses of intentional content, especially varieties of vagueness and ambiguity, and the misunderstanding of nominal definitions.

Of special interest here is the discussion of epistemology, which has implications for logic proper. Despite the authors' basic rationalism, they allow for knowledge grounded in sensation. At the basis of sensory knowledge is a distinction between essential and contingent truth. Knowledge of essential truths and the axioms of science, both of which are understood to be necessarily true, are describe as being justified for the most part by the apprehension of clear and distinct ideas. Knowledge of contingent truth, however, is grounded in sensation. The distinction between necessary and contingent truth has important implications for semantic theory. In particular, the truth-conditions for affirmative propositions must be qualified so that if a proposition describes a contingent fact, its terms must refer to existing things. Contingent truths, in short, carry existential import. On the other hand, essential truths, which describe inclusion relations among idea-contents, may be true even if their terms fail to signify existing things.

Part IV may be divided into three parts. In the early sections the authors abstract the argument forms appropriate to science. These are of two types: arguments appropriate to scientific discovery, and arguments used in promulgating and teaching scientific knowledge. The middle sections of Part IV focus on the importance of conceptual clarity in science. These portions elaborate the role of clear and distinct ideas in justifying scientific axioms and give advice on the careful selection of nominal definitions. It is here that the *Logic* proposes its rules for definitions, axioms, demonstration, and method. The final sections of Part IV concern the difference between scientific and contingent truth. This chapter will concentrate on the first two topics: the role of logic in scientific arguments and the importance of clear definitions. Chapter 6 will discuss essential and contingent truths, and their truth-conditions.

In the early sections of Part IV, the authors select from a cornucopia of then contemporary views to formulate a distinctly Cartesian approach to method. The discussion begins by distinguishing scientific from sensory knowledge. Science, the authors hold, consists of self-evident "axioms" and their logical consequences. Knowledge of contingent truths, on the other hand, is justified by sensation and concerns particular events and individuals.

Method is relevant to the former. It consists of the rules and customs for obtaining and imparting scientific knowledge. From the perspective of modern logic, what the *Logic* says about method, like the formal logic in Part III, is of little technical interest from the perspective of modern logic. It is, however, interesting from the perspective of philosophical logic due to the way it marshals the forms of syllogistic reasoning as part of philosophical analysis.

Since antiquity, logicians, mathematicians, and philosophers had speculated about the investigative procedures (the "method") appropriate for the discovery of scientific knowledge and, once discovered, for its presentation and instruction. Acquisition and instruction of scientific knowledge were clearly understood to be human activities. Method was intended to provide guidance to these behavioral practices. The practice itself as part of life was often described as a habit or craft—the Stoics called it *technē*. Despite being an activity, however, in the two hundred years prior to the *Logic* method was explained abstractly in terms of argument forms. These arguments had a specific syntactic structure, the various parts being intended to represent aspects of the investigative procedures. In an argument representing acquisition, the premises stood for knowledge acquired earlier in the discovery process. Such premises were usually about observable particulars—things or events. The argument's conclusion then stood for the knowledge that was literally derived as part of the discovery process. The conclusion was thought to be a causal law capturing a universal truth of nature.

Arguments representing instruction and presentation—the two were discussed as one—had a form that revered the pattern of arguments representing acquisition. The premises of the argument were supposed to represent general laws previously derived in the acquisition process, while the conclusion represented the particular facts these laws explain. The *Logic*'s discussion of method follows this tradition.

The use of formal logic to describe methodological practice is curious. It presents an example of formal logic—in this case syllogistic arguments—being applied to the explanation of a philosophical topic outside logic proper. In this instance formal logic "explains" scientific discovery and exposition. The particular argument forms that the *Logic* elects for this purpose are also intriguing due to the logic involved. By and large, the relevant logical patterns were not original to the *Logic* and had been applied to this purpose by others before—another example of the *Logic*'s authors appropriating earlier logic when useful. An understanding of the particular syllogistic forms employed to represent methodological practice requires some discussion of their historical background. First, however, it is necessary to describe the argument forms themselves.

Part IV opens by endorsing the standard view that method divides into two parts: analysis and synthesis. Analysis is the method by which the truths of science are discovered; it is also referred to as resolution and the method of discovery. Analysis is said to consist of reasoning from effect to cause, and from the more specific to the more general. More abstractly, analysis consists of the argument forms in which general laws are deduced from descriptions of particular events. Because an effect follows from its cause, analysis is said to be *a posteriori*.

Synthesis is what we would call today the explanation of facts. It is defined as the method appropriate for demonstrating that the previously observed properties of some particular thing or event follow from a general causal law. Formally, synthesis is analysis in reverse. It reasons from cause to effect and is called the method of composition. Synthesis is the form of scientific knowledge that is exhibited in instruction and persuasion, and in the statement of explanations in scientific treatises. More abstractly, synthesis is identified with the argument form in which a description of an observable event is deduced from a general law. Such a deduction constitutes an explanation of why a particular event occurred. Because causes are prior to effects, synthesis is said to be *a priori*.

Analysis

Analysis is understood as the method by which one acquires knowledge of causes from effects or, equivalently, of the more general from the specific. In this way of speaking, causation is conflated with generality, a view common in early philosophy. Aristotle, for example, thought of a genus as the formal cause of its species, and Neoplatonists believed that higher hypotheses, which were more general in their causal properties, generated lower ones. When analysis is conceived as describing the discovery of essential truths, it is understood as taking the investigator from knowledge of species lower in the tree of Porphyry to knowledge of a higher genus.

It must be said that, to a modern reader, the method of analysis seems to be based in a logical confusion. The apparent suggestion in analysis is that it is possible to "deduce" a cause from an effect, or a general law from its instances; it appears to claim, in effect, that induction from a few particular cases to a general law is a valid logical argument. To make sense of this claim, absurd on its face, some history is necessary. The account starts with Plato and undergoes maturation in Renaissance logic.

In the 15th and 16th centuries, discussions of method referred back to Plato. In the *Phaedrus*, Socrates says "I am myself a great lover of these processes of division [*diairesis*] and generalization [*synagōgē*]."[1] The classical example of division is the Stranger's definition of *angler* in the *Sophist* (218e ff.). The Stranger arrives at a characterization of *angler* by progressively dividing larger groups starting with "art in general." Generalization was understood as the process of division in reverse.

What appears to be the first application of argument forms to explain analysis and synthesis is found in Euclid, in lines interpolated into texts as remarks on Proposition 13 of Book I of the *Elements*. Heath speculates that the insertion dates from as late as the first century AD. The text reads:[2]

> Analysis is the assumption of that which is sought as if it were admitted <and arrived at> by means of its consequences at something admitted to be true. Synthesis is an assumption of that which

---

1 265d, Jowett trans.
2 *Euclid 1956*, p. 442.

is admitted <and arrival> by means of its consequences at something admitted to be true.

A more complete statement of the same distinction is found somewhat later in the geometry of Pappus (c. 340):[3]

> Analysis, then, takes that which is sought as if it were admitted and passes from it through its successive consequences [*akolouthōn*] to something which is admitted as the result of synthesis; for in analysis we assume that which is sought as if it were already done (γεηονοός), and we inquire what it is from which this results, and again what is the antecedent [*proēgoumenon*] cause of the latter, and so on, until by so retracing our steps we come upon something already known or belonging to the class of first principles, and such a method [*ephodos*] we call analysis, as being a solution backwards [*anapalin lysin*].
>
> But in synthesis, reversing the process, we take as already done suppose that which was last arrived at in the analysis and, by arranging in their natural order as consequences [*epomena*] what before were antecedents [*proēgoumena*], and successively connecting them one with another, we arrive finally at the construction of what was sought; and this we call synthesis.
>
> Now analysis is of two kinds, the one directed to searching for the truth, being called *theoretical*, the other directed to finding what we are told to find and called *problematical*. (1) In the theoretical kind we assume what is sought as if it were existent and true, after which we pass through its successive consequences, [*akolouthōn*], as if they too were true and established by virtue of our hypotheses, to something admitted: then (*a*), if that something admitted is true, that which is sought will also be true, but (*b*), if we come upon something admittedly false, that which is sought will also be false. (2) In the *problematical* kind we assume that which is propounded as if it were known, after which we pass through its successive consequences, taking them as true, up to something admitted: if then (*a*) what is admitted is possible and obtainable, that is, what mathematicians call *given*, what was originally proposed will also be possible, and the proof will again correspond in the reverse order to the analysis, but if (*b*) we come upon something admittedly impossible, the problem will also be impossible.[4]

Here proofs in geometry provide the paradigms. Analysis is the seeming paradoxical process by which the investigator proceeds from "what is to

---

3 Heath 1921, vol. 2, pp. 399–400.
4 Compare the translation in *Hintikka 1974*, pp. 8–10.

be proven" to the propositions "from which it can be proven." Synthesis is the process in reverse—the investigator produces the proof from premises, taken as given, to a desired conclusion, which, as such, is a theorem. Under this description, synthesis seems to be an abstraction from proofs like those of the *Elements*, which are recognizable similar to proofs in modern mathematics. From a modern vantage point, it is not unreasonable to consider a proof in Euclid as a presentation of a knowledge that has been discovered together with the proof serving as its justification. Such a proof is also suitable for instruction. Analysis, on the other hand, is rather different. It seems to approximate what in modern times Schiller called "the logic of scientific discovery."[5] Here an investigator speculates about a proposition that might be true. He or she then applies analysis in steps that lead to a more general explanatory principle. We are familiar in modern times with attempts at a "logic of discovery"—abduction, inference to the best explanation, inductive logic, and even probability theory. A major oddity in Pappus' account is that he clearly seems to have thought that synthesis was deductive, that one can reason deductively from a theorem to be proven to the propositions that entail it. As we shall see, what seems to be a similar logical error affects the version of analysis and synthesis in the *Port Royal Logic*. How students of method in the centuries prior to the *Logic* marshaled syllogistic logic to solve this conundrum makes an interesting story. The solution they arrived at appears in the *Logic*'s own version of analysis and synthesis. Technically, the logic employed, although subtle, is not difficult. It consists of simple syllogisms marshalled symmetrically.

Historically, Pappus' distinction survived the Middle Ages. Neither analysis nor synthesis themselves were standard topics in medieval logic.[6] They are not mentioned, for example, in Ockham's *Summa Logic* or Buridan's *Summulae*. When they were discussed by name, they were abstracted from geometry and conceived of as applying to knowledge in general. In these instances analysis and synthesis were discussed as methods for knowledge acquisition and instruction broadly conceived. Aquinas draws the distinction as follows:[7]

> The first is the method of analysis, by which we go from what is complex to what is simple or from a whole to a part, as it is said in

---

5 Schiller 1917.
6 *Diogenes Laertius* 1970, III.25, pp. 298–299; *Proclus* 1970, 211, pp. 163–164.
7 *Thomas Aquinas* 1961, *Commentary on the Metaphysics*, Book II, p. 278. See also *Thomas Aquinas* 1964–1980, *Summa theologiae* Ia.II.q15.a5.
   Una quidem per modum resolutionis, secundum quam procedimus a compositis ad simplicia, et a toto ad partem, sicut dicitur in primo physicorum, quod confusa sunt prius nobis nota. Et in hac via perficitur cognitio veritatis, quando pervenitur ad singulas partes distincte cognoscendas. Alia est via compositionis, per quam procedimus a

Book I of the *Physics* that the first objects of our knowledge are confused wholes. Now our knowledge of the truth is perfected by this method when we attain a distinct knowledge of the particular parts of a whole. The other method is that of synthesis, by which we go from what is simple to what is complex; and we attain knowledge of truth by this method when we succeed in knowing a whole. Thus the fact that man is unable to know perfectly in things a whole and a part shows the difficulty involved in knowing the truth by both of these methods.

This account exhibits two technical features that were to persist. First, analysis and synthesis are described abstractly as arguments. Despite the fact that discovery and instruction were human activities, habits, and skills, they are described in terms of formal arguments. Second, Aquinas follows Pappus in describing both analysis and synthesis as deductive.

As Pappus explicated it, both analysis and synthesis proceed from propositions to their "consequences" [*akolouthōn*]. It makes perfect sense, then, to regard the sequence of propositions in a Euclidian proof as deductive because they are similar to proofs in modern geometry proceeding from premises to a conclusion by steps of logical reasoning. The case for analysis is otherwise. As Pappus describes analysis, it proceeds from a theorem to the propositions from which it is proven. It seems inappropriate, if not simply mistaken, to think of this process as deductive. A theorem does not usually logically entail its premises. There is no mistaking Pappus' intention. He says, "If we come upon something admittedly false, that which is sought will also be false." A proposition cannot be shown false by its logical relation to another false proposition unless that relation is one of logical entailment. Pappus' view would be tenable if he also held that a theorem and its premises mutually entail one another, that they were logically equivalent. But theorems in geometry are seldom equivalent to the propositions from which they are proven.

The doctrine that one can reason backwards by valid steps of entailment from the theorems of geometric proof to the premises from which they are deduced, odd as it seems, persisted in the logical tradition, as the quotation from Aquinas shows. The view is endorsed by Arnauld and Nicole in their explanation of analysis. In Part IV, they say:

> This is the way to understand the nature of analysis as used by geometers. Here is what it consists in. Suppose a question is presented to them, such as whether it is true or false that something is a theorem,

---

simplicibus ad composita, qua perficitur cognitio veritatis cum pervenitur ad totum. Sic igitur hoc ipsum, quod homo non potest in rebus perfecte totum et partem cognoscere, ostendit difficultatem considerandae veritatis secundum utramque viam.

or whether a problem is possible or impossible; they assume what is at issue and examine what follows from that assumption. If in this examination they arrive at some clear truth from which the assumption follows necessarily, they conclude that the assumption is true (*s'ils arrivent dans cet examen à quelque vérité clair dont ce que leur proposé soit une suite nécessaire, ils en concluent, que ce qui leur est proposé est vrai*). Then starting over from the end point, they demonstrate it by the other method which is called *composition*. But if they fall into some absurdity or impossibility as a necessary consequence of their assumption, they conclude from this that the assumption is false and impossible.[8]

Renaissance logicians found a solution to this logical conundrum in a distinction of Aristotle's. The details of how they appropriated the distinction to explain analysis is found in the *Logic*'s own account. The first step, which is illustrated in Aquinas' text, was to abstract analysis from geometry and to apply it to science more generally. It then became possible to apply Aristotle's distinction to science at large.

At one point in the *Posterior Analytics*, Aristotle remarks that there are two sorts of demonstration. In one, we start with what is better and immediately known, typically an observation of particulars. We then reason to a causal law that explains what we observed. In a second sort of demonstration, we reason deductively from this same causal law to the particular observed effect. In medieval logic, the first sort of demonstration was later called reasoning "from effect to cause," or a *demonstratio quia*, and the second was called reasoning "from cause to effect," or a *demonstratio propter quid*. Aristotle draws the distinction as follows:[9]

> Knowledge of the fact differs from knowledge of the reasoned fact. To begin with, they differ within the same science and in two ways: (1) when the premises of the syllogism are not immediate (for then the proximate cause is not contained in them—a necessary condition of knowledge of the reasoned fact): (2) when the premises are immediate, but instead of the cause the better known of the two reciprocals is taken as the middle; for of two reciprocally predicable terms the one which is not the cause [i.e. the observed effect] may quite easily be the better known and so become the middle term of the demonstration [the demonstration *quia*]. Thus (2) (a) you might prove as follows that the planets are near because they do not twinkle [the effect]: let C be the planets, B not twinkling, A proximity [the cause]. Then B is predicable of C; for the planets do not twinkle.

---

8 LAP IV.2, KM V 367, B 238.
9 *Aristotle Posterior Analytics*, I.13, 78a23–38, trans. G.R.G. Mure.

But *A* is also predicable of *B*, since that which does not twinkle is near—we must take this truth as having been reached by induction or sense-perception. Therefore *A* is a necessary predicate of *C*; so that we have demonstrated that the planets are near. This syllogism, then, proves not the reasoned fact but only the fact; since they are not near because they do not twinkle, but, because they are near, do not twinkle.

The major and middle of the proof, however, may be reversed, and then the demonstration will be of the reasoned fact [a demonstration *propter quid*]. Thus: let *C* be the planets, *B* proximity [the cause], *A* not twinkling [the effect]. Then *B* is an attribute of *C*, and *A*—not twinkling—of *B*. Consequently *A* is predicable of *C*, and the syllogism proves the reasoned fact, since its middle term is the proximate cause.

The passage describes two syllogisms that are formally related. Their major premises are converted relative to one another—their subjects and predicates are reversed—and the minor premises and conclusions are switched. Moreover, their explanatory intentions are reversed as well. In a sense that will be exploited by the students of method, the first syllogism argues from an observed event as premise to a law that explains it as conclusion, and the second argues in reverse, from an explanatory law to an observed event. The two syllogisms are the following:

Demonstration Quia *(from observed fact to its reason):*

Everything that does not twinkle (observed effect) *is proximate* (cause)	AMP	effect-cause	commutable
<u>*Every planet does not twinkle*</u> (observed effect)	<u>ASM</u>	subject-effect	
∴ *Every planet is proximate* (cause)	ASP	subject-cause	

Demonstration Propter Quid *(from reason observed fact):*

Everything proximate (cause) *does not twinkle* (observed effect)	AMP	cause-effect	commutable
<u>*Every planet is proximate*</u> (cause)	<u>ASM</u>	subject-cause	
∴ *Every planet does not twinkle* (observed effect)	ASP	subject-effect	

As the displays indicate, the major premises in the syllogisms are converses of each other. It is strange to think that both could be true simultaneously. For both to be true—in medieval terms, for them to be convertible—their subjects and predicates would have to be coextensive. This is a dubious assumption that will be considered in a moment.

It will be helpful to elucidate in colloquial terms what the arguments are intended to show. Each syllogism can be expressed in a single sentence expressing a kind of explanation. The first says that the reason that (*"propter quid"*) planets do not twinkle is that they are close. The second says that because (*"quia"*) planets are close, it is an interesting fact that they do not twinkle.

These syllogisms provided models for analysis and synthesis. Analysis and synthesis as such, however, were not widely discussed in medieval logic. Aristotle's distinction, however, and the two syllogisms above were a standard topic. Aquinas draws the distinction this way:[10]

> There are two kinds of demonstration. One kind is through a cause and is called a demonstration *propter quid*—and this sort of demonstration is through things that are prior, absolutely speaking. The second kind is through an effect and is called a demonstration *quia*—and this sort of demonstration is through things that are prior with respect to us. For since an effect is more apparent to us than its cause, we proceed through the effect to a cognition of the cause.
>
> Now from any effect it can be demonstrated that a cause proper to it exists—as long as its effects are more known to us. For since effects depend on a cause, it follows that once an effect is posited, it must be that its cause exists prior to it. Hence, insofar as it is not known to us *per se* there is a God, this is demonstrable though effects that are known to us.

Ockham adds to the terminology by describing a demonstration *quia* as *a priori*, and a demonstration *propter quid* as *a posteriori*:[11]

> In light of this, it is important to see that some demonstrations are such that their premises are absolutely prior to the conclusion; and

---

10 *Thomas Aquinas 1888, Summa theologiae* I.q2.a2:

> Respondeo dicendum quod duplex est demonstratio. Una quae est per causam, et dicitur propter quid, et haec est per priora simpliciter. Alia est per effectum, et dicitur demonstratio quia, et haec est per ea quae sunt priora quoad nos, cum enim effectus aliquis nobis est manifestior quam sua causa, per effectum procedimus ad cognitionem causae. Ex quolibet autem effectu potest demonstrari propriam causam eius esse (si tamen eius effectus sint magis noti quoad nos), quia, cum effectus dependeant a causa, posito effectu necesse est causam praeexistere. Unde Deum esse, secundum quod non est per se notum quoad nos, demonstrabile est per effectus nobis notos.

11 *William of Ockham 1974, Summa Logicae*, III.1, Chapt. 17, p. 533:

> Propter quod oportet scire quod quaedam est demonstratio cuius praemissae sunt simpliciter priores conclusione, et illa vocatur demonstratio a priori sive propter quid. Quaedam est demonstratio cuius praemissae non sunt simpliciter priores conclusione,

these are called *a priori* or *propter quid* demonstrations. Other demonstrations are such that their premises are not absolutely prior to the conclusion but are nonetheless better known [than the conclusion] to the one who is constructing the syllogism, with the result that it is through these premises that the one constructing the syllogism comes to a cognition of the conclusion; and these are called *quia* or *a posteriori* demonstrations.

John Buridan devotes chapters to the distinction in the *Summulae*.[12]

In the Renaissance, interest revived in method, and with it interest in analysis and synthesis. Method was understood as a description of behavior, the habit or "art," for first obtaining knowledge (*inventio*) and then, once knowledge was obtained, for its instruction and dissemination. Training in method was thought to be practical. It was an aid to research and instruction and was regarded as more useful than the formal study of scholastic logic. In practice, however, method continued to be explained, as Pappus did, in terms of mathematical paradigms. Directions for investigators and teachers were set out in rules or pointers for the formation of syllogism. This formalist approach was later followed by Descartes in his *Regulae* and *Discourse on Method* and by the authors of the *Logic* in the discussion of Part IV.

In his influential *On Methods*, Jacabo Zabarella (1533–1589) applied Aristotle's account of demonstration to Pappus' distinction between analysis and synthesis. In so doing, he provided an explanation of the puzzle of how in analysis a theorem can be "deduced" from its premises:[13]

> It happens, therefore, that in every syllogism constructed for the sake of knowing scientifically, it is necessary that progression

---

sunt tamen notiores sic syllogizanti, per quas devenit sic syllogizans in notitiam conclusionis, et talis demonstratio vocatur demonstratio quia sive a posteriori.

12 *John Buridan 2001, Summulae* 8.7.10 to 8.9.3.
13 *Zabarella 2013, On Methods*, Book III, Chapt. IV.4, vol. 2, pp. 22–25:

> Hinc fit ut in omni syllogismo sciendi gratia constructo necesse sit vel à causa ad effectum vel contrà ab effectu ad causam progressum fieri, aliud genus scientifici syllogismi et ex propositionibus eo modo necessariis constituti non inveno. Cùm enim in propositione maiore medium et maior extremitas collocentur et necessum sit alterum alterius causam esse, medium quidem maioris causa si fuerit, syllogismus est à causa ad effectum; si verò maior extremitas sit causa medii, est ab effectu ad causam. Duae igitur scientificae methodi oriuntur, non plures, nec pauciores, altera per excellentiam demonstrativa methodus dicitur, quam Graeci, κυρίως ἀπόδειξιν vel ἀπόδειξιν τοῦ διότι vocant, nostri potissimam demonstrationem vel demonstrationem propter quid appellare consueverunt. Altera, quae ab effectu ad causam progreditur, resolutiva nominatur, huiusmodi enim progressus resolutio est, sicuti à causa ad effectum dicitur compositio, methodum hanc vocant Graeci, συλλογισμὸν τοῦ ὅτι vel διὰ

occurs either from cause to effect or, on the contrary, from effect to cause. I do not find another kind of scientific syllogism also constituted from premises [that are] necessary in this way. For since the middle [term] and the major extreme are included in the major premise, and it is necessary that one be the cause of the other, then, of course, if the middle [term] was the cause of the major, the syllogism would be from cause to effect; and if the major extreme were the cause of the middle [term], it would be from effect to cause. Two scientific methods, therefore, arise—neither more nor fewer. One, which the Greeks call *kurios apodeixis* (demonstration of the strongest sort) or *apodeixis tou dioti* (demonstration of the on-account-of-which), and we have been accustomed to call demonstration *potissima* or demonstration *propter quid*, is said to be demonstrative method *par excellence*. The other, which progresses from effect to cause, is named resolutive. For a progression of this type is a resolution, just as composition is said to be from cause to effect. The Greeks call this method *syllogismos tou hoti* (syllogism of the that-it-is-the-case) or *dia semeion* ([syllogism] by means of signs). We [call it] demonstration *quia* or syllogism *a signo* or demonstration of the second degree.

Zabarella conceives of method as a research practice for obtaining knowledge and, once obtained, for its instruction. He calls it the "way of doctrine."[14] The preceding text, however, is typical of his practice. He abstracts from human behavior to discuss method in terms of argument forms. The initial stage of scientific inquiry, called analysis, consists of reasoning from what we see to a causal law that explains it. It is represented by a demonstration *quia*. In this syllogism, what is to be explained is expressed in the minor premise, *every S is M*, in which S names the subject under investigation and M the property that is to be explained. The major premise *every M is P* is a hypothetical causal law in which the major term P names the causal property. Here the middle term M assumes the role of an effect brought about by the causal property P. The conclusion *every S is P* follows in the mood *Barbara*. It asserts that the observed subject S has the required causal property P needed to explain what was observed.

As we shall see below, as formulated in analysis, the major premise *every M is P* says that everything effected P has the causal property P. This premise says that M cannot fail to have the causal property P. In other words and somewhat paradoxically, the more general M falls under

---

σημείων nostri demonstrationem quia vel syllogismum à signo vel secundi gradus demonstrationem.

14 On Zabarella see *Gilbert 1960*, pp. 167–176.

the less general *P*. This is the converse of what we normally think of as the causal order *every P is M*, which says that everything that has the causal property *P* has the property *M* that results from it.

Viewed abstractly, once the situation to be explained *every S is M* is posited as a minor premise in analysis, the completed analysis in *Barbara* can be constructed with a causal law *every M is P* as major premise by choosing any property whatsoever as the major term *P*. To be plausible as an explanation, however, the choice of *P* needs to be true and necessary. What constrains the choice of *P* depends on an author's wider view of science. We shall see below that the authors of the *Port Royal Logic* impose the condition that the causal law *every M is P* has been previously established by a prior analysis, or if it is new, *M* must be a clear and distinct idea and *P* must describe its content.

The second part of science, Zabarella explains, is instruction. It is represented by a demonstration *propter quid* or a synthesis. He provides directions for its construction from a prior demonstration *quia*. The goal is to prove, by a syllogism in *Barbara*, the conclusion *every S is M*, which says that the subject *S* has an observed property *M*. The construction posits as its major premise the causal law *every P is M*, which is the converse of the law in the prior analysis. Its minor premise is *every S is P*, which asserts that the subject *S* has the relevant causal property *P*. The argument as a whole represents a causal explanation of the observed fact.

To modern eyes, the convertibility (equivalence) of the two causal laws represents a resurfacing of the difficulty that afflicts Pappus' account. For the desired conversion of the major premises to be plausible, it is necessary that the causal property and its effect be coextensive. Each must determines the other. In Aristotelian terminology, the observed property cannot be merely an accident of the subject—it must be a necessary property, a *proprium*, characteristic of it. The problem is equivalent to the one in Pappus' account of analysis in which a derived theorem is regarded as logically equivalent to the principles from which it was proven. For Aristotle's technique to work, it seems, an effect must be coextensive with its cause or, alternatively, that a species must be coextensive with its genus.

It is instructive to look at a formally identical example of this sort of "backwards" reasoning in the logic of the period. It occurs in the medieval doctrine of topics or "places" (*topoi, loci*). Topics were techniques for constructing, from an incomplete enthymeme, a valid syllogism that completes an explanation. The general form of the enthymeme is "*S is P, because every M is P*." A standard "topic" is a set of instructions for completing the enthymeme by converting it into the valid syllogism in *Barbara: every M is P, every S is M, therefore every S is P*."

There are two topics in particular that have the same form as a demonstration *quia* or analysis. The first topic is called "from the effect to the efficient cause." The task in this case is to complete the enthymeme, *S is P because P causes M*. The second is the topic called "from the species to the genus." In it the task is to complete the partial argument, *S is in the genus P because M is a species of P*.

Paired with each of these is a complementary topic, called respectively "from the efficient cause to the effect" and "from the genus to the species." In each pair the completed syllogism of the first topic bears the same formal relation to that of the second topic as a demonstrations *quia* does to demonstrations *propter quid*.

The topics and their syllogistic completions are displayed below. Beneath each enthymeme is its completed syllogism. To their right are those formally similar to demonstrations *quia* and analysis, and to the left are those formally similar to demonstrations *propter quid* or synthesis. As in the syllogisms representing analysis and synthesis, the terms of the major premises of each pair are reversed, and the minor premise and the conclusion switch places. The examples are from Peter of Spain:[15]

From the Effect
Enthymeme:
The knife is good

Therefore, the knife is caused by the smithy

From the Cause

Everything good is caused by the smithy
Therefore, the knife is caused by the smithy

Syllogism:
Everything good is caused by the smithy
The knife is good
Therefore, the knife is caused by the smithy

Everything caused by the smithy is good
The knife is caused by the smithy
Therefore, the knife is good

From the Species
Enthymeme:
Socrates is a man
Therefore, Socrates is an animal

From the Genus

Socrates is an animal
Therefore, Socrates is a man

Syllogism:
Every man is an animal
Socrates is a man
Therefore, Socrates is an animal

Every [rational] animal is a man
Socrates is a [rational] animal
Therefore, Socrates is a man

The construction of the syllogisms on the right from those on the left follows exactly that of a demonstration *propter quid* from a demonstration

---

15 *Peter of Spain* 2014, pp. 212–213, 218–219.

quia. As in the case of the causal laws, in the construction of a demonstration *propter quid* from a demonstration *quia*, the effect must be coextensive with the cause, and the species with the genus.

Odd as it may seem, Aristotle at times assume that an efficient cause and its effect are convertible—that they "determine each other" (*allēlōn antia*).[16] If the context is right, it may also be appropriate to consider a species as coextensive with its genus if, for example, the assumption is made that the only members of the genus that are relevant are those of the species.

The account in the *Port Royal Logic* falls squarely within this tradition. The purpose of analysis, they argue, is knowledge acquisition—to discover the truth (*découvir la vérité*).[17] It proceeds "from what is better known to what is less well known," and from the particular to the general—from "*vérités connues dans l'examen particulier*" to "*conaissances générales*"—and from effect to cause.[18] Moreover, as in Pappus and Zabarella, the derivation relation in analysis is logical entailment. The derivation of the general from the particular, and of the cause from the effect, follows by necessity.[19]

In Chapter 2 of Part IV the authors provide two examples of analysis. In the first, an investigator discovers that a subject under investigation has St. Louis as a remote ancestor. St. Louis, his progenitor, is in a sense his "cause."[20] When spelled out, the underlying logic consists of a series of syllogisms in *Barbara*.

A series of syllogisms is constructed working backward from the subject to his father, grandfather, and earlier progenitors. In each syllogism the minor premise affirms of a subject (the minor term) that he is the descendant of his father (the middle term). An auxiliary major premise is needed for the inference to go through. This affirms of the subject's father that he is the descendant of his grandfather (the major term). The conclusion affirms that the subject is the descendant of his grandfather.

The authors remark that auxiliary major premises of this sort are typical of analysis: "in analysis we introduce clear and evident maxims only to the extent that we need them."[21] Coming to realize that the extra premise is needed, and that the extra premise is true, is part of the discovery process of analysis.

This pattern is repeated for each generation working backward from the subject. The conclusion of the last syllogism in the series affirms that

---

16 See *Metaphysics* D, 1013b9; *Physics* II.3, 195a11.
17 *LAP* IV.2, *KM* V 361, *B* 233.
18 *LAP* IV.2, *KM* V 362, 366, *B* 234, 237.
19 *LAP* IV.2, *KM* V 367, *B* 238.
20 Ibid.
21 *LAP* IV.2, *KM* V 366, *B* 237.

the subject is a descendant of St. Louis. The full analysis spelled out looks like this:

every descendant of B is a descendant of C, A is a descendant of B/∴ A is a descendant of C
every descendant of C is a descendant of D, A is a descendant of C/∴ A is a descendant of D
every descendant of D is a descendant of E, A is a descendant of D/∴ A is a descendant of E
every descendant of E is a descendant of St. Louis, A is a descendant of E/∴ A is a descendant of St. Louis

The explanation proceeds in a sense from the particular to the general because increasingly earlier ancestors have increasingly more descendants. Thus, each succeeding predicate has a broader extension, and the final predicate *is a descendant of St. Louis* is the "most general" of all.

The corresponding synthesis is the series in reverse order. As in the earlier examples, the causal premise must be converted on the assumption, evidently, that this particular chain of descendants is linear. It would look like this:

every living descendant of St. Louis is a living descendant of E, A is a living descendant of St. Louis /∴ A is a living descendant of E
every living descendant of E is a living descendant of D, A is a living descendant of E/∴ A is a living descendant of D
every living descendant of D is a living descendant of C, A is a living descendant of D/∴ A is a descendant of C
every living descendant of C is a living descendant of B, A is a living descendant of C/∴ A is a living descendant of B

The *Logic* offers a second example of reasoning from effect to cause. It is also reasoning from species to genus.[22] In this series too, each syllogism makes use of a hypothetical major premise needed to make the inference complete. The example represents the reasoning process in which it is discovered that the soul is immortal. The formal logic is the following:

Thinking things are immaterial. The soul is a thinking thing. /∴ The soul is immaterial.
Anything that is immaterial is indestructible. The soul is immaterial. /∴ The soul is indestructible.
Anything that is indestructible is immortal. The soul is indestructible. /∴ The soul is immortal.

22 Ibid. Cf. Descartes, Synopsis of Second Meditation, §13, *Descartes 1985b*, II.9.

In general, the authors claim that "it is impossible to know a species properly without knowing the genus."[23] Although the authors themselves do not provide an example that reasons explicitly from genus to species, it will be instructive to contrive one illustrating their point:

> every human is an animal, Socrates is a human/∴ Socrates is an animal
> every animal is a living creature, Socrates is an animal/∴ Socrates is a living creature
> every living creature is a body, Socrates is a living creature/∴ Socrates is a body
> every body is a substance, Socrates is a body/∴ Socrates is a substance

In the technical language of the *Logic*, this series unpacks the comprehension of the idea *human*. The sequence begins in the first syllogism by affirming of *Socrates* the restricted predicate *human*, which has the comprehension {rationality, self-motion, life, corporeality, being}. In the subsequent syllogisms, species of increasingly less restricted comprehensions are predicated of Socrates. The sequence terminates by predicating of Socrates the most general genus.

The corresponding synthesis reasons in the reverse direction. It explains why Socrates is a human by reasoning from his most general properties. Its containment premises would be conversions of those in the prior analysis. This unlikely convertibility would be plausible in the case of a genus-species pair only on the assumption that the causal sequence running from genus to species leads in a direct line to a specific individual. It would look like this:

> All individuals in (the genus) substance are individuals in (the species) body. Socrates is an individual in (the genus) substance. /∴ Socrates is an individual in (the species) body.
> All individuals in (the genus) body are individuals in (the species) living creature. Socrates is an individual in (the genus) body. /∴ Socrates is an individual in (the species) living creature.
> All individuals in (the genus) living creature is an individual in (the species) animal. Socrates is an individual in (the genus) living creature. /∴ Socrates is an individual in (the species) animal.
> All individuals in (the genus) animal are individuals in (the species) human. Socrates is an individual in (the genus) animal. /∴ Socrates is an individual in (the species) human.

The analysis-synthesis distinction of the Renaissance morphed over time into the analytic-synthetic distinction of modern analytic philosophy.

---

23 *LAP* IV.3, *KM* V 368, B 238.

Hobbes' version of analysis and synthesis is formulated in terms of causal relations but is otherwise similar to the *Logic*'s.[24] Spinoza's notion of causation was essentially Neoplatonic, but he is known to have possessed the *Port Royal Logic* in his library.[25] Spinoza subscribed to his own version of the thesis, that the order of cause to effect was the same as the order in logic of subject to predicate, of the sort represented in the preceding synthesis.

In various papers Leibniz explored versions of analysis that are essentially more formal versions of the *Logic*'s.[26] It was typical of Leibniz to symbolize the predicate of a universal affirmative as a series $P_1 \ldots P$ of concatenated terms. In his notation the term letters are intended to stand for modes definitive of an idea, much like the *Logic*'s species-comprehensions. In a typical example Leibniz lays down an initial premise S is $P_1 \ldots P_k$. The "analysis," then, is a deduction that proceeds by the application of a simplifying inference rule that deletes terms from the predicate. In the deduction, each new line's predicate is therefore more general. The deduction terminates in a line with only the most general predicate of all. The inference rule, which deletes a term, may be defined as follows:

$$S \text{ is } X_1 \ldots X_n \vdash S \text{ is } X_1 \ldots X_{n-1}.$$

An example of a deductive analysis in Leibniz' style sort would be:

S is P_1, P_2, P_3, P_4
S is P_1, P_2, P_3
S is P_1, P_2
S is P_1

It is possible to see how the terminology evolved over time. According to the *Logic*, if the premise unpacked the content of an idea, it would be

---

24 Hobbes 1992, *De Corpore*, I.6.1, p. 66.
25 See *Offenberg 1973*.
26 Leibniz explains his notion of analysis as follows:

> I hold that every true proposition is either *immediate* or *mediate*. An immediate proposition is one that is true by itself, i.e. a proposition whose predicate is explicitly contained in its subject; I call truths of this sort "identical." All other propositions are mediate; a *true* proposition is mediate when its predicate is included virtually in its subject, in such a way that analysis of the subject, or of both predicate and subject, can ultimately reduce the proposition to an identical truth. That's what Aristotle and the scholastics mean when they say "the predicate is in the subject."

> Leibniz to Arnauld, 14.vii.1686 (unsent draft), *Bennett 2017*, p. 33. For examples of analysis within the context of a logical system see *De arte combinatoria* in *Parkinson 1966*, and *Swoyer 1995*.

necessarily true. That premise and the lines deduced from it would be analytic in Kant's sense. If the soul experienced the idea as clear and distinct, this demonstration is *a priori*, in Ockham's sense, and would also be known *a priori* in Kant's sense. In this way, medieval *a priori* analysis morphed into Kant's *analytic a priori*. The *Logic*'s use of these terms lies in the middle of this historical evolution.

Logically, of course, the inferential steps employing Leibniz' rule, and even syllogisms in the mood *Barbara*, are extremely simple-minded. As explained in Chapter 3, the *Logic*'s authors were not concerned that anybody would make mistakes doing syllogisms. In keeping with the emphasis on intentional content, they thought it more probable that people would make mistakes about the meaning of words. Accordingly, when they give advice on analysis, they give rules, which they borrow from Descartes, that do not talk about logical forms or fallacies—after all, anybody can reason in *Barbara*. All they say, in effect, is that in formulating one's premises, one ought to be careful not to add or to omit content to an idea's intention.[27]

Demonstration

The *Logic* discusses demonstration or deductive reasoning under the rubric of synthesis. The detailed discussion begins in Chapter 3 of Part IV. The core idea is similar to that of earlier writers. Synthesis is the "reverse" of analysis. Its premises are causal or generic laws, and its conclusions are descriptions of observations about particulars.

Like Zabarella, Arnauld and Nicole conceived of synthesis as the formal converse of analysis. The authors might have simply restricted their remarks to directions for converting an analysis into a synthesis. Instead, they go into details that explain their understanding of the process of logical reasoning.

Descartes seemed to have regarded valid logical reasoning as completely intuitive. The *Logic*'s authors, on the other hand, define logical demonstration formally, as steps that conform to syntactic paradigms. In doing so, they are following Pascal, who was not only a fellow Jansenist at Port Royal but a mathematician.

Although the authors regarded logic as formal, the logic they had in mind was the traditional syllogistic and its extensions of Part III, which they regarded as straightforward, even trivial. Nevertheless, it is the syllogistic logic of Part III that the authors employ to explain synthesis. Syllogisms marshaled in the appropriate way constitute what they called *demonstration*. Syllogistic demonstration, in other words, is the format for the statement of scientific knowledge, as it appears, for example, in scientific treatises, and as it is used in instruction. Its premises are causal

---

27 *LAP* IV.2, *KM* V 364–365, *B* 235–236; cf. Rules XIII, *AT* X 435–436, *Descartes 1985a*, pp. 54–55.

laws. These laws are required to be necessary truths. The most important of these are essential truths or real definitions, a view that dates to Aristotle in the *Posterior Analytics*.[28] The authors follow Descartes in regarding geometry as a model both for the certainty of its axioms and for the deductive nature of its proofs.[29]

Viewed in isolation from its theoretical context, the *Logic*'s description of demonstration is not unlike modern logic's. In a formal system today, a theorem is defined as either an axiom or a formula that follows from previously proven theorems by the rules of logic. The authors' formulation is similar and is a version of Pascal's rule describing reasoning in geometry. Pascal's rule reads:[30]

> Prove all propositions, using in for their proof only axioms that are perfectly self-evident or propositions already demonstrated or granted.

The *Logic* abstracts from Pascal's rule to a description of demonstration in general:[31]

> Prove all slightly obscure propositions, using in the proof only preceding definitions, axioms that have been granted, propositions that have already been demonstrated, or the construction of the thing itself that is in question whenever there is some operation to be done.

In generalizing the account to science more broadly, the rule omits constructions peculiar to geometry—the use of drawing and figures in proofs. Nominal definitions, however, remain important. The *Logic*'s rule appropriate for all science reads:[32]

> Prove all propositions that are even slightly obscure, using in their proofs only definitions that have preceded, axioms that have been granted, or propositions that have already been demonstrated.

---

28 For Aristotle, scientific demonstrations are sound syllogistic arguments. He says:

> Demonstrative knowledge must proceed from premises which are true, primary, immediate, better known than, and prior to, and causative of the conclusion (71b20). The knowledge of immediate premises is not by demonstration [72b20]. It is evident that scientific demonstrations are concerned with essential attributes and proceed from them [75a30].

29 Rules II, *AT* X 365, *Descartes 1985a*, p. 12. Descartes even speculates that there could be a single general science embracing all mathematics (a *mathesis universalis*) formulated in deductive arguments with premises that are either intuitively certain or previously proven. Rules VI, *AT* X 378, *Descartes 1985a*, p. 19.

30 *Pascal 1963b*, p. 357; *Pascal 1952*, p. 443.

31 *LAP* IV.4, *KM* V 369, *B* 240.

32 *LAP* IV.11, *KM* V 394, *B* 259.

The *Logic*'s account differs from Descartes' more intuitive demonstration in two way: in what counts as a premise and in the nature of inference. Descartes is clear that the only propositions that are certain in themselves are those that are grasped by what he calls intuition. Intuition for Descartes is a primitive epistemological faculty, which he does not explain in the *Discourse on Method* or in the *Regulae* where he addresses these issues. Presumably, a clear intuition is the same as having an understanding of a clear and distinct idea, but that experience also is epistemically primitive. In a Cartesian demonstration, each premise is grasped, one by one, by intuition. A proof of this sort unfolds over time. Descartes allows that in some cases by going over the completed proof repeatedly, the entire proof may be grasped in a single instantaneous intuition. He does not, however, say anything about the particular logical rules that should be applied at each step. He requires only that each line must itself be grasped intuitively.[33] Indeed, in his entire corpus Descartes has very little to say about formal logic. He is, however, clear on one point, which he shares with the authors of the *Logic*: training in logic, in the detailed rules of the syllogism, or in other branches of technical logic is often as much of a hindrance as a help in doing proofs.[34] No training, he believes, is necessary for accurate logical intuition. As a result, Descartes has little to say about the nature of demonstration other than that each step of a proof, and possibly the whole, must be grasped by intuition. He does not explain what intuition is, nor does he provide any analysis of the logical form of inferential steps.[35] The account of demonstration in the *Logic*, on the other hand, is much more complete—as one would hope in a treatise on logic. It explains both which premises are acceptable and what formal logic, albeit trivial, is to be applied in making inferential steps.

Premises are acceptable only if they are certain. The *Logic* spells out three categories of admissible premises: propositions that affirm the content of a clear and distinct idea, nominal definitions, and previously proven propositions.[36] By far the most important of these are those justified by clear and distinct ideas. These and the epistemology in support of them are discussed in detail in Chapter 6.

The *Logic* devoted Part III to detailing the rules of logic. These consist of the traditional categorical syllogistic and various extensions familiar in the logic of the period. In Part IV, the authors are assuming that the logic applied in demonstration is that of Part III. Unlike Descartes, who

---

33 Rules III, *AT* X 368–370, *Descartes 1985a*, pp. 14–15; Rules XI, *AT* 407–409, *Descartes 1985a*, pp. 37–38.
34 Rules II, *AT* X 365, *Descartes 1985a*, p. 12; Rules IV, *AT* X 372, *Descartes 1985a*, p. 16; Rules VII, *AT* X 389, *Descartes 1985a*, p. 26.
35 See *Gaukroger 1989*.
36 *LAP* IV.8, *KM* V 384, *B* 251.

regards the inferential steps in a demonstration as intuitive, the *Logic*'s authors make the point that they are formal:

> A true demonstration requires two things: one, that the content include only what is certain and indubitable; the other, that there is nothing defective in the form of the argument.[37]

Moreover, a demonstration begins, as does a synthesis for Zabarella, with premises about the genus. It concludes with the properties of the species.[38] The step-by-step syllogistic reasoning within the proof is via a "middle term":

> if we need some other idea besides the idea of the thing, the proposition must be demonstrated. . . . a demonstration requires some new middle term which the axioms do not clearly contain . . . it must be demonstrated, by using some other ideas to show the connection.[39]

Therefore, the steps in a demonstration are understood to be validated by the formal logic of the period.

On the other hand, the authors had warned, "There is little value in knowing the rules of the syllogism."[40] They regarded the application of formal logical rules as "natural" and easy. Like Descartes, they think logic "does not need to be studied." On logical errors, they observe "it is almost impossible for a person of average intelligence who has some insight ever to fall into them."[41]

Thus, according to the authors, the logic employed in science is the syllogistic and its extensions, which they regard as essentially trivial. One of the ironies in the history of logic is that, on the one hand, philosophers since Aristotle had been advocating the syllogistic for its scientific use, but on the other, scientists themselves never bothered to put arguments in syllogistic form. This failure of classical and medieval logic to affect science is especially glaring in geometry, the science with the most developed use of proof. As famously argued by Bertrand Russell,[42] one reason was probably the difficulty of representing relations in the syllogistic's subject-predicate syntax.

In the 16th century there was a serious attempt by Christian Herlinus and Conrad Dasypodius (1566) to state the proofs of Euclid's

---

37 *LAP* IV.8, *KM* V 384, *B* 251.
38 *LAP* IV.9, *KM* V 391, *B* 257; cf. Descartes *Rules AT* X 380–387, *Descartes 1985a*, pp. 20–24; *LAP* IV.11, *KM* V 394, *B* 259. Cf. *AT* X 18–19, *Descartes 1985a*, p. 20.
39 *LAP* IV.6, *KM* V 379–380, *B* 248–249.
40 *LAP* IV.Introduction, *KM* V 354, *B* 227.
41 *LAP* IV.8, *KM* V 384–385, *B* 252.
42 See *Russell 1902*, pp. 221–226, and *Russell 1992*.

Elements in syllogistic form.[43] Although many of their revised proofs appear valid in the sense that the lines of the proofs appear to follow from one another, the arguments they put forward as syllogisms are not genuine syllogisms in the strict sense. They employed relational expressions that, strictly speaking, do not conform to the subject-predicate grammar. An example of their proofs is given in the Appendix. The attempt is interesting because it illustrates the difficulty of formulating mathematical reasoning, especially relational issues, in the limited syntax of the syllogistic.

In summary, then, the discussion of demonstration in Part IV looks both forward and backward. It offers a general characterization of a proof as a series of lines that are either axioms, previously proven, or follow formally from earlier lines. This formulation was arrived at under the tutelage of Pascal. It is formal and rather modern. On the other hand, the formal logic assumed is traditional, with little promise that it could live up to the goal of capturing all scientific demonstrations.

Definition, Division, and Equivocation

It was not the logical inferences in scientific demonstrations that the authors thought people erred in using. Any simpleton, so they professed, could reason in syllogisms. They were much more concerned about the premises in the demonstrations. These are the basic laws of science. In Part IV the authors devote considerable discussion to their epistemological status. In doing so, they go into some detail about the more obscure parts of Cartesian epistemology, especially the difference between, on the one hand, certain knowledge, which is grounded in clear and distinct ideas, and on the other hand, knowledge based on sensation and faith. Definition plays a key role. The premises of scientific demonstration are either previously proven or they are "definitions."

Definitions fall into two types: real and nominal (*définition de chose* and *définition de nom*). Both are used to express certain knowledge, but equally important, each is subject to its own variety of abuse and error. Numerous sections of Part IV are devoted to characterizing the knowledge associated with definitions and giving advice for avoiding errors. Indeed, there may not have been a work since Aristotle that has focused so clearly on the verbal mistakes in the formation of premises in syllogistic reasoning.

In their account, the authors acknowledge that they are drawing heavily on a then unpublished essay by Pascal.[44] In Pascal's account of demonstration and definition, he argues that logic should follow the practices

---

[43] Herlinus 1566.
[44] *LAP* Premier Discour, *KM* V 110, *B* 10.

of geometry. Four of his five rules concern definition and equivocation.[45] The authors abstract from Pascal's list to formulate their own rule set applicable to all science generally. What they regard as important can be gauged from the fact that seven of their eight rules are about definition and equivocation. The *Logic*'s rules read:[46]

1. Leave no term even slightly obscure or equivocal without defining it.
2. In definitions, use only terms that are perfectly known or have already been explained.
3. In axioms, require everything to be perfectly evident.
4. Accept as evident what needs only a little attention to be recognized as true.
5. Prove all propositions that are even slightly obscure, using in their proofs only definitions that have preceded, axioms that have been granted, or propositions that have already been demonstrated.
6. Never exploit the equivocation in terms by failing to substitute mentally the definitions that restrict and explain them.
7. Treat things as much as possible in their natural order, beginning with the most general and the simplest, and explaining everything belonging to the nature of the genus before proceeding to particular species.
8. Divide each genus as much as possible into all its species, each whole into all its parts, and each difficulty into all its cases.

Real Definitions

Definitions are classified as either real or nominal. Real definitions are the more important because they express necessary laws of nature and essential truths. They are closely connected to classification. Plato described his practice in the *Sophist* (218e) as division and generalization. When method became an important topic in the Renaissance and 16th-century logic, classification and definition were subjects of special concern. Peter Ramus (1515–1572) was perhaps the most prominent exponent of classification. He held that method consisted largely of dividing a subject into categories:

> the disposition of many things from universal and general principles to the subordinate and singular parts, by means of which the whole subject may be more easily taught and perceived.[47]

---

45 These are cited in *LAP* IV.3; *Pascal 1963a*, pp. 356 and 257; and *Pascal 1952*, pp. 442–443.
46 *LAP* IV.11, *KM* V 393, *B* 259.
47 *Methodus doctrinae*, quoted in *Gilbert 1960*, p. 42.

Although his classification schemes were popular at the time, they are of little interest today. More relevant is what Zabarella had to say. Zabarella explains that classification, which consists of assigning subjects to the proper genus and species, determines which definitions play a role as premises in analysis and synthesis.[48] Definition plays a similar role in the demonstrations in the *Logic*. What it has to say sheds light on intentional content.

Part IV builds on the discussion in Part II, Chapters 15–16, where the authors introduced classification and definition as part of a broader discussion of propositional types. The account there says essentially that classification is determined by intentional content. An idea's content determines its division into immediately subordinate species ideas—usually two in number, although possibly more. These subordinate ideas must have extensions that jointly partition the extension of the idea being classified. As in modern logic, the partition must meet three conditions: the extensions of the subordinates must be disjoint, their joint extensions must be exhaustive of the extension of the idea being classified, and together the subordinate extensions must not include anything outside the extension of the idea being classified. Since subordinate ideas have disjoint extensions, they are contraries ("opposites").

The *Logic* divides classification into four kinds. The first three consist of different ways in which a genus may be partitioned: into its species, into the differentiae of its species, or into a set of exhaustive accidents. A fourth variety is the partition of an accident into a group of subordinate but exhaustive accidents.[49] Normally classification is into just two subordinate ideas. In that case the division is easier to understand, the authors say, if both contraries are "positive" (e.g. *left* and *right*), but often one is positive and the other is its privative negation (e.g. *rational* and *irrational, man* and *brute*).

Thus, classification is determined by what was referred to in Chapter 3 as the structure of ideas. This structure, the authors attest, "depends on what is contained in the true idea of a thing."[50] In other words, it depends on intentional content. In the *Logic*'s technical jargon, an idea's content is identified as its comprehension if it is a substantive and as its secondary signification if it is an adjective. The importance of real definitions to classification lies in the fact that they are the mental propositions that describe conceptual containments. Thus, classification is a consequence of the containment relations described by real definitions. According to

---

48 See especially "On Methods," in *Zabarella 2013*, vol. 2, Chapts. 16–17, pp. 254–263.
49 Since, according to Part II, a species and its difference have the same extensions, the only difference between classification of an idea by its subordinate species and classification by their differences is that the intentional contents of the subordinate ideas differ from those of their differences.
50 *VFI* Chapt. 6, *KM* I 209, *G* 76.

II.16, a real definition is a universal affirmative that characterizes one idea in terms of others that are necessarily true of that ideas' extension. These characterizing predicates may be *propria*, but in its strictest sense, a real definition has a species as its subject term and a predicate that consists of it a genus restricted by a difference. The comprehension of the species must consist of the union of the comprehensions of the genus and the secondary signification of the difference. In the language of Chapter 1, the species "contains" the genus and the difference. It follows that a real definition is necessarily true. It is said to describe the species' nature and essence. The examples of real definitions the authors provide include *man is a rational animal; time is the measure of motion;*[51] *the mind is a substance that thinks*; and *body is an extended substance.*[52] Fonseca gives a nice account of the sort of classification by definition that the *Logic* assumes:[53]

> Plato proposed two methods, which thought in general and science share, namely division and collection. Although Aristotle never propose this, he does teach that definition can be investigated in two ways, namely by division and collection. By division in this way: in the first step, he says, the thing being defined [call is *S*] is grouped together in its most general collection (its genus) [call it *G*]. It is then clear how its definition should proceed: the genus is next itself divided as follows:

---

51 *LAP* I.12, *KM* V 171, *B* 61.
52 *LAP* II.16, *KM* V 244, *B* 126.
53 Fonseca 1964 [1575] Liber V, Caput 7, pp. 304–306:

> Duas methodos ponebat Plato, quibus omnis rerum cognitio, et scientia contineretur, Divisivam scilicet, et Collectivam. Aristoteles vero etsi non omnino hoc probat, docet tamen hisce duobus modis investigari posse definitionem, divisione inquam, et collectione. Divisione quidem hoc modo, Sumatur, ait, primum, id quod communius est, latiusque patet quam res definienda: deinde illud ipsum dividatur: mox differentia quae rei convenit, addatur primo attributo: rursus, si nondum oratio reciprocabitur cum re proposita, dividatur id totum, quod assumptum est, tandemque eo usque fiat progressio dividendo, donec oratio propria efficiatur, quae nullam in rem aliam transferri possit. Exempli causa si hominem definire velis, accipies primo loco aliquod genus hominis, verbi gratia substantiam, quae omnium latissime patet, dicesque Homo est substantia. Deinde, quia sustantiarum quaedam sunt corporis expertes, ut intelligentiae quaedam corporatae, qualis est homo, addes: Corporata. Sed quia corporatae substantiae partim interire non possunt, ut caeli, partim possunt, e quibus est homo, addes, Quae interire potest. Rursus, quia earum subtantiarum, quae intereunt, quaedam non vivunt, ut lapides, aliae sunt viventes, in quibus est homo, addes, Vivens. Verum ne id quidem satis est. Viventium enim quaedam nil sentiunt, ut plantae, quaedam sentiunt, in quibus homo numeratur. Quare adiungendum est, Sentiens. Sed commune adhuc. Nam eorum, quae sentiunt, quaedam sunt expertia rationis, quaedam rationem participant, ut Socrates, et Plato. Addes igitur, Rationis particeps: quod satis erit. Nam totum hoc, substantia corporata, quae interire potest, vivens, sentiens, et rationis particeps soli homini convenit, et cum eo reciprocatur.

the difference characteristic of the thing [call it *D*] is added [to the definition] as the thing's first attribute [*Every S is a DG*]. If the resulting sentence does not describe exactly the thing being defined [i.e. if *S* is not co-extensive with *DG*], then the genus is divided into a new whole which is then taken up, until by this progressive division a sentence results that does not fit any other thing. For example, if you wish to define *man* you first choose a genus for *man*, for example substance, which clearly is the broadest of all, and you say *man is a substance.* Then, because some substances are incorporeal, like those that are intelligent, and some are corporeal, which is what men are, you add: *corporeal*. But because one portion of corporeal substances cannot perish, like heavenly bodies, but another portion can, among which is man, you add *who can perish*. Again, because among substances that can perish some are not alive, like stones, and other are alive, among them man, you add *living*. But that is not enough, for among the living some are not sentient, like plants, and some have sensation, included among them is man. This is why *sentient* should be added, as has been the common practice. Now, of those who are sentient some are irrational and some exhibit reason, like Socrates and Plato. Therefore, you add *exhibits reason*, and this is enough. Now the entire thing is this: *man alone is a corporeal substance that can perish, live, have senses, and exhibit reason*, and this fits man exactly.

Real definitions, however, are not obvious. On the other hand, a demonstration requires premises that are "perfectly evident"; they cannot be formulated in terms of ideas that are even "slightly obscure." Because real definitions report facts of conceptual containment, they are about nature independent of the will, even though that nature is conceptual. For this reason real definitions are not, in general, immediately obvious or known to be true. If the definition serves as a premise in scientific demonstration, it must be "supported by reasons." The strongest source of support consists in the intellectual understanding of the idea itself, in its apprehension as a clear and distinct idea. In such an apprehension the soul is aware of the idea's content vividly and clearly. In this case, the proposition that predicates this content of the idea is known with certainty and qualifies to serve as an "axiom" in a scientific demonstration:

> A definition must be clear, that is, it must furnish us a more clear and distinct idea of the thing being defined, and it must help us understand its nature as much as possible, so that we can make sense of its principal properties. This is primarily what we should consider in definitions.[54]

---

54 LAP II.16, KM V 245, B 127.

On the other hand, if a premise is not supported by a clear and distinct idea it must be supported by a prior demonstration.

A serious source of intellectual error that Part IV wants to correct is the misuse of real definitions. Defective definitions include those that are circular and those in which the terms in its *definiens* are obscure. The *Logic* cites examples of defective definitions from Aristotle's psychology and physics:[55]

> the soul is the first form of a natural organic body, which has life potentially; motion as the act of being in potency insofar as it is in potency; dryness as being easily retained within its boundaries, and with difficulty within the boundaries of another body; moistness as being easily retained in the boundaries of another body, and with difficulty in its own; heat as that which unites similar bodies and separates dissimilar ones; cold as that which unites dissimilar bodies and separates similar ones.

A more serious error is the attempt to employ a purported real definition of a confused idea. A confused idea is one that has a content that consists of incompatible modes. These are called *false ideas*, and figure prominently in Chapter 6 in the discussion of contingent truth. The *Logic* provides several examples of real definitions that are faulty because they contain a false idea: *fire* as *the material cause of the sensation of heat* and *rock* as *the material cause of the sensation of weight*.[56]

Nominal Definitions

Real definitions are entirely mental. They associate a species with a difference and genus. All three (genus, species, and difference) are ideas in the mind; they are terms in mental language. A second kind of definition, called a *nominal definition*, explains spoken language. It fixes a spoken word to the idea it "signifies." In both medieval logic and in the authors' usage, signification is a technical term with a fluid sense. In its primary medieval sense, signification refers to the relation between a concept and the things in the world that the concept stands for. This too is its normal sense in the *Logic*, as, for example, when the text says that a substantive signifies those things that satisfy the modes in its comprehension or that a connotative term primarily signifies those things that satisfy the modes in its secondary signification. But in another sense, a spoken term is said to be a sign for a mental term and a written term for a spoken term. What is important is that the relation between the verbal sign and its idea is

---

55 *LAP* II.16, *KM* V 245–246, *B* 127–128.
56 *LAP* I.12, *KM* V 173, *B* 62.

a contingent matter determined by convention. The role of a nominal definition is to declare the conventional pairings of a spoken word with an idea:[57]

> we consider only the sound, and then determine this sound to be the sign of an idea we designate by other words.

Because nominal definitions are arbitrary agreements among language users, once fixed they cannot be contested without vitiating that agreement. As statements of these conventions, they may serve as unproven premises or "axioms" in scientific demonstration:

> From this it follows: first, that nominal definitions are arbitrary, and real definitions are not. Since each sound is indifferent in itself and by its nature able to signify all sorts of ideas, I am permitted for my own particular use, provided I warn others, to determine a sound to signify precisely one certain thing, without mingling it with anything else.... Second, it follows from their arbitrariness that nominal definitions cannot be contested.... It follows, third, that every nominal definition can be taken for a principle, since it is not contestable.[58]

In his essay on method, Pascal argues that logic should resemble geometry more closely in its practice of demonstration and definition. Of special interest are his remarks on what we would call today eliminable definition.[59] In medieval logic, the central utility of nominal definitions was considered to be their use as abbreviations for complex concepts or phrases in mental language. Buridan, for example, says that in the strict sense, nominal definitions are verbal abbreviations of complex concepts.[60] A spoken term may be assigned by a nominal definition to signify a mental complex consisting of the restriction of one concept by another. In this case, an occurrence of that spoken term may be replaced in speech by a longer spoken phrase in which each of its component terms stands in a one-to-one relation to the ideas that enter into the formation of the complex idea in the mind, each to a component that enters into the mental restriction. In this case, the structure of spoken replacement parallels the structure of the mental complex that it signifies.

Unlike the *Logic*'s authors, in his essay on geometric method Pascal sees little use for real definitions as explications of "natures." He emphasizes

---

57 *LAP* I.1, KM V 128–129, B 26–27; compare *Peter of Spain 2014*, Chapt. 1, pp. 101–102; *John Buridan 2001*, 1.1.6, pp. 10–14, and 11th Conclusion, *Sophismata*, p. 840.
58 *LAP* I.12, KM V 172, B 61.
59 *Pascal 1963a*, p. 350; *Pascal 1952*, p. 433.
60 *John Buridan 2001*, 11th Conclusion, *Sophismata*, p. 840.

instead the use of nominal definition in mathematics. One of his rules of demonstration stresses their eliminability: "Always substitute mentally the definitions in place of the thing defined."[61] The *Logic*'s authors adopt this advice as their 6th rule in the list quoted earlier.[62] They then devote an extended discussion to the technique of checking for equivocation by replacing every occurrence of a defined term in a proof by its *definiens*.[63] They argue that if Euclid had replaced every occurrence of *angle* by its *definiens*, or *ratio* by its definition, or if Simon Stevin had replaced *number* by its *definiens*, various equivocations would have been detected.

By eschewing real definitions and stressing the replacement of defined terms, Pascal may appear to be thinking of something like eliminable definitions in a modern axiom system. Because the *Logic* follows Pascal, its account too may seem "modern." The similarity, however, is misleading. A modern eliminable definition in an axiom system is purely syntactic—an occurrence of a defined string of signs is replaceable by a shorter syntactic proxy that represents a longer syntactic expression. In principle, the finished system written in defined terms represents a hypothetical system in which each of these terms is replaced by the expression it abbreviates. The replacement process has a specific order. Starting with the last theorem of the system and working forward to the axioms, and starting with the last term in the list of defined expression and continuing backwards through the list, each occurrence of each defined term is replaced by the expression it abbreviates. In this way each occurrence of a defined term is replaced by its longer *definiens*. As a result, the entire axiom system is reformulated into so-called primitive notation; no theorem contains a defined term. For the assignment of eliminable definitions to be formally acceptable, it must satisfy a condition of non-creativity: it must not be possible to prove anything from expressions written in defined terms that cannot be proven when expressions are replaced by the expressions they abbreviate.[64]

Nominal definitions as described both in the writings of Pascal and in the *Logic* fall well short of this picture. In their view, nominal definitions are understood in the medieval way. They are assignments of corporeal representatives to ideas. A single sign can replace a longer spoken phrase in a speech because the two have been paired by an accident convention. Although authors describe scientific knowledge as ordered in demonstrations, this order does not approach an axiom system with eliminable

---

61 *Pascal 1963a*, p. 357; *Pascal 1952*, p. 443. On Pascal's influence on the *Logic*'s account of definitions (I.12–13, IV.3–5, II.16, I.14) see *Miel 1969*; and *Nuchelmans 1998*, p. 114.
62 *LAP* IV.11, *KM* V 394, *B* 259.
63 *LAP* IV.4, *KM* V 370, *B* 241–243.
64 There are additional requirements as well (e.g. non-circularity). See *Suppes 1960*, pp. 16 and 17.

definitions. In particular, they do not consider reformulating the statement of scientific knowledge by replacing longer spoken expressions that parallel conceptual structure one to one by shorter spoken abbreviations. Nor do they mention non-creativity.

There is a deeper way in which the *Logic*'s account of nominal definitions differs from both modern logic's and Pascal's. At issue is the relation of intentional content to equivocation. The definition of equivocation had been settled since Aristotle.[65] The *Logic* explains it as follows:

> Different ideas are connected to a single sound so that the same sound applies to several things, not according to a single idea but by different ideas.[66]

An equivocal word is paired with distinct ideas in such a way that there is "no natural relation between them." The authors offer the example of *canon*, which in French means both a weapon and a statute in church law. Equivocation in a secondary sense is called *pros hen* equivocation by Aristotle (*focal meaning* in modern literature) and "analogous" equivocation by the *Logic*'s authors:[67]

> a word connected primarily to a given idea is joined to another idea merely because there is some relation between the ideas, such as cause, effect, sign, or resemblance. Equivocal words of this sort are called *analogues*. An example is the word "healthy" when attributed to animals, the air, and food. The main idea joined to this word is health, which applies only to animals. But it is connected to another idea close to that one, namely the cause of health, which makes us say that air and food are healthy, because they help us conserve our health.[68]

Switching the meaning of terms in mid argument is, of course, a traditional fallacy, as the authors had pointed out in Part III. But it is more than just one fallacy among many. Equivocation, the authors hold, is

---

[65] The first sentence of the Categories, (1a1) reads (*Aristotle 1938*, Cooke trans.):

> Things are equivocally names, when they have the name only in common, the definition (*logos*) or statement of essence (*ousia*) corresponding with the name being different.

[66] *LAP* I.6, *KM* V 144, *B* 39.

[67] On the fallacy of equivocation see *Sophistical Refutation* XIX; on *pros hen* equivocation see *Metaphysics* 1003a33–34. The distinction was standard. See, for example, *Peter of Spain 2014*, Chapt. 7.24, p. 269; Ockham *Summa Logic*, I.13; *Conimbricenses 1617*, Caput I, Ques I, Art III, pp. 302 and 321; *Eustachio de S. Paulo 1648*, Pars Prima, Quaestio IIII, pp. 17 and 19. Both the latter use the terminology *analogical equivocation*. Both Peter and Eustachio use the example of *healthy*.

[68] *LAP* I.6, *KM* V 144–145, *B* 39.

the source of most errors in logic, and by extension in metaphysics and ethics:

> It is also easy to show that we will never commit an error in the form of an argument as long as well observe the second rule, which is never to exploit the equivocation in terms by failing to substitute mentally the definitions that restrict and explain them.[69]

The reason the *Logic* attaches hyperbolic importance to equivocation is that it is an abuse of intentional content. Earlier accounts had explained equivocation errors in terms of signification: a single spoken term mistakenly represents two concepts that signify distinct kinds of things in the world. The *Logic* provides a fuller explanation by appeal to intentional content. A spoken term is paired with distinct ideas defined by distinct mode-sets. Hence the two ideas are true of distinct ranges of signification.

The root cause of equivocation is that the thinker is unclear about what ideas a term is paired with or, in other words, is unclear about the idea's content.[70] As part of its methodological advice, the *Logic* proposes two means of avoiding equivocation, both of which turn on intentional content.

The first is a test for equivocation, which they incorporate into their rules for demonstration. It is designed to achieve two goals: that a spoken sign is paired with a single idea and that that idea itself is clear and distinct. An idea is clear and distinct if the soul is aware of its intentional content. This content must be internally consistent. Its modes must not logically contradict each other and it must be physically possible for them to be instantiated together in the natural world. The test of internal compatibility of an idea's modes turns on eliminability. All ideas have definitions of sorts. Species have real definitions, and other ideas have comprehension or secondary significations that are expressible in mental language as a conjunction of modes or, grammatically, as a restriction of a substantive by adjectives. The compatibility test consists of replacing a term by a complex expression that details the list of modes in its content. For any spoken terms, "It is then possible to substitute mentally the definitions that restrict and explain them."[71] "Eliminating" a term in this way avoids both sorts of error of equivocation because when mentally replacing an idea by its *definiens*, it is necessary both to have identified what idea or ideas the terms stands for and to have a clear understanding of their defining modes.

---

69 *LAP* IV.8, *KM* V 384, *B* 252.
70 *LAP* I.12, *KM* V 172–174, *B* 62.
71 Rule 6, *LAP* IV.11, *KM* V 394, *B* 259.

The second technique for avoiding equivocation is linguistic reform.[72] For clarity, explicit agreements should be struck among language uses. In particular, if a spoken expression is new to usage, all must agree on its definition:

> The best way to avoid confusion in words encountered in ordinary language is to create a new language and new words that are connected only to ideas we want to represent. But in order to do that it is not necessary to create new sounds, because we can avail ourselves of those already in use, viewing them as if they had no meaning. Then we can give then the meaning we want them to have, designating the idea we want them to express by other simple words that are not at all equivocal.

An issue left unaddressed by Pascal and the *Logic*'s authors, however, is the compatibility of old with new usage. They allow, for example, that we could strip the word *parallelogram* of its usual meaning and replace it with that of *triangle*,[73] but they do not comment on the consequences of doing so in linguistic practice. In particular, they do not mention what may be called the need to preserve extensions. When advancing a new analysis in the empirical sciences or when defining an eliminable term in an axiom system, if the term receiving the new definition has a previous history, it is normally required that the extensions of the old and new meanings be roughly the same. But preserving extensions by selecting the right modes is often difficult. In short, it is not very easy to reform language by agreeing on intentional content.

A more serious issue is whether the new idea can be used in serious thought at all. By abstraction and restriction we possess the capacity to form new ideas. If we form an idea by defining in terms of a set of logically compatible modes, it exists and is unique. Moreover, because we are fashioning it ourselves, we can be relatively certain of its intentional content. It follows that the proposition that predicates of the idea its content would be necessarily true. There is, however, a difficulty. The idea formed may be faulty. Although the idea itself exists as a mode of the soul, what it signifies is often less so. It may describe a so-called being of reason, like *chimera*,[74] because it contains physically incompatible modes, or like *golden mountain*[75] it may contain modes that are contingently false of every existing thing. Whether propositions with faulty ideas of this sort can be true or serve as terms in genuine knowledge claims is addressed in Chapter 6.

Closely related to the issue of equivocation proper is the problem the authors call equivocation by error. This refers to cases in which speakers

---

72 *LAP* I.12, *KM* V 70–71, *B* 60.
73 *LAP* I.12, *KM* V 172, *B* 61.
74 *LAP* I.12, *KM* V 172, *B* 62.
75 *LAP* I.1, *KM* V 131, *B* 28; *LAP* I.2, *KM* V 136, *B* 320.

agree about what idea a term is paired with and also about the modes that make up its intentional content, but disagree on what the term signifies. In other words, there is a disagreement over what entities in the world satisfy the term's defining modes. Disputes of this sort, according to Arnauld and Nicole, are less likely to arise if the defining modes are sensible qualities, which are easily confirmed empirically. An example of an easily confirmed idea is *six feet tall*. Disputes, however, are typical if the defining modes are theoretical, or as they put it, "judged not by the senses but only by the mind."[76] The authors offer examples from ethics, interpretation, history, and theology: *valiant men, an author's meaning, Aristotle's opinion, prince of philosophers, true religion, the son of Philip, the word of God.*[77]

This chapter has reviewed how the *Logic* adapts method understood as analysis and synthesis in its account of scientific knowledge. The most important propositions in science are real definitions because they are necessarily true and affirm of a species its nature and essence. Synthesis provides the structure to the body of propositions that make up scientific knowledge. In synthesis, propositions are deduced by the logic of Part III from various necessary propositions. Among acceptable unproven premises are propositions that affirm the content of clear and distinct ideas. These are certain. Nominal definitions may also serve as unproven premises, but only with care. They must signify a single idea with a clear intentional content. In particular, care must be taken to avoid equivocation, which is a frequent source of error in logic, and by extension in physics and morality. The knowledge described has been that of science, which consists of axioms that affirm the content of clear and distinct ideas, nominal definitions, and propositions deducible from these. Not included are the uncertain reports of sensation. Chapter 6 considers the possibility of such contingent knowledge. There the *Logic* finds a place for sensation and contingent truth. The account, moreover, has important implications for logic. The resulting theory of contingent truth requires a revision in the truth-conditions for contingent affirmative categorical propositions: they must be supplemented with a clause requiring that their terms carry existential import.

References

Aquinas, Thomas. 1888. *Summa theologiae*. Roberto Busa, S.J. (translator).
Aquinas, Thomas. 1961. *Commentary on the Metaphysics*, Chicago. Joseph Kenny, O.P. (ed.), John P. Rowan (translator). Priory of the Immaculate Conception: Washington, D.C. http://dhspriory.org/thomas/english/Metaphysics2.htm.

---

76 *LAP* I.8, *KM* V 153, *B* 46.
77 *LAP* I.8, *KM* V 153–155, *B* 46–48.

Aquinas, Thomas. 1964–1980. *Summa theologiae*, New York, McGraw-Hill [1964–1980].
Aristotle. Posterior Analytics. Mure, G.R.G. (translator). http://classics.mit.edu/Aristotle/posterior.mb.txt. The Internet Classics Archive by Daniel C. Stevenson, Web Atomics.
Aristotle. 1938. *The Categories*, Cambridge, MA, Harvard University Press. Cooke, Harold P. (translator).
Bennett, Jonathan. 2017. *The Correspondence Between Leibniz and Arnauld*. www.earlymoderntexts.com/assets/pdfs/leibniz1686a_2.pdf.
Buridan, John. 2001. *Summulae de dialectica*, New Haven, Yale University Press. Klima, Gyula (translator).
Conimbricenses. 1617. *Commentarii collegii conimbricensis societatis iesu in tres libros de anima, aristotelis stagiritae*, Colonia [Cologne], Lazarus Zetznerus.
Descartes, Rene. 1985a. *Rules for the Direction of the Mind*, Cambridge, Cambridge University Press. Cottingham, John, Robert Stoothoff, and Dugald Murdoch (translators).
Descartes, René. 1985b. *Meditations on First Philosophy*, Cambridge, Cambridge University Press. Cottingham, John, Robert Stoothoff, and Dugald Murdoch (translators).
Euclid. 1956. *The Thirteen Books of the Elements*, New York, Dover, 2nd ed. Heath, Thomas L. (translator).
Eustachio de S. Paulo. 1648. *Summa philosophiae quadripartita, de rebus dialecticis, ethicis, physicis et metaphysicis*, Cantabrigia [Cambridge], Rogerus Danielis.
Fonseca, Pedro da. 1964 [1575]. *Instituciões dialéctica [Institutionum dialecticarum libri octo]*, Coimbra, Universidade de Coimbra.
Gaukroger, Stephen. 1989. *Cartesian Logic*, Oxford, Oxford University Press.
Gilbert, Neal W. 1960. *Renaissance Concepts of Method*, New York, Columbia University Press.
Heath, Thomas L. 1921. *A History of Greek Mathematics*, London, Oxford University Press.
Herlinus, Christian and Conrad Dasypodius. 1566. *Analysis Geometricae sex libroroum Euclidis. Elementum Primum VIII*, Strasbourg, Iosia Richelius.
Hintikka, Jaakko and Unto Remes. 1974. *The Method of Analysis*, London, Dordrecht, D. Reidel, pp. 8–10.
Hobbes, Thomas. 1992. *De corpore*, Routledge and Thoemmes Press. Molesworth, William (ed.).
Laertius, Diogenes. 1970. *Lives of Eminent Philosophers*, Cambridge, MA, Harvard University Press. Hicks, R. D. (translator).
Miel, Jan. 1969. Pascal, Port-Royal, and Cartesian Linguistics. *Journal of the History of Ideas*, 30, 261–271.
Nuchelmans, Gabriel. 1998. Logic in the Seventeenth Century: Preliminary Remarks and the Constituents of the Proposition. In: Garber, Daniel and Michael Ayers (eds.) *The Cambridge History of Seventeenth-Century Philosophy*, Cambridge, Cambridge University Press.
Offenberg, Adri K. 1973. Spinoza's Library. The History of a Reconstruction. *Quaerendo*, 3, 309–322.
Parkinson, G.H.R. 1966. *Leibniz, Logical Papers*, Cambridge, Clarendon Press.

Pascal, Blaise. 1952. "*On Geometrical Demonstration,*" Section II, Concerning the Art of Persuasion, Chicago, William Pention, Encyclopedia Britannica. Hutchins, Robert Maynard (ed.), Scofield, Richard (translator).

Pascal, Blaise. 1963a. De l'Esprit géométrique et de l'Art de Persuader. In: *Œuvres complètes*, Paris, Seuil.

Pascal, Blaise. 1963b. *Œuvres complètes*, Paris, Seuil.

Peter of Spain. 2014. *Tractatus*, Oxford, Oxford University Press. Copenhaver, Brian P., Calvin Normore, and Terence Parsons (eds. and translators).

Proclus. 1970. *Proclus: A Commentary on the First Book of Euclid's Elements*, Princeton, NJ, Princeton University Press.

Russell, Bertrand. 1902. *Principles of Mathematics*, New York, Norton.

Russell, Bertrand. 1992. *A Critical Exposition of the Philosophy of Leibniz*, London, Routledge.

Schiller, F.C.S. 1917. Scientific Discovery and Logical Proof. *Studies in the History and Method of Science*, 1, 235–289.

Suppes, Patrick. 1960. *Axiomatic Set Theory*, Princeton, Van Nostrand.

Swoyer, Chris. 1995. Leibniz on Intension and Extension. *Nous*, 29, 96–114.

William of Ockham. 1974. *Summa Logicae*, St. Bonaventura, NY, Franciscan Institute. Boehner, Philotheus (ed.), Freddoso, Alfred (translator).

Zabarella, Jacopo. 2013. *On Methods*, Cambridge, MA, Harvard University Press. McCaskey, John P. (translator).

6 The Semantics of Discourse. Existential Import[1]

Introduction

Chapter 5 explored the *Logic*'s account of scientific knowledge in which justification is understood as *a priori*. Scientific belief there is grounded in the apprehension of the intentional content of clear and distinct ideas and in deductions from them. Scientific knowledge is, therefore, independent of sensation. Because scientific knowledge is grounded in reason alone, it is fair to think of Arnauld and Nicole as rationalists. The *Logic*, however, also allows for knowledge of contingent truths, which are grounded in sensation. The rudiments of the account of contingent truth are sketched in the *Logic*'s Part IV, with a more complete explanation set out in *On True and False Ideas*. The account draws on both ontological considerations and the authors' philosophical psychology. It also appeals to logic, in particular, to two doctrines in the semantics of mental language: that the content of sensations accurately correspond to worldly events and that the propositions describing these events carry existential import.

The discussion in this chapter is in two parts. First is a review of the *Logic*'s account of sensation in terms of intentional content. This is followed by a discussion of implications for the theory of truth. The semantic details concern the nature of "correspondence to the world" in the case of contingent truth, the account of which entails that the truth-conditions of Part II for contingent affirmations must be revised to require existential import.

In an effort to refute Malebranche's Neoplatonic vision of perceptual representationalism, Arnauld developed a version of direct perception that appeals to intentional content. The mechanisms of sensation, moreover, ensure that there is a difference between, on the one hand, essential definitions of science, which are necessary, and, on the other hand, true reports of sensation, which are contingent.

---

1 This chapter draws on material from *Martin 2011*.

Sensation

Arnauld defends an account of direct perception. The theory of direct perception holds that during sensation, the mind is aware of things in the world and various properties instantiated in them. The view is distinguished from perceptual representationalism, which holds that, in sensation, the mind is not aware of properties of things outside the mind, but only of representations of them. These representations, moreover, are ontologically distinct from the things in the world that they represent. Arnauld developed his views in an efforts to refute Nicolas Malebranche, who held an Augustinian version of representationalism. Malebranche believed that in sensation God causes a mode to be instantiated in the soul. The instantiation of this mode constitutes a state in which the soul is imperfectly aware of an idea in God's mind.[2] In the tradition of Augustine, Malebranche called this awareness "illumination." This divine idea, moreover, functions as a representation of things in the world because in creation, God's ideas are the seminal causes of material things. In the creative process, God causes material things to "imitate" his ideas in a Neoplatonic way. The material substance literally instantiates imperfectly the properties possessed by the idea that is its seminal cause. This view is supplemented by a version of occasionalism. On the occasion in which the body appears to be affected by a material substance in sensation, God causes the soul to experience a state of illumination, in which the soul is made directly aware of the seminal cause in God's mind.

Arnauld rejected this view out of hand as violating principles of parsimony. In contrast, Arnauld's ontology is simpler, consisting only of substances and their modes, which are either material or spiritual. During sensation, material modes are physically transferred by causation from the object of perception to the body of the perceiver. These, in turn, cause "motions" in the brain, which themselves consist of material modes inhering in a material substance. At this point, Arnauld too invokes occasionalism. On the occasion of the motions in the perceiver's brain, God causes a spiritual mode to be instantiated in the soul. This mode, moreover, consists of a state of understanding that Arnauld explains by appeal to intentional content. The mode in the perceiver's soul that is caused by

---

2 On The *Logic*'s view on occasionalism see in *LAP Discours* II 1.1, *KM* V 132–133, *B* 29–30; I.3 *KM* V122, *B* 33; I I.9, *KM* V 157–158, *B* 49–50, I.11, *KM* V 168–170, *B* 58–60. In *VFI* see Chapt. 6, *KM* I 204, *G* 71–71; Chapt. 27, *KM* I 349–350, *G* 208; and Chapt. 28. On Malebranche's representationalism within his Neoplatonic semantics see *Martin 2014*. There has been a long discussion in the literature about whether Descartes was a perceptual representationalist. The prevailing view at one time was that he was. See, for example, *Stroud 1984*, pp. 33–34. More recently, the prevailing opinion has been that he was not. See, for example, *Kemp-Smith 1952, O'Neil 1974, Yolton 1975, Normore 1986, Nadler 1989, Brown 2007,* and *Alanen 1990*.

God—in other words, the perception—consists of a vivid awareness of a series of modes that make up the "content" of the perception. Some of these modes are material and are actually instantiated in the material object being sensed. These material modes tend to be quasi-geometric modes typical of Cartesian physics, such as motion, relative size, and position. Some of the modes, however, are "sensory," being true not of the object of sensation but of the soul. Included among the sensory modes are color, taste, feel, and smell.

In *On True and False Ideas*, Arnauld refers to the modes that make up perceptual content as "objective being." As explained in Chapter 1, objective being was typically postulated in the Middle Ages to serve as that entity "understood" when the soul understands an abstract idea or, in an alternative use of objective being, as the object of perception in the case of illusions. Chapter 2 describes how the *Logic* employs objective being in semantics to determine the signification of substantives and adjectives. Ideas signify those things in the world that satisfy the modes in their "objective being." In Part IV, the authors appeal to objective being as the content of perception. In doing so, the authors are clear that objective being is not an entity with a special ontological status, nor is it representational in nature, functioning as an intermediary between the soul and the world. Instead, Arnauld and Nicole hold that objective being is simply perceptual content: the fact that an idea possesses objective being consists of the fact that it has an intentional content. Ontologically, objective being consists of a series of modes: some material, some spiritual. Because the soul of the perceiver is brought into direct awareness of the material modes instantiated in the object of perception, the doctrine qualifies as one of direct perception. The combination of material modes that God causes the soul to be vividly aware of on the occasion of sensation are the very modes that are instantiated in the object of perception.

The clearest texts explaining Arnauld's view occur in *On True and False Ideas*. There he attempts to clarify his version of "direct perceptual realism." During the perceptual experience associated with sensation, Arnauld claims that the perceiver has a direct experience of the object itself outside the mind:

> in order to see the object [of vision], it is necessary that it be before our eyes. This is what they [i.e. all men] call "presence," and this is what makes them consider this "presence of the object" to be a necessary condition of sight.[3]

---

3 Author's translation. *VFI* 1, *KM* I 190, *G* 58.

> il falloit que l'objet fût devant nos yeux, afin que nous le pussion voir: ce qu'ils ont appelé *présence*, &c c'est ce qui leur a fait regarder cette présence de l'objet comme une condition nécessaire pour voir. L'autre, qu'on voyoit aussi quelquefois les

In the following passage, Arnauld makes the case against Malebranche's version of perceptual representationalism in which the soul directly perceives only ideas in God's mind. Arnaul explains why ideas cannot be representatives of things in the world as believed by Malebranche:[4]

> . . . it follows that, since every perception is essentially representative of something, and accordingly is called an *idea*, it cannot essentially be reflecting on itself, that its immediate object cannot be this idea, that is, what my soul is said to perceive is *the objective reality* of the thing. For example, if I think of the sun, the objective reality of the sun, which is present to my soul, is the immediate object of this perception; and the possible or existing sun, which is outside my soul, is its mediated object, in a manner of speaking. And thus, without recourse to *representative beings* distinct from perceptions, one sees, clearly, in this sense, not only with regard to material things but generally with regard to all things, that it is our ideas that we see *immediately*, and which are *the immediate object of our thought*: and this does not prevent us from also seeing the object by means of the ideas, which formally contain only what is in the idea objectively [*ce qui n'empesche pas que nous ne voyions aussi par ces idées l'objet, qui contient formellement ce que n'est qu'objectivement dans l'idée*]. For example, I do not conceive the formal being of a square, which is objectively in the idea, nor the perception that I have of a square.

In the passage, Arnauld breaks the perceptual process down into two logically distinct stages, the first being a necessary condition of the second. The prior condition requires that the soul be aware that it is having

---

choses visibles dans les miroirs, ou dans l'eau, ou d'autres chose qui nous les repésentoient; & alors ils ont cru, quoique par erreur, que ce n'etoit pas les corps même que l'on voyoit, mais leur images.

4 Author's translation. *VFI* 6, *KM* I 204–205, G 71–72.

. . . il s'ensuit, que toute perception étant essentiellement représentative de quelque chose, & selon cela s'appellant *idée*, elle ne peut être essentiellement réfléchissante sur elle-même, que son objet immédiat ne soit cette *idée*; c'est-à-dire, *la réalité objective* de la chose que mon esprit est dit apercevoir: de sort que, si je pense au soleil, la réalité objective du soleil, qui est présent à mon esprit, est l'objet immédiat de cette perception; & le soleil possible ou existant, qui est hors de mon esprit, en est l'objet médiat, pour parler ainsi. Et ainsi, l'on voit, que, sans avoir recours à des *êtres représentatifs*, distingués des perceptions, il est très-vrai en ce sens, que, non seulement au regard des choses matérielles, mais généralement au regard de toutes choses, ce sont nos idées que nous voyons *immédiatement*, & qui sont *l'objet immédiat de notre pensée*: ce qui n'empêche pas que nous ne voyions aussi, par ces idées, l'objet qui contient formellement ce que n'est qu'*objectivement* dans l'idée: c'est-à-dire, par exemple, que je ne conçoive l'être formel d'un quarré, qui est *objectivement* dans l'idée, ou la perception que j'ai d'un quarré.

a perceptual experience. The second stage consists of apprehending the modes in the content of the perception as instantiated in a particular configuration in the object perceived. The two stages occur simultaneously and are thus only logically distinct.

In the text Arnauld explicitly appeals to objective being. The sense of objective being he is invoking is the medieval notion explained in Chapter 1, which we would today call intentional content. Thus, "direct perception" works as follows. In the case of an abstract idea, the soul is aware of modes that inhere outside the mind signified by that idea. In this case, the soul "understands" what the *significata* of the idea are "like": it understands what modes characterize that sort of object. In perception, the soul is directly and vividly aware of modes that make up the perception's content. If some of these modes are material, they are in general "veridical"; they are true of the object being sensed. It had been the standard view in medieval logic that the content of perception, which was called an "intuition," was always of an individual thing. The properties sensed were sufficiently detailed so as to be true of only that individual.[5] The *Logic*'s authors no doubt shared this view. They probably believed that material modes in the content of the perception were of sufficient detail to pick out a single individual or event.

It should be stressed that the understanding that occurs in perception is different from the understanding of an abstract idea. In the case of abstract ideas, if the awareness of the modal content of an idea's objective being is clear and distinct, that awareness *ipso facto* constitutes an understanding that the things the idea signifies possess the modes in the idea's content. In the case of perception, the awareness of the modal content associated with a sensation *ipso facto* constitutes a direct perception of the individual outside the mind in the sense that the soul is brought into direct awareness of those material modes inhering in that material object in a certain configuration. Upon the occasion of perception, these modes are actually true of, and inhere in, the perceived material substance in that configuration. In Aristotle's terminology, the soul is directly aware of what is "true in" the substance. If, moreover, the soul understands the substance abstractly, it may also understand its nature or, in Aristotle's terms, what is "true of" the substance. Thus, contrary to Malebranche, who held that a perception in the soul signifies a representational idea in God's mind, Arnauld held that, generally speaking, a sensory experience is a state of direct awareness of a thing outside the mind through a direct experience of the modes instantiated in it.

The interpretation of sensation just sketched is reinforced by two remarks in the key passage just quoted. The first remark concerns the fact that ideas are self-reflective. For a Platonist like Malebranche, the

---

[5] See for example *William of Ockham 1981, Reportatio*, Book II, Question XIII.

object of intellectual awareness is the idea itself. The entire experience of illumination consists of being aware of the idea as the object of intellection. Having an idea consists of being aware of the idea's properties. On the other hand, the fact that something in the world has its the properties depends on an external cause. Its properties derive from the properties from its cause. A triangle in the world is three-sided because the idea of triangle is three-sided. There is no further explanation for why this idea has its properties other than it has the properties it does. The idea of triangle is three-sided because it is three-sided. There is no more explanation of understanding, on Malebranche's account, than the understanding of the idea itself. In illumination, the experience of the idea is exhausted in self-reflection, much as there is no further explanation of God's existence other than God himself. God is his own cause. In his case and in the case of ideas, the causal relation is reflexive.

Arnauld grants that understanding is self-reflective. It consists in part awareness of the experience itself. More formally, the awareness relation is reflexive: x is aware of y only if x is aware of x. Understanding entails an awareness of content, and the modes in content are in general not modes of the idea itself. In Arnauld's words, the reflective awareness of the idea itself is "immediate" and the perception of content is "mediated" (*médiat*). He is stressing the priority of the awareness of experience itself to the direct perception of the modes of the individual outside the mind, but this priority is logical rather than temporal. A necessary condition for the sensation of an object is the fact that the soul is having a sensory experience. It is part of the "essence" of sensation that the soul is aware that experience is occurring, but—this is Arnauld's point—it is also an essential feature of perception that it has a content consisting of modes that inhere not in the soul but in the object of perception:[6]

> our thought or perception is essentially reflective upon itself; or, as it is said rather better in Latin, *est sui conscia*. For I do not think without knowing that I think; I do not know a square without knowing that I know it; I do not see the sun or, to avoid, any doubt, I do not imagine I see the sun, without being certain that I imagine I see it.

---

6 VFI 6, KM I 204, G 71:

> notre *pensée ou perception* est essentiellement réfléchissante sur elle-même; ou, ce qui se dit plus heureusement en latin, *est sui conscia*; car je ne pense point, que je ne sache que je pense. Je ne connois point un quarré que je ne sache que je le connois: je ne vois point le soleil, ou pour mettre la chose hors de tout doute, je ne m'imagine point voir le soleil, que je ne sois certain que je m'imagine de le voir.

See also the description of abstraction in VFI 6, KM I 207–208, G 74–75, and the discussion in *Dominicy 1984*, p. 36.

Objective being is part of the explanation. The reason an idea consists in an awareness of objective being is that it directly understands or perceives (it is "of") those things that satisfies the modes detailed in its objective being. Conception of an abstract idea and perception associated with sensation are both self-reflective processes in the sense that the soul is aware that the conception or perception is taking place. Both acts, nevertheless, are in general directed to objects other than the mind itself.

In the final sentence in the earlier passage, Arnauld makes use of the technical terminology "formal being," which was discussed at some length in Chapter 1. An idea's formal being is the being it possesses because it is a mode of the soul. Arnauld makes the point that in understanding it is not formal being that the soul understands or perceives. It is not the idea *qua* mental act that is understood or perceived. Rather, the soul understands and perceives objects outside the mind as possessing material modes.

In sum, Arnauld is arguing against Malebranche's Platonic representationalism. He is making the point that understanding and perception do not consist of self-reflexive awareness alone. Both processes require that the soul be aware of the content of objective being.

A second remark in the passage quoted merits more detailed discussion. This is Arnauld's description of perception as a relation. He says that a perception is "present to the soul." He goes on to explain what he means:[7]

> I have said that I take *perception* and *idea* to be the same thing. It must nevertheless be noted that, while this thing is single, it stands in a twofold relation, to the soul that it modifies, and to the thing perceived in so far as this latter is objectively in the soul, and the word "perception" more directly refers to the former relation, the word "idea" to the latter.

The relation of perception, Arnauld contends, holds between the soul, on the one hand, and the object that possess the material modes contained in the perception's objective being, on the other. In the *Logic*, very little use is made of the various distinctions among Aristotle's nine non-substance categories. The concept of relation in particular is seldom mentioned. Its use here, however, would have had implications for then contemporary readers.

In premodern logic, the preferred vocabulary of science, according to philosophers, was the subject-predicate syntax of the syllogistic. Syllogistic syntax, however, lacks modern logic's expressive power for

---

[7] *VFI* 5, KM I 198, G 66. Compare *Raconis 1651, De principiis entis* a. 3, p. 827.

relations. In the logic of the day, expressions that refer to a binary relation were often reduced to deeper, non-relational subject-predicate propositions. These substance-mode facts that hold of the respective *relata* were thought to capture what was intended by the relational expression. A binary relation holds between two individuals, the doctrine claimed, because each possessed a non-relational, one-place mode characteristic of the relation from the perspective of that individual. On this analysis, Adam bears the fatherhood relation to Abel because Adam possess the mode "paternity with respect to Abel" and Abel possess the mode "sonhood with respect to Adam."[8]

The *Logic*'s substance-mode ontology accords well with the analysis of perception as a relation. According to Arnauld, when a perception obtains, the soul instantiates a mode, namely, an idea possessing an intentional content. Simultaneously, the object sensed instantiates its own modes, among which are those that impact the body's sense organs. That the soul and the material object each possess their respective modes constitutes the relational fact. Understood in the medieval manner, the fact that the modes are instantiated in the respective *relata* constitutes the relational fact that the one is perceiving the other. The analysis fits the *Logic*'s ontology. Ontologically, there is nothing more to direct perception than substances having modes. In the world outside the mind, the object sensed possesses the relevant Cartesian material modes. At the same time, the soul experiences a perception with a certain content. This mental act is a spiritual mode.[9]

As detailed in Chapter 5, the awareness of objective being has epistemic consequences both for ideas and sensation. If the soul's awareness of the content of an abstract idea is clear and distinct, the soul knows with certainty that objects signified by that idea possess those particular properties. In the case of sensation, because God is not a deceiver, the soul is able to know with confidence that the quasi-geometric material modes that make up the content of a perception are true of the object perceived. While Aristotle attributed the veridical nature of sensation to a reliable mechanism by which information from the external world is causally transferred to the soul, Arnauld, in keeping with Descartes, justifies sensation by an *a priori* argument

---

8 See, for example, the discussion in *Mugnai 1992*.
9 The reduction of relations to one-place modes can also be extended to the relation that holds between a mental act and its content. Ideas and perceptions, which are modes of the soul, stand in the relation of containment to their contents: an idea or perception "contains" the modes in its content. Containment is a binary relation and may be analyzed in terms of properties of the *relata*, in this case a mental act on the one hand and the modes contained on the other. These modes would be second-order, or in the language of the *Logic*, mode of second-intension.

based on God's veracity. The following demonstration ensures that sensory perception is reliable:

> It is certain, whether by reason, supposing God is not a deceiver, or at least by faith, that I have a body and that the earth, the sun, the moon, and many other bodies that I know exist outside my mind actually do exist outside my mind.... When my senses cannot assure me of the existence of external things reason will convince me, by adding the fact that God is not a deceiver. And if I cannot be entirely assured by reason, I can at least be assured by faith.... Hence to me, since I have faith as well as reason, it is very certain that when I see the earth, the sun, the stars, and people who converse with me, these are not imaginary bodies or people that I see, but the works of God, and they really are men whom God has created just as He has created me ... the bodies that I believe I see are as a rule actual bodies that exist outside me.[10]

God's benign nature entails that he accurately coordinates the properties of worldly events with the contents of the soul's perceptions. Thus Arnauld, true to the rationalist program, provides an *a priori* justification of empirical knowledge.

In the final sections of Part IV, the *Logic* addresses the epistemological basis of religious faith. Curiously, perhaps, the argument advanced is also *a priori* and formally the same as the argument justifying the veridicality of sensation. God, who is not deceiver, would not allow religious authorities to teach what is false:[11]

> The first is knowledge we have of it ourselves, from having recognized and examined the truth either by the senses or by reason. This can generally be called *reason*, because the senses themselves depend on a judgment by reason, or *science*, taking this name here more generally than it is taken in the Schools, to mean all knowledge of an object derived from the object itself. The other path is the authority of persons worthy of credence who assure us that a certain thing exists, although by ourselves we know nothing about it. This is called faith or belief,
>
> ...
>
> But since this authority can have two sources, God or people, there are also two kinds of faith, divine and human.
>
> ...

---

10 *VFI* 5, *KM* I 201 and 202, *G* 68 and 69. See also Chapt. 27, *KM* 355, *G* 213–214, and Chapt. 28, *KM* I 355, *G* 213–214.
11 *LAP* IV.12, *KM* V 395, *B* 260 and following.

> Divine faith cannot be subject to error, because God can never deceive us nor be deceived.
>
> ...
>
> since God is truth itself, he could not deceive us in what he reveals to us about his nature or his mysteries.
>
> ...
>
> it is more certain that what God says is true than what our reason convinces us of, because God is less capable of misleading us than our reason is of being misled.

Although this defense of faith is far removed from formal logic in the modern sense, it played an influential role historically in the development of Arnauld and Nicole's positions. As mentioned in the Introduction, the *Logic* was reprinted and translated many times and served as the model for many subsequent textbooks, coming to represent its own variety of "Cartesian logic," contrasted with so-called Aristotelian and Ramist logics. These rival "logics" rejected dualism and were thought by subsequent students to be sympathetic to empirical science. Aristotelian texts tended to be formal and stress the syllogistic. Ironically, some putative Aristotelian texts also came to include material from the *Port Royal Logic*, such as its rules for the valid syllogisms. So-called Ramist logic stressed classification methods, which were considered sympathetic to empirical science despite being weak in formal logic. In contrast, Cartesian logic was seen as more *a priori* due to its emphasis on knowledge based on clear and distinct ideas. It was also more pious due to its defense of faith and tradition. It was adopted by religious conservatives, not only by Jansenists and other Catholics, but also by dissenting Protestants in mainland Europe, England, and America. Cartesian logic, for example, was taught by the Protestant divines at Harvard for two centuries.[12]

Existential Import

Sensation as explained in Part IV has implications for logic as such because the semantic mechanism that makes veridical sensations possible has implications for the truth-conditions of categorical propositions. The distinction the *Logic*'s authors draw between the general truths of science discussed in Chapter 5 and the particular truths of sensation presuppose another distinction, that between essential truth, on the one hand, and contingent truth, on the other. All truths are constrained by the structure

---

12 On the popularity of the *Logic* in Europe in the years after its publication see *Auroux 1993*. On the importance of Cartesian logic in conservative religious circles see *Kennedy 1995*. Jonathan Edwards, for example, thought that *the imminence of the end of the world* and that *the Pope as the Antichrist* were clear and distinct ideas. See *Marsden 2003*.

of ideas, as detailed in Chapter 3, but contingent truths are further constrained by various contingent facts of nature exhibited in the structure of significance ranges and extensions. Of particular importance is the special case in which the subject term of a contingent affirmative proposition fails of reference. In this case the subject term is a "false idea" and the proposition is automatically false. The authors draw the distinction between essential and contingent truth in this way:[13]

> The first reflection is that it is necessary to draw a sharp distinction between two sorts of truths. First are truths that concern merely the nature of things and their immutable essence, independently of their existence. The others concern existing things, especially human and contingent events, which may or may not come to exist when it is a question of the past. I am referring in this context to the proximate causes of things, in abstraction from their immutable order in God's providence, because on the one hand, God's providence does not preclude contingency, and on the other, since we know nothing about it [i.e. contingent creation], it contributes nothing to our beliefs about things.
>
> For the first kind of truth, since everything is necessary, nothing is true that is not universally true. So we ought to conclude that something is false if it is false in a single case.

On the one hand, there are what are called variously essential, general, immutable, and necessary truths. Knowledge of an essential truth is justified by a clear and distinct idea or by a deduction from other known necessary propositions. Such essential propositions are distinguished from truths about individuals and singular events. The latter are grammatically singular in form and contingent in truth-value. Knowledge of these is, by and large, independent of essential truths; they are justified rather by sensation.

What is important for logic is that essential and contingent truths differ in truth-conditions. These differences are major. As we shall see, they entail that corrections must be introduced to the truth-conditions for contingent categorical propositions as detailed in Chapter 4.

The truth-conditions for affirmative categorical propositions as explained in Chapter 4 do not require that their subject terms signify something that exists. If extensions are sets of ideas, they can contain one another and overlap even if they do not signify anything in the world. On the other hand, it is a clear implication of the *Logic*'s doctrine of "false ideas" that the terms in contingent propositions carry existential import. False ideas do not make any sense otherwise. An idea is not false unless

---

13 *LAP* IV.13, *KM* V 398, B 263. See also *LAP* II.13.iv, *KM* V 234, B 118.

it fails to signify, and a proposition with a false idea would not be false, as the *Logic* requires, unless its subject were a false idea. As we shall see, the truth-conditions of Part II continue to apply to contingent propositions but with the qualification that its terms signify existing things. What remains of this chapter will explore the relevant semantic revisions, first for essential propositions and then for contingent propositions. In each case, the issue of existential import has a background history that has shaped the *Logic*'s own position.

Essential Truth

The issue of whether essential truth carries existential import can be traced to Aristotle. In the *Topics* he makes clear that an essential truth, understood as a truth that states the nature of a substance, is necessary:[14]

> Now attributes attaching essentially to their subjects attach necessarily to them: for essential attributes are either elements in the essential nature of their subjects or contain their subject as elements in their own nature.

To the extent that essential truths are demonstrable, he believed, they are also eternal.[15] In Aristotle's era, it was uncontroversial that an essential definition was necessary and eternal because the natural world was thought to be eternal. Aristotle further held that a necessary condition for knowing something's nature was knowing that the thing existed:[16]

> He who knows what human—or any other—nature is, must know also that man exists; for no one knows the nature of what does not exist—one can know the meaning of the phrase or name "goat-stag" but not what the essential nature of a goat-stag is.

This text was historically interpreted as maintaining that the subject term of an essential truth must refer to existing things. The assumption of the eternity of the world became problematic for Christians, who believed, on the one hand, that God's knowledge was eternal but, on the other, that the world had a beginning in time. It was agreed that the ideas in God's mind, which serve as the seminal causes of things, are eternal, as Augustine explained:

> Ideas are certain principal, stable and immutable forms or reasons of things. They are not themselves formed, and hence they are eternal

---

14 *Aristotle 1928b*, Topics I.6 74b7.
15 Topics I.8 75b22.
16 *Posterior Analytics*, Book II.7 92a34–92b18.

and always stand in the same relations, and they are contained in the divine understanding. And although they neither arise nor perish, nevertheless everything that is able to arise and perish, and everything that does arise and perish, is said to be formed in accordance with them.[17]

While God's ideas were understood to be eternal, essential definition posed a problem. It seemed that essential definitions must have been true prior to creation even though their subject terms could not have referred to anything real.

William of Sherwood (c. 1200–c. 1272) addressed the issue with a distinction that was to resonate later. On this view, the copula in a universal affirmative is ambiguous. On the one hand, it functions in contingent truths about the actual world. These conform to Aristotle's view that affirmatives carry existential import. The copula in this case attributes "actual being" (*esse actuale*) to the subject. The subject term carries existential import in the sense that the proposition is true only if its subject exists. The copula in necessary propositions functions otherwise. In essential predications, a genus is affirmed of a species. The predicate declares the essence or nature of the subject, and the copula attributes being in a second sense called "habitual being" (*esse habituale*). In these cases the proposition does not entail the subject's actual existence. Sherwood draws the distinction in a discussion of an argument relative to the essential truth *every man is an animal*:

> But again, consider this counterargument: "every animal is, every man is an animal; therefore every man is." The first premise is true, and the second is necessary, [it is claimed] since the genus is predicated of a species. [In response to this] we must point out that the argument is not valid [*non valet*], for when one says "every animal is" one predicates *actual* being [*esse actuale*]—i.e., existence. But when I say "every man is an animal" *relational* being [*esse habituale*] is predicated.

Here the copula is equivocal because it is used in its actual sense in the major premise, the habitual sense in the minor, and the actual sense in the conclusion.

---

17 *Augustine 1975*, Q. 46.2, Spade trans. In *Spade August 29, 1985*, vol. II, text 3, p. 7. See also *Augustine 1894*, *De genesi ad litteram*, vi.10.

Sherwood remarked, moreover, that the copula does not require the subject's existence. This conclusion follows, he says, from the fact that the categorical proposition is equivalent to a conditional:

> and insofar as it [namely, "every man is an animal"] is necessary it has the force of this conditional: "if it is a man it is an animal" (*si homo est, animal est*). For when "is" is placed as a kind of mean between the extremes "a man" and "an animal" it declares an inter-relation between the two (*dicit habitudinem mediam inter haec duo*). Thus it is clear that the signification of "is" in the first proposition differs from that in the second. Therefore the conclusion "every man is" does not follow.[18]

Sherwood reasons, on the one hand, that the conditional and the universal affirmative categorical proposition are equivalent and, on the other, that there are cases in which the conditional is true although its antecedent is false. It follows in these cases that the universal affirmative is also true and that its subject term does not signify an actual thing.

Note that while the universal affirmative is said to be equivalent to a conditional, Sherwood cannot be proposing something like the modern first-order analysis of a universal affirmative as a universally quantified material conditional $\forall x(Sx \rightarrow Px)$ because the modern formula does not carry existential import. As the terminology *habitual* suggests, the conditional he has in mind is a variety of dispositional counterfactual, and as such it is non-extensional in the modern sense. Suárez would later make a similar point.

Regardless of Sherwood's proposal, the standard view in the Middle Ages was that the subject terms of a universal affirmative, including essential definitions, carries existential import. Since universal affirmatives entail particular affirmatives, they too carry existential import.[19] Ockham was a strong defender of the standard view. He rejected the claim that a universal affirmative was ever equivalent to a conditional:[20]

> on the assumption that there are no donkeys, they deny this syllogism, "Every animal is a man; every donkey is an animal; therefore every donkey is a man." They claim that the verb "to be" is

---

18 William of Sherwood 1937, *Introductiones in logicam* I.14; English text *Sherwood 1966*, pp. 124–126. Klima also mentions a text to the same effect from Garland the Computist (11th century) cited in *Henry 1984*, pp. 85–86. See also *de Rijk 1962–1967*, II.2, p. 730, and the discussion in *John Buridan 2001*, Introduction, xlv–xlvii.
19 Others in addition to Ockham include Roger Bacon (see *Braakhuis 1977*) and Robert Kilwardby (see *Ebbesen 1986*).
20 William of Ockham 1980, *Summa Logicae*, I.14, p. 123.

> equivocal in these syllogisms, since in the major premises it is taken for an operation of a being—and this is the "to be" of what exists—whereas in the minor premises it is taken for the "to be" of condition or consequence. The verb "to be" in this sense occurs when one says: "If it is white, then it is colored." This claim is completely irrational, for it amounts to destroying every syllogistic form. For whenever it pleases me, I will say that "to be" is equivocal in the propositions, and I will ascribe at will a fallacy of equivocation to every syllogism.

Here Ockham rejects Sherwood's conditional reading because it vitiates the validity of any syllogism stated in terms of universal affirmatives. This is alleged to be the case because the reading is open to the charge of equivocation on the copula. Ockham seems to assume that neither the syntax nor the speech content provides a way to distinguish which of the two senses would be intended.

Ockham argues by example that a universal affirmative is not equivalent to a conditional:[21]

> Hence, distinctions such as that between the "to be" which is an operation of a being and the "to be" of condition are frivolous, and they are posited by those who do not know how to distinguish between a categorical proposition and a conditional proposition. Hence, these propositions are distinct: "A donkey is an animal" and "If a donkey exists, an animal exists." For the one is categorical and the other is conditional and hypothetical—and they are not interchangeable. Rather, one can be true while the other is false. In the same way, "A non-creating God is God" is now false, and yet these conditionals are true: "If a non-creating God exists, then God exists" and "If this is a non-creating God, then it is God."

On the one hand, Ockham holds that some essential universal affirmatives have an empty subject term and are therefore false (*à la* Aristotle). His example is *a non-creating God is a God*. On the other hand, the conditional in medieval logic was normally understood to affirm a "consequence," i.e., an inference in which the antecedent necessarily implies the consequent for reasons of logic or nature. On this reading, the conditional may be true even though its antecedent is false. The example Ockham furnishes is the conditional *if there were a non-creating God, he would be God*, which understood as a consequence is true.

Ockham remarks that the standard reading has what may appear to be counterintuitive consequences, which were to trouble its future defenders.

---

21 *William of Ockham 1980, Summa Logicae*, II.4, pp. 98–100.

For example, he grants that *a chimera is a chimera* is false even though it appears to be a tautology.[22]

Sherwood, however, was one of a series of logicians to draw a distinction between necessary and contingent propositions in terms of existential import. John Buridan is a case in point; he granted that, in the ordinary case, it is assumed that the subject term of a universal proposition signifies something that exists. In this case, Buridan agrees with Ockham that propositions like *a chimera is a chimera* are false.[23] But he also held that there are cases in which terms are used in what he called *natural supposition*, in which terms signify in a way that abstracts from time so that if the proposition is true, it is true timelessly:[24]

> Again, just as the intellect is able to conceive of man and animal without any distinction of time by means of the concepts whence the terms "man" and "animal" are imposed, so it is likely that it is able to form a complexive concept without any distinction of time. But then the mental proposition [formed with this concept] will be indifferent with respect to all present, past and future times, and so also [its] terms will supposit for everything from those times indifferently. But we do not have an utterance properly imposed to signify such a mental copula, so we can use the verb "is" by convention [*ad placitum*] to signify such a copula by which the present time will no more be signified than is the past or the future; indeed, [it will signify] no time at all, and so there will occur a natural supposition of the terms.

A timeless proposition is "eternally true;" in this sense it resembles what Quine refers to as an eternal statement:[25]

> In fact, perhaps we can show from our faith that we are able to form such mental propositions. For God could preserve all things in rest, without motion (I mean all things other than motion). So let us suppose that He does so. Then nothing would be time, if every

---

22 William of Ockham 1980, *Summa Logicae*, II.14, p. 123.

> any affirmative proposition in which the name "chimaera" or one just like it, taken significatively, is either the subject or the predicate is, strictly speaking, false ... if the terms supposit significatively, then "A chimaera is a chimaera" is, strictly speaking, false.

Here the predicates re attributed *true* and *false* as applied to terms, the derivative sense later found in Descartes and Arnauld.

23 Buridan 2001, p. 834. *Summulae, Sophismata*, Chapt. 1, Sophism 6, 5th Conclusion. See the discussion in Ashworth 1977.

24 *John Buridan 2001, Summulae* 4.3.4, p. 261.

25 Ibid.

time is motion, as Aristotle shows in bk. 4 of the *Physics*. Nevertheless, the souls of the blessed would know and understand by mental propositions that God is good and that they are present to Him; and by the copulas of those mental propositions they would not co-understand [*cointelligerent*] time, for they would also know that there is no time, and so they would know that neither they themselves nor God did exist in the present time, and that they did not coexist with the present time either. And it appears to me that a spoken copula imposed precisely to signify such a complexive concept would be purely syncategorematic, while others, which connote a certain time, already share [the characteristics of] categorematic [terms], in that beyond their concept they also signify an external thing conceived besides the things signified by the subject and the predicate, namely, time.

As an example, Buridan gives the proposition *God is good*, which he suggests would be true and known to the blessed in heaven even if God caused motion, and hence time, to cease to exist. In such a case, *every man is an animal*, which is the paradigm of an essential definition, would also be true timelessly.

Perhaps the fullest development of Sherwood's suggestions is found in Suárez. His views are seen to be much like those of Arnauld and Nicole, and he accepts the dual senses of the copula:[26]

> It seems to me that this controversy derives entirely from the multiple signification of the copula *is* which joins the extremes of these propositions, for it can be taken in two ways.

The first sense is the standard one used to describe contingent facts. In this sense, the subject term of an affirmative proposition carries existential import:[27]

> [The copula in this sense] signifies the actual and real conjunction of the extremes that exists in the thing itself, for example, when *man is an animal* is said, it is signified that the thing itself exists (*significetur reipsa ita esse*); . . . the proposition's truth depends without doubt on the existence of the extremes because the union does not remove the tense from the signification of the word *is*, or—what is the same thing—*is* signifies a real and actual duration. For when existence [at a time, as indicated by its present tense] is taken away, there is nothing there [*nulla est*]; and therefore, such a proposition is false

---

[26] Suárez 1856–1878, *Disputationes Metaphysicae* (hereinafter *DM*) XXXI.12.44, p. 296.
[27] Suárez 1856–1878, *DM* XXXI.12.44 cont.

because it is affirmed of a subject that does not stand for anything [*non-supponente*].

Suárez grants that Aristotle was correct about ordinary usage, in which the subject term stands for something that exists. If it does not, the proposition is false:[28]

> when existence is taken away from an actual thing, it is denied that propositions are true in which essential predicates in this sense are said of subjects, for, as it is true, as it says in *Categories* in the chapter on substance, "when primary substance is taken away, it is impossible that anything remains."

In the copula's second sense, however, the proposition's subject does not stand for something in the world but for a *ratio*. In this case the copula "signifies that the predicate exists as the subject's *ratio*, whether or not the extremes exist."[29] It follows that the subject term lacks existential import:[30]

> propositions are true even if the extremes do not exist, and in this sense they are necessary and perpetual truths, for since the copula *is* in this sense does not signify existence, it does not attribute actual reality to the extremes in themselves, and therefore does not require for its truth either existence or actual reality.

Suárez explains in greater detail than does Sherwood why an essential truth is equivalent to a conditional, or to what the logic of the period called a hypothetical:[31]

> propositions in this sense are reduced to a hypothetical or conditioned sense [*sensum hypotheticum seu conditionatum*], for when we abstract from a tense and say that man is an animal, we say only the nature of man is such that it would not be possible for a man to exist unless it was an animal. . . . Hence, just as the conditional *if it is a man, it is an animal*, is perpetual or *if it runs, it is moved*, so too this is perpetual: *man is an animal*, or *running is a motion*.

According to Suárez, *man is an animal* asserts that no man could have been brought into existence without being an animal. The proposition is

---

28 *Suárez 1856–1878, DM* XXXI.12.44 and 45; pp. 296–297.
29 *Suárez 1856–1878, DM* XXXI.12.44 cont.
30 *Suárez 1856–1878, DM* XXXI.12.45 cont.
31 Ibid.

equivalent to the perpetually true conditional *if it is a man, it is an animal*. Similarly, *running is a motion* is perpetually true and is equivalent to the conditional *if it runs, it is moved*.

Like Sherwood and Buridan, Suárez holds that essential truths do not presuppose that their subject terms refer. He does so by explaining how essential truths describe God's knowledge prior to creation. They are true even though their subject terms stands for things that have not yet been caused to exist:[32]

> For both of these conditionals are equally true: *if a stone is an animal, then it is sensible*, and *if a man is an animal, it is sensible*. Also, therefore, this proposition *every animal is sensible* does not [for its truth] depend, in itself [*per se*], on a cause that can affect an animal. Hence, if *per impossibile* there were no efficient causes [and hence no actual entities or actual truths], that sentence would nevertheless be true, just as this would be true: *a chimera is a chimera*, and similar examples.

The *consequentiae* here are true even if their terms do not refer. To use Suárez' own words, they are true even if their referents lack "efficient causes":[33]

If a stone is an animal, then it is sensible
If a man is an animal, then it is sensible

These conditionals do not require that an animal "has been caused" to actually exist. Likewise if the universal affirmative *every man is sensible* and *every chimera is a chimera* are understood as equivalent to conditionals in this way, it is not required for their truth that their subjects refer to actual existents.

On Suárez' analysis it is also clear why essential truths understood as *consequentiae* are dispositional (*habituale*), as Sherwood suggested earlier. They are non-truth functional and, therefore, not equivalent to the universally quantified material conditionals of modern logic. The proof is by examples. On the one hand, the consequence *if a stone is an animal, then it is sensible* is true. Furthermore, it is equivalent to the universal affirmative *every animal is sensible* because the term *stone* functions like a free variable in modern logic and stands for anything whatever. On the other hand, the consequence *if a stone is a plant, then it is sensible* is false. But it is equivalent to *every plant is sensible*. Thus, although the conditionals as a whole have different truth-values, their parts, namely

---

32 Ibid.
33 Ibid.

their antecedents and consequences, have the same truth-values. They are all false. Therefore, although the parts of the conditional have the same truth-values, the wholes do not. Thus the truth-values of the parts of the conditionals do not determine the truth-values of the wholes. Hence the conditionals are non-truth-functional.

It is clear, then, that Suárez has presented a detailed account of the difference between essential truths and more ordinary contingent truths. The distinction later drawn in the *Port Royal Logic* is similar, but its explanation is briefer. What is particularly relevant is that Suárez goes on to explain essential truths in terms of objective being.

An essential truth, he holds, does not corresponds to things in the world, not to what he calls "real being" (*esse reale*):[34]

> The first thing to be established is that the essence of a creature, or the creature as such prior to being brought into being by God [*priusquam a Deo fiat*], has in itself no true real being [*esse reale*], and in this sense, namely "the being of existence [*esse existentiae*]," it is not any existing thing, but is entirely nothing [*omnino esse nihil*].

Suárez, nevertheless, subscribes to a correspondence theory of truth. The entities that an essential truth corresponds to, however, are not real being; they are what he calls the subject's *ratio* or essence. They exist "objectively" in the intellect:[35]

> To which [it is replied as follows]: if the essence of a creature is considered as a being in act [*actu ens*], taken precisely, on its own and not as a something made, it is either: attributed to some [other and relating] being in act [*actu esse*], or it is considered not as something in itself [*in se*], but relative to its cause [*in causa*], [and as such] it does not possess any real being [*esse reale*] apart from that of its cause, or if understood as having being in itself in the way that something true does [*sic verum est*], then, on this understanding, it is not a real being [*ens reale*], but a being of reason [*ens rationis*], because it does not exist in itself, but only objectively [*objective*] in the intellect.

Here Suárez employs the language of earlier logic. He is suggesting that an essential truth accurately corresponds to relations holding in "objective being" or "being of reason" that exist "objectively in the intellect." Chapter 1 describes how the authors of the *Port Royal Logic* later appropriated a version of objective being as a way to analyze the intentional

---

34 Suárez 1856–1878, DM XXXI.2.1, p. 229.
35 Suárez 1856–1878, DM XXXI.2.10, p. 232.

content of ideas, but were careful to reject a view that attributed to objective being a special ontological status distinct from material and spiritual substances and their modes. For Arnaud and Nicole, an essential truth is simply that affirmation of an idea's content as predicate of that idea as subject.

What is relevant about Suárez view of essential truths for the *Logic* is that he ascribes to them a special semantic status, which differs from that accorded to contingent truths. What makes them different is explained in terms of objective being. We shall see shortly that the authors of the *Logic* accept both of Suárez' points but subscribe to a different, ontologically neutral understanding of objective being.

Descartes had a more immediate influence on the *Port Royal Logic* than Suárez. Like Suárez, he distinguishes necessary from contingent truth. Although he refers to necessary truths as "eternal truths," Descartes is well-known for endorsing the view that God's will alone determines whether a proposition is eternally true. God, he believed, could will any proposition, even truths of logic and mathematics, to be false.[36] In *Meditation* V he maintains, nevertheless, that these truths are about immutable nature. More relevant to the *Logic* is their semantics. Descartes holds that terms in eternal truths do not carry existential import. The *Logic* later adopted the view that terms in essential truths do not have existential import. Descartes held eternal truths to be true, even if the entities ideas refer to "don't exist anywhere outside me":[37]

> The most important point is that I find in myself countless ideas of things that can't be called *nothing*, even if they don't exist anywhere outside me. For although I am free to think of these ideas or not, as I choose, *I didn't invent them*: they have their own true and immutable natures, which are not under my control. Even if there are not and never were any triangles outside my thought, still, when I imagine a triangle I am constrained in how I do this, because there is a determinate nature or essence or form of *triangle* that is eternal, unchanging, and independent of my mind.

On this view of semantics, a universal affirmation may be true even if its subject term fails to stand for something that actually exists.

Although not required to refer to actual existents, eternal truths are not without ontological presuppositions. Descartes makes the rather obscure claim that what their terms signify is "not nothing." This expression is

---

36 *Descartes 1967*, vol. 2. Response to 6th Objection, p. 238; AT 7 431–433.
37 *Meditation* V.05, AT 7 64 76–77. English translations of the *Meditations* here and below are from *Descartes 1967*.

brought forward from *Meditation* III, where he uses it to refer to objective being. He says there:

> however imperfect may be the mode of existence by which a thing is objectively in the understanding by its idea, we certainly cannot, for all that, allege that this mode of existence is nothing.[38]

What Descartes appears to be saying is that when something is understood through an idea, "what is understood" is something that exists "objectively in the understanding." Moreover, Descartes seems to regard objective being as possessing a special mode of existence distinct from existence in the actual world. As discussed in Chapter 1, one of the historical motives for positing objective being as a distinct entity was to identify it with "what is understood" when we understand an abstract idea—such was Ockham's reason for positing "*ficta*." Descartes' objective being functions in this regard like Suárez' *esse reale*.[39] Descartes and Suárez take the position that an essential truth can be true even if its terms fail to signify anything in the world. In both cases, the explanation of truth appeals to objective being.

With this background it is now possible to situate the *Logic*'s own position on the existential import of essential truths. Its authors side with Descartes and Suárez in that an essential truth can be true even if its terms fail to signify anything in the world. Moreover, they explain essential truth by appeal to objective being or, in the language of the *Logic*, by appeal to the "content" of ideas.

Part II sets out in detail the inclusion and exclusion conditions that must be met for the four types of categorical proposition to be true. These truth-conditions apply correctly the essential truths of Part IV that serve as the axioms of scientific demonstration. In particular, the conditions apply to real definitions. Real definitions describe "what is contained in the true idea of a thing," they are "universal," and they "explain the nature of a thing by its essential attributes."[40] If the terms signify existing things, the conditions apply in a straightforward way: if the proposition is a universal affirmative, it is true if the extension of the subject is included in that of the predicate; if it is a particular affirmative, the two extensions share an idea that signifies at least one existing thing; if it is a universal negative, the extensions are disjoint; and finally, if it is a particular negative, the extension of the subject is not included in that of the predicate.

---

38 *Meditation* III.14, AT 7 41 26–29; III.6, AT 7 37–36. See also *Meditation* V, AT 7 65 2–6 and 7 64 6–9.
39 See *Suárez 1856–1878*, DM XXXI.12.46, p. 298.
40 *LAP* II.16, *KM* V 243–244, *B* 126.

The problem cases are those in which the terms do not refer. The *Logic*'s authors discuss these in terms of possibility. In the case of an essential truth, if it is possible, it is true:[41]

> possibility is a sure mark of the truth with respect to what is recognized as possible, whenever it is a question only of the essence of things. For the mind cannot conceive anything as possible unless it conceives it as true according to its existence. Thus when a geometer conceived that a line could be described by four or five different motions, he never took the trouble actually to draw the line, because it was enough for it to be possible in order for him to consider it as true, and to reason based on this assumption.

Here the authors are making a point in modal logic. A proposition that is about essence, like a real definition, is a law of nature, and as such, it is either necessarily true or necessarily false. If a proposition is either necessarily true or necessarily false, and is possibly true, then it is necessary:[42]

$(\Box P \vee \sim \Box P) \wedge \Diamond P \models P.$

In the case of a proposition with non-referring terms, what indicates possibility is content inclusion. The hierarchy of genera and species carves up the world according to a necessary structure imposed by God. If the defining properties of a species S possibly include those of the genus G, the proposition *every S is G* is possibly true. Here possibility is to be understood in the sense of natural possibility as constrained by Providence to conform to the tree of Porphyry. Real definitions are then understood as the laws describing the structure of nature. Accordingly, any purported real definition is either necessary or impossible. It follows that if a real definition is possible, it is necessary. Moreover, if the soul is vouchsafed a clear and distinct idea of S as P, it knows that the

---

41 *LAP* IV.13 first edition of 1662, KM 398, B 263.
42 This is not the only time that the authors resorts to modal logic to justify axioms in demonstrations. In Part IV they allow "true and certain" premises based on a geometric "construction":

> the construction of the thing itself in question, whenever there is some operation to be performed. This should also be as indubitable as the rest, since the construction should have been previously shown to be possible, if there had been any doubt about it. *LAP* IV.8, KM 384, B 251.

This seems to be a case of possible $\Diamond P \models \Box \Diamond P$. In the case of geometry, if it is possible to construct a figure, that possibility is sufficient evidence for admitting that possibility as a demonstrative premise in science, which requires only necessary propositions as axioms.

proposition is true, regardless of whether its terms refer. If it is clear that the genus is not in the content of the species, it knows that the proposition is necessarily false.

Possibility is conditional existence. The *Logic*'s position on essential truth, then, is conditional, somewhat in the manner of Sherwood and Suárez. If the terms of a real definition do in fact refer, the truth-conditions of Part II obtain. The tree of nature then mandates that anything the species signifies, the genus also signifies. If terms signify actual things, conceptual inclusion entails actual extensional inclusion because, as Chapter 3 explains, there is an order-inverting mapping from idea-contents to idea-extensions. If the content of idea G is included in that of S, then the extension of S is included in that of P. The truth-conditions of Part II then dictate that *every S is P* is true, and similarly for the other categorical propositions.

The truth-conditions of Part II also apply to contingent propositions. Here, however, issues of existential import are relevant. As will be explained below, a term that fails to refer to an actually existing thing is a "false idea." False ideas, moreover, have a role in establishing truth-conditions: any affirmative categorical proposition with a false idea as subject term is false. As in the case of essential truths, the doctrine's history shaped the *Logic*'s own version.

Contingent Truth

This chapter begins with a long quotation that is the *Logic*'s clearest commitment to contingent truths. They are described there as referring to "existing things, especially human and contingent events, which may or may not come to exist when it is a question of the past."[43] That contingent truths pertain to "existing things" has implications for truth-conditions. An affirmation with a subject term that fails to signify (a "false idea") is automatically false.

An early account of false ideas is found in Aristotle. As in modern logic, Aristotle recognized that in their primary senses *truth* and *falsity* are terms that apply to propositions, not to the ideas or concepts that make up propositions:[44]

> where the alternative of true or false applies, there we always find a putting together of objects of thought in a quasi-unity. . . . For falsehood always involves a synthesis; for even if you assert that what is white is not white you have included not white in a synthesis. It is possible also to call all these cases division as well as combination.

---

43 *LAP* IV.13, *KM* V 398, B 263.
44 Aristotle 1952, *De Anima*, III.6, 430a25–b6, trans. J.A. Smith.

Moreover, the terms that make up a proposition have no independent truth-value but are only rendered true or false in the context of the larger proposition in which they are found and which determine their meaning:[45]

> As there are in the mind thoughts which do not involve truth or falsity, and also those which must be either true or false, so it is in speech. For truth and falsity imply combination and separation. Nouns and verbs, provided nothing is added, are like thoughts without combination or separation; "man" and "white," as isolated terms, are not yet either true or false. In proof of this, consider the word "goat-stag." It has significance, but there is no truth or falsity about it, unless "is" or "is not" is added, either in the present or in some other tense.

Aristotle holds that it is propositions that are true or false in the first instance, but that a term may be described as *false* in the derivative sense if the corresponding proposition predicating the existence of that term is false. The term *goat-stag* is false because the proposition *a goat-stag exists* is false. Likewise, Aristotle describes perceptions and imaginations as false in a derivative sense. Although he held sensations to be veridical because they were generally caused by things that exist, he also allowed that imaginations (*phantasiai*) could be false if they do not correspond to existing things. "All sensations," he says, "are true, but most imaginations are false."[46] Moreover, he blames error on "false imaginations" (*pseudetai*):

> for while the perception that there is white before us cannot be false, the perception that what is white is this or that may be false.[47]

By Aquinas' time, the secondary usage of *true* and *false* was well established. The terms apply in the first instance to propositions, but they can be extended in analogical senses, first to *rationes* or definitions, next to things outside the mind, and lastly to people:[48]

> And so it is that truth is found in a prior sense in the composition and division of the intellect. Secondarily, however, the quiddities

---

45 Aristotle 1928a, *De Interpretatione*, 16a13, trans. E. M. Edghill.
46 *De Anima*, III.3, 428a12.
47 *De Anima*, III.3, 428b22.
48 Thomas Aquinas 2006 [1970], *De veritate*, q. 1, a.3 co; 51615.

> Et inde est quod veritas per prius invenitur in compositione et divisione intellectus. Secundario autem dicitur verum et per posterius in intellectu formante quiditates

of things or definitions are called true by being forming afterwards in the intellect. Hence a definition is called true or false by reason of a true or false composition, as when a definition is called false because it is of something that does not exist, for example, if to *triangle* is assigned the definition *circular* or when the parts of the definition cannot be combined together, or if it were said that the definition of a particular animal was *insensible*, for the composition implied, namely that *some animal is insensible*, is false. And so a definition is not said to be true or false unless it is the result of composition, and a thing likewise is called true through the disposition of the intellect. It is clear from what has been said, therefore, that the "true" is what is prior in composition or division of the intellect, second it is said of the definition of things according to the true or false composition implicated in them, third it is said about things according to the degree they are match the divine intellect [*adaequantur intellectui divino*] or that they match by natural design human intellect [*adaequari intellectui humano*]; fourth it is said of a man if he is judged true fellow or because there is a true or false appraisal of him or others on account of what he says or does.

It is the sense of "false" *ratio* or definition that is relevant here. A false definition is one that fails to refer. The examples in Aquinas are of a triangle defined as circular and of an animal defined as insensible. Because there are no circular triangles or insensible animals, the propositions *every triangle is circular* and *every animal is insensible* is false. Because these propositions are false, the definitions *circular triangle* and *insensible animal* are false. They are false because the parts that make them up "cannot be combined" (*partes definitionis non possunt componi*

---

rerum vel definitiones; unde definitio dicitur vera vel falsa, ratione compositionis verae vel falsae, ut quando scilicet dicitur esse definitio eius cuius non est, sicut si definitio circuli assignetur triangulo; vel etiam quando partes definitionis non possunt componi ad invicem, ut si dicatur definitio alicuius rei animal insensibile, haec enim compositio quae implicatur, scilicet aliquod animal est insensibile, est falsa. Et sic definitio non dicitur vera vel falsa nisi per ordinem ad compositionem, sicut et res dicitur vera per ordinem ad intellectum. Patet ergo ex dictis quod verum per prius dicitur de compositione vel divisione intellectus; secundo dicitur de definitionibus rerum, secundum quod in eis implicatur compositio vera vel falsa; tertio de rebus secundum quod adaequantur intellectui divino, vel aptae natae sunt adaequari intellectui humano; quarto dicitur de homine, propter hoc quod electivus est verorum vel facit existimationem de se vel de aliis veram vel falsam per ea quae dicit vel facit.

See the similar discussion at *Summa theologiae* 1, q. 17, a. 13, r. 2.

ad invicem). He makes this point explicitly in his commentary on the *Metaphysics*:[49]

> complex terms have truth and falsity through affirmation or negation. And here affirmation is called combination because it signifies that a predicate belongs to a subject, whereas negation is called separation because it signifies that a predicate does not belong to a subject.

In these texts Aquinas employs the notions of *false ratio* and *false complex term* to refer to what later philosophers, including Suárez, Descartes, and the *Logic*'s authors, call "beings of reason" or "false ideas." Later philosophers drew a semantic thesis from such accounts. An idea is false and fails to signify because the properties that define it fail to be jointly true of anything in the actual world.

Like his views on eternal truths, Descartes' remarks on false ideas are echoed in the *Logic*. In the *Meditations*, Descartes explains how he was "beset by false ideas":[50]

> But with regard to light, colors, sounds, odors, tastes, heat, cold, and the other tactile qualities, they are thought with so much obscurity and confusion, that I cannot determine even whether they are true or false; in other words, whether or not the ideas I have of these qualities are in truth the ideas of real objects [*an ideae, quas de illis habeo, sint rerum quarundam ideae, an non rerum*]. For although I before remarked that it is only in judgments that formal falsity, or falsity properly so called [*falsificatem proprie dictam, siue formalem*], can be met with, there may nevertheless be found in ideas a certain material falsity [*falsitas materialis*], which arises when they represent what is nothing as if it were something [*cum non rem tanquam rem repraesentant*]. Thus, for example, the ideas I have of cold and heat are so far from being clear and distinct, that I am unable from them to discover whether cold is only the privation of heat, or heat the privation of cold; or whether they are or are not real qualities: and since, ideas being as it were images, there can be none that does not

---

49 *Thomas Aquinas 1961, Commentary on the Metaphysics*, Book 6 lib. 6, l. 4, n. 1, trans. John P. Rowan:

> Voces enim incomplexae neque verum neque falsum significant; sed voces complexae, per affirmationem aut negationem veritatem aut falsitatem habent. Dicitur autem hic affirmatio compositio, quia significat praedicatum inesse subiecto. Negatio vero dicitur hic divisio, quia significat praedicatum a subiecto removeri.

50 *Meditations* III.19–20, AT VII 43–44.

seem to us to represent some object, the idea which represents cold as something real and positive will not improperly be called false, if it be correct to say that cold is nothing but a privation of heat; and so in other cases.

To ideas of this kind, indeed, it is not necessary that I should assign any author besides myself: for if they are false, that is, represent objects that are unreal [*nullas res repraesentent*], the natural light teaches me that they proceed from nothing; in other words, that they are in me only because something is wanting to the perfection of my nature; but if these ideas are true, yet because they exhibit to me so little reality that I cannot even distinguish the object represented from non-being, I do not see why I should not be the author of them.

Consistent with Aristotle, the medieval tradition, and modern logic, Descartes held that in their primary sense, truth and falsity are properties of propositions, not ideas:[51]

Now, with respect to ideas, if these are considered only in themselves, and are not referred to any object beyond them, they cannot, properly speaking, be false.

He goes on to say, "it is only in judgments that formal falsity, or falsity properly so called [*falsificatem proprie dictam, siue formalem*], can be met with." But the meaning of *false* can be extended: "There is, however, a derived sense in which ideas can be false." He inquires of colors, sounds, odors, tastes, heat, cold, and the other tactile qualities, "whether or not the ideas I have of these qualities are in truth the ideas of real objects [*an ideae, quas de illis habeo, sint rerum quarundam ideae, an non rerum*]." He goes on to apply the term *false* to ideas saying that false ideas "represent objects that are unreal [*nullas res repraesentent*]." He cites *goat* as an example of a true idea and *chimera* as a false idea.[52]

It is clear that by false idea Descartes means an idea that fails to signify something in the actual world. He describes this failure of signification as a relational property of ideas:[53]

Considering ideas if they are inspected only in themselves, I will not admit what they are related to, they cannot on their own be false. [*Iam quod ad ideas attinet, si solea in se spectentur, nec ad aliud quid illas reseram, falsae proprie esse non possunt*]. . . . If I were only

---

51 *Meditations* III.06, *AT* VII, 13, 37.
52 *Meditations* III.15, *AT* VII 37.
53 *Meditations* III.6, *AT* VII 37 25.

to consider ideas as modes of my thought, not refer to what they are related (*ad quidquam aliud*), they can hardly present to me any matter for error. [*si tantum ideas ipsas ut cogitationis meae quosdam modos considerarem, nec ad quidquam aliud referrem, uix mihi ullam errandi materiam dare possent.*]

Here Descartes is using the standard Latin jargon for a relation, *ad aliud*. A true idea is one that signifies something. He expresses this fact negatively: "ideas are . . . related to [*ad aliud*] that to which bind them, they can't be false." Falsity is the relational property of signification failure. Falsity is defined relationally just as truth is defined in terms of correspondence.

In the text, Descartes explicates this position in medieval terminology. It is correct, he contends, to refer to propositions as true or false in the primary sense. They can possess what he calls "formal falsity." Ideas can further possess these properties in a secondary sense, which he calls "material falsity" (*falsitas materialis*). Falsity in this sense occurs when ideas represent "what is nothing as if it were something [*cum non rem tanquam rem repraesentant*]."

The terminology of formal and material truth and falsity derives from medieval supposition theory, in which it was employed to make a distinction similar to the use-mention distinction in modern logic.[54] If a term has formal supposition, it signifies what it normally does; if used with material signification, it signifies itself. A proposition is formally true if it is true when terms are used in formal signification. Some examples will help to illustrate this point. In the normal case, the term *man* signifies what it usually does, namely men in the actual world. In this case, the proposition *a man is an animal* is formally true and *man is not an animal* is formally false. However, if *man* is used in material supposition to signify itself, *man is not a species* is false, while *man is a species* is true.

In the preceding text Descartes is extending material falsity to apply to ideas in cases of reference failure. In normal cases of successful reference, there exists a correspondence between the formal truth of an affirmation and the material truth of a metalinguistic statement that states that its terms signify the appropriate things in the world. For example, the proposition *men are animals* is formally true with *men* under formal supposition if, and only if, the proposition *man signifies what animal signifies* is materially true with *man* under material supposition. In a similar manner, *chimerae are animals* is formally false with *chimera* in formal

---

54 On material supposition see *William of Ockham 1974 [ca. 1323], Summa Logicae* I. 67, p. 197; *Walter Burley 1996, Treatise on Properties of Terms*, 1.1.1, p. 81 ff., Spade trans.; *John Buridan 2001, Summulae* 4.3.2, p. 254; *Fonseca 1964 [1575]*, 8.21 a–d, pp. 282–284. Both Burley and Fonseca distinguish formal supposition from material.

supposition if, and only if, *chimera signifies what animal signifies* is materially false with *chimera* in material supposition. Descartes extends the usage of false proposition to false idea. In such cases, the idea *chimera* is materially false. The idea is described as materially false because it fails of reference. Moreover, due to the meaning of *chimera*, any similar affirmation that has *chimera* as its subject and a term that signifies actual things as its predicate will be formally false. Accordingly, as he says above:

> Ideas can possess in the secondary sense "material falsity [*falsitas materialis*], which arises when they represent what is nothing as if it were something [*cum non rem tanquam rem repraesentant*].

Descartes holds false ideas to be a cause of error in ordinary life. This view is suggested in the earlier texts of Aristotle and Aquinas.[55] It is at root a semantic thesis because the error in question results from the fact that the ideas in question fail of reference. This analysis was later adopted by the authors of the *Logic* and given an important place in their epistemology. Descartes writes:[56]

> But the chief and most ordinary error consist in this that I might judge that ideas, which are in me, are similar to things posited as external to me but without conforming [to them]. [*Praecipuus autem error et frequemtissimus qui possit in illis reperiri, consistit in eo quod ideas, quae in me sunt, iudicem rebus quibusdam extra me positis similes esse siue conformes.*]

Although Descartes does not disambiguate what is meant here by "conform to things," he seems to be saying that an idea is false because its content fails to be true of anything in the world.

The *Logic* expands on the semantics of false ideas and the mechanism by which they lead to error. False ideas are introduced in the second chapter of Part I, and the doctrine is developed throughout the work. False ideas are described from the outset in semantic terms: they are understood to be terms in mental language that fail to signify anything in the actual world. In modern parlance, they are "empty terms"; they fail of reference:[57]

> Whether they be substances or modes, if the objects represented by these ideas are represented to us as they are in fact, one calls them true [*véritables*]. If they are not such, they can only be false [*elles sont*

---

55 *Meditations* III.6, AT VII 37.
56 *Meditations* III.6, AT VII 37.
57 *LAP* I.2, *KM* V 136, *B* 32, author's translation. See also *LAP Discours* I, *KM* V 110, *B* 9–10; I.9, *KM* V 157–178, *B* 49–50; and I.11, *KM* V 168–170, *B* 58–60.

fausses en la maniere qu'elles les peuvent être], and this is what one calls in the School beings of reason, which usually consist of the combination that the soul makes from two ideas real in themselves, but which are not joined in truth to form a single idea. An example is the one that can be formed from a mountain of gold. It is a being of reason, because it is composed of two ideas, of mountain and of gold, which it represents as one even though they would not really be so.

Here a false idea is described as a "combination" of two ideas which, taken individually, are usually "true" because they "represent things as they are"; the combination of the two ideas, however, is false because it represents things in a way that they are not. Over the course of the text the authors elaborate upon this doctrine, explaining how ideas are combined, how they signify substances and modes, and why in some cases this signification fails. Ideas are combined by restriction. Terms signify those entities that satisfy the modes in their intentional contents – comprehensions in the case of nouns, and secondary significations in the case of adjectives. If there is no entity that satisfies this content, then the term fails to signify anything real.

The preceding text cites *golden mountain* as an example of a false idea. It is formed by restricting the substantive *mountain* by the adjective *golden*. Both of the ideas *golden* and *mountain* have contents by which they signify those things that possess the modes in their contents. They succeed in signifying actual mountains and golden things, respectively. The restricted term *golden mountain* has a comprehension that consists of all the modes in the contents of *mountain* and *gold*. Because there is nothing in the world that jointly satisfies these modes, the combined term fails to signify anything at all.

Adopting a technical notion from earlier logic, the text describes a false idea as "being of reason." As explained in Chapter 1, when a concept failed to signify anything in the world, its objective being was sometimes called a being of reason. Philosophers like Suárez held objective being to occupy an ontological status distinct from both ideas and the actual world. The *Logic* likely follows in this tradition in understanding "being of reason" as objective being. In doing so, however, they mean by "objective being" the idea's intentional content, which consists of material and spiritual modes that, in general, inhere in things other than the idea itself. They authors are committed only to the existence of souls, material things, and their modes.

Chapter 7 of Part II acknowledges, as in earlier logic, that truth and falsity are in the first instance properties of propositions. Falsity, it says, is "usually encountered only in propositions." It goes on to say that there is a sense in which it applies to some "complex terms," by which it means idea formed by restriction. It cites examples that consist of a head noun restricted by an "explicative" relative clause. The complex idea is false "if there is some [false] judgment in the complex term, or some affirmation, either explicit or implicit." It refers to the associated affirmation as the term's *subordinate proposition*: the "attribute of the subordinate proposition is affirmed of the subject to which the noun refers." In other worlds, the complex term *AB* presupposes a background or "subordinate" proposition: *every A is B*. The authors provide an example:[58]

> In "Alexander who is the son of Philip," I affirm of Alexander, albeit only incidentally, that he is the son of Philip, and consequently there is some falsity in that if it is not the case.

The case described is the following. Suppose (contrary to fact) that Alexander was not the son of Philip. In that case, the proposition *Alexander is the son of Philip* would be false. It would follow in a derivative sense that *Alexander, the son of Philip* is a false idea.

The doctrine of false ideas has both philosophical and logical implications. The philosophical implications are epistemological. False ideas are a major source of false belief. The *Logic*'s authors adopt this view from Descartes, but in doing so they add a semantic explanation of the error. The fault lies in the intentional content of a false idea. As uncritical children we form beliefs that falsely affirm one idea of another. The examples that particularly concern the *Logic*'s authors are ones that affirm a spiritual mode of a corporeal substance. From the affirmation we form a complex false idea by combining the subject and the predicate:[59]

> Because we were children before we became adults, and because external things acted on us, causing various sensations in the soul by the impressions they made on the body, the soul saw that these sensations were not caused in it at will, but only on the occasion of certain bodies, for example, when it senses heat in approaching the fire. But it was not content to judge merely that there was something outside it that caused its sensations, in which case it would not have been mistaken. It went further, believing that what was in these objects was exactly like the sensations or ideas it had on these *occasions*. From these judgments the soul formed ideas of these things, transporting the sensations of heat, color, and so on, to the things themselves outside the soul. These are *the obscure and confused* ideas we have of sensible qualities, the soul adding *its false judgments* to what nature caused it to know.[60]

---

58 *LAP* II.7, *KM* V 209, *B* 92.
59 *LAP* I.9, *KM* V 157, *B* 49–50.
60 *LAP* I.10, *KM* V 157–158, *B* 49–50. The text continues *LAP* 1.11, *KM* V 169–170, *B* 59–60:

> But all error derives only from judging badly, in concluding, for example, that the sun is only two feet in diameter because the great distance causes the image it forms

Although the two simpler ideas may be "true" in the sense that separately the modes in their contents are jointly true of the entities they signify, the combined idea is false because the modes in its newly specified content are not jointly true of anything.

The preceding passage continues with examples from physics about the material world and with further examples from morality. It is common, the authors say, to form false ideas about bodies by combining an idea true of material substances with another true of sensations. The idea *hot fire* falsely combines *fire*, a corporeal phenomenon, with the sensation *heat*, which is a property of the soul. Likewise *bodily pain* combines the idea of *body*, which describes material substance, with the sensation *pain*, which is a spiritual mode. *Gravity* and *magnet* are false ideas because they combine an idea true of bodies with the idea of something that moves with a purpose, which is something only a soul can do.[61] Chapter 10 continues with false ideas dealing with morals. People naively combine the spiritual idea of moral goodness with material power and wealth and the idea of happiness, which is a property of the soul, with worldly regard or with physical valor. What is important from a logical perspective are the implications of the view for the truth-conditions for categorical affirmatives.

As in the tradition that preceded it, the *Logic*'s doctrine of false ideas entails that an affirmation about the world with a false idea as subject is false. The idea *SP* and its subordinate proposition *every S is P* are false if, as Aristotle says, the proposition "*SP* exists" is false. It follows that the truth-conditions for affirmative propositions about contingent facts must be qualified. They must include a clause to the effect that the subject term signifies an existing thing; if the subject term of an affirmative signifies something, the predicate must also. To ensure that the standard logical relations of the Square of Opposition hold—subalternation, contradictoriness, contrariety, and subcontrariety—the truth-conditions of the two negative categoricals must also be revised to include a clause stipulating that if the subject fails to signify something real, the proposition is true.

It should be stressed that it was standard in medieval logic to add these existence conditions, both positive and negative, to the truth-conditions of categorical propositions, and in this way to guarantee the Square's

---

in the back of the eye to be almost the same size as the one produced by an object of two feet at a distance more proportional to our usual manner of seeing. But because we have made this judgment since childhood and we are so accustomed to it that we do it at the very instant we see the sun, practically without reflecting, we attribute it to sight, and we say that we see small or large objects depending on whether they are nearer to or farther from us. Despite this, it is the mind and not the eye which judges their smallness or largeness.

61 See also *LAP* I.9, *KM* V 160–161, *B* 52–53.

logical properties. Aristotle probably held that an affirmative categorical proposition is true only if the subject term stands for an existing thing, and that a negative categorical is true if its subject does not.[62] These conditions became standard in medieval logic. They persisted and were standard among the *Logic*'s contemporaries.[63]

In sum, the standard truth-conditions laid out in Part II for categorical propositions, which are stated only in terms of inclusion and exclusion relation on term extensions, must be qualified by conditions on existential import. Revisions are necessary for contingent propositions.

The truth-conditions for categorical propositions from Part II as formulated in Chapter 4 are sufficient for the case of essential propositions. They are sufficient because the conditions of conceptual containment or overlap that hold among intentional contents in the case of an essential truth entail corresponding conditions of containment or overlap in significance ranges and extensions of their terms. Because the idea *animal* is contained in that of *man*, the significance range of *animal* contains that of *man*, and hence the extension of *animal* contains that of *man*. Thus the proposition *every man is an animal* is therefore true by the

---

62 Read 2015, 2017, and the discussion in *Martin 2004*, footnote p. 6.
63 See *Ashworth 1973*. Jean-Claude Pariente (*Pariente 1985*, pp. 246–247) argues that neither affirmative carries existential import in the *Logic*. He rejects the analysis of truth-conditions that holds that an affirmative categorical proposition is false if it has a subject term that is a false idea, i.e., a term that fails to signify. His argument is based on what he reads as a counterexample in the *Logic*'s discussion (II.7) of the proposition *Alexander, who was the son of Philip, defeated the Persians*. The discussion posits:

Alexander, who was the son of Philip, is defeated the Persians is true,
Alexander was the son of Philip is false,
Alexander defeated the Persians is true, and the subject term *Alexander, who was the son of Philip* is a case of explication.

Pariente argues that this is a counterexample because the subject term *Alexander, who was the son of Philip* is a false idea but that the whole proposition *Alexander, who was the son of Philip, defeated the Persians* is true. Pariente, however, misinterprets the example. The intent of the discussion is that because the case of restriction employed is explication and not determination, the subject term is not a false idea. The subject has the same comprehension as *Alexander*. Accordingly, the proposition *Alexander, who was the son of Philip, defeated the Persians* has the same truth-value as its contained part *Alexander defeated the Persians*. In other words, in mental language two propositions are being asserted, *Alexander was the son of Philip* and *Alexander defeated the Persians*. By hypothesis, the first is true and the second is false, and in both cases the subject term signifies Alexander. The term is not a false idea in either proposition. In other words, the issue of false ideas is irrelevant.

It may be doubted that the authors of the *Logic* thought much about the properties of the empty set. However, from the perspective of modern theory, there would be an obvious reason for incorporating existential import into the truth-conditions of contingent affirmatives, for otherwise, given the truth-conditions of Chapter 4, any propositions with a false idea as subject would be true because its extension would be empty, and therefore a subset of the extension of any predicate.

truth-conditions of Part II. In addition, because the structure of ideas constrains nature, an essential proposition—for example, a real definition of a species—is either necessarily true or false. Therefore, an essential proposition is necessarily true if it is possibly true.

The qualification required for contingent propositions is one requiring existential import: a contingent affirmation is true if, and only if, its subject term signifies at least one existing thing and, in addition, the truth-conditions specified in Part II are met. A negative contingent proposition is true if, and only if, its contradictory is false. It follows that a negative categorical proposition is automatically true if its subject term fails of reference.

In both essential and contingent truth, truth-conditions appeal to intentional content, although in different ways. In the case of essential propositions, an affirmative is true because the intentional content of the predicate is included in that of the subject. This condition makes requirements on the world outside the mind and on the possible configuration of significance ranges and extensions. In cases in which the subject term of a true essential affirmation refers to existing things, these conceptual constraints on possibility force corresponding inclusion and exclusion in the world outside the mind. In the case of a merely contingent proposition, on the other hand, correspondence to the world is a function of facts in the world that although constrained by conceptual possibility are not entailed by them. A contingent affirmation is true, first, because the modes in the intentional content of the subject term are contingently true of at least one thing and, second, because the modes in the contents of its terms contingently stand in right inclusion or overlap relations.

Throughout the *Logic*, semantics is alleged to have important implications for epistemology. Knowledge of both essential and contingent truths is in part a function of intentional content. Essential truths—for example, real definitions—directly describe inclusion and exclusion relations on the sets of ideas that make up intentional content. These truths are, in general, difficult to know. Scientific knowledge requires demonstrations that have certain axioms as premises. These premises are either the conclusions of prior demonstrations or are certain in themselves. They are certain in themselves if the soul has the relevant clear and distinct idea. Having a clear and distinct idea is explained in terms of intentional content. The proposition *every S is P* is true and known with certainty if the soul has a clear idea of the intentional content of S as including that of P. Knowledge of these inclusion relations, however, is not easy to come by.

Contingent truths are known in two ways, either by direct deduction from essential truths (e.g. as a special case of a general law) or through sensation. Sensation is explained in part in terms of intentional content. A sensation consists of a mental act in which the soul is vividly aware of a content consisting of modes. These modes are of two kinds. Some are material modes that, in general, are true of the material substance that is affecting the body's sense organs and brain, and some are spiritual modes true of the soul itself. The material modes are, in general, true of the material substance then affecting the body because God is not a deceiver. In like manner, the authors hold that the orthodox teachings of religion are true because, again, God is not a deceiver. Part IV concludes the *Logic* on this happy note. Science, although difficult, is accessible through reason; contingent knowledge of individuals and events is secure because God ensures that sensation is veridical; and God's goodness, likewise guarantees the truth of Port Royal's particular version of religious faith. The *Logic* has argued for these truths within its semantics of mental language made consistent with Descartes' dualism. It has done so largely by the special role of intentional content.

References

Alanen, Lilly. 1990. Cartesian Ideas and Intentionality. In: Haaparanta, L., M. Kusch, I. Niiniluto (eds.) *Language, Knowledge and Intentionality*, Helsinki, Acta Philosophical Fennica.

Aquinas, Thomas. 1961. *Commentary on the Metaphysics*, Chicago. Joseph Kenny, O.P. (ed.), John P. Rowan (translator). Priory of the Immaculate Conception: Washington, D.C. http://dhspriory.org/thomas/english/Metaphysics2.htm.

Aquinas, Thomas. 2006 [1970]. *De veritate (Textum Leoninum Romae)*, Fundación Tomás de Aquino OCLC nr. 49644264. Roberto Busa, S.J. and Enrique Alarcón (eds.).

Aristotle. 1928a. *De Interpretatione*, Oxford, Oxford University Press. Ross, W. D. (ed.), Edghill, E. M. (translator).

Aristotle. 1928b. *Topica*, Oxford, Oxford University Press. Ross, W. D. (ed.), Pickard-Cambridge, W. A. (translator).

Aristotle. 1952. *On the Soul*, Chicago, Encyclopaedia Britannica. Hutchins, Robert Maynard (ed.), Smith, J. A. (translator).

Ashworth, E. J. 1973. Existential Assumptions in Late Medieval Logic. *American Philosophical Quarterly*, 10, 141–147.

Augustine, St. 1894. De Genesis Ad Litteram Imperfectus Liber. In: Zycha, Joseph (ed.) *Corpus Scriptorum Ecclesiasticorum Lantinorum*, Arbeitsgruppe CSEL, Universität Salzburg.

Augustine, St. 1975. On Eighty-Three Different Questions. In: Mutzenbecher, Almut (ed.) *Sancti Aurelii Augustini de diversis quaestionibus octoginta tribus, De octo dulcitii quaestionibus*, Turnholt, Brepols.

Auroux, Sylvain. 1993. *La Logique des Idées*, Montréal, Paris, Bellarmin, Vrin.

Braakhuis, H.A.G. 1977. The Views of William of Sherwood on Some Semantical Topics and Their Relation to Those of Roger Bacon. *Vivarium*, 15, 111–142.

Brown, Deborah. 2007. Objective Being in Descartes: That Which We Know or That by Which We Know? In: Lagerlund, Henrik (ed.) *Representation and Objects of Thought in Medieval Philosophy*, Aldershot, Ashgate.

Buridan, John. 2001. *Summulae de dialectica*, New Haven, Yale University Press. Klima, Gyula (translator).

Burley, Walter. 1996. *On the Properties of Terms*, MS, Philosophy Department, Indiana University. Spade, Paul Vincent (translator).

de Rijk, Lambertus Marie. 1962–1967. *Logica Modernorum, a Contribution to the History of Early Termist Logic*, Assen, Van Gorcum.

Descartes, René. 1967. *Objections*, Cambridge, Cambridge University Press. Haldane, Elizabeth S. and G.R.T. Ross (eds.).

Dominicy, Marc. 1984. *La Naissance de la Grammaire moderne*, Bruxelles, Pierre Mardaga.

Ebbesen, Sten. 1986. The Chimera's Diary. In: Knuuttila, Simo and Jakko Hintikka (eds.) *The Logic of Being*, Dordrecht, Reidel.

Fonseca, Pedro da. 1964 [1575]. *Instituciões dialéctica [Institutionum dialecticarum libri octo]*, Coimbra, Universedade de Coimbra.

Kemp-Smith, Norman. 1952. *New Studies in the Philosophy of Descartes*, London, Macmillan.

Kennedy, Rick (ed.). 1995. *Aristotelian & Cartesian Logic at Harvard*, Boston, Colonial Society of Massachusetts (distributed by University of Virginia).

Marsden, George M. 2003. *Jonathan Edwards, a Life*, New Haven, Yale University Press.

Martin, John N. 2004. Aristotle's Natural Deduction Reconsidered. In: *Themes in Neoplatonic and Aristotelian Logic*, Aldershot, Ashgate.

Martin, John N. 2011. Existential Import in Cartesian Semantics. *History and Philosophy of Logic*, 32:2, 1–29.

Martin, John N. 2014. Malebranche's Neoplatonic Semantic Theory. *The International Journal of the Platonic Tradition*, 8, 33–71.

Mugnai, M. 1992. *Leibniz' Theory of Relations*, Stuttgart, F. Steiner.

Nadler, Steven M. 1989. *Arnauld and the Cartesian Philosophy of Ideas*, Manchester, Manchester University Press.

Normore, Calvin. 1986. Meaning and Objective Being: Descartes and His Sources. In: Rorty, Amélie Oksenberg (ed.) *Essays on Descartes' Meditations*, Berkeley, University of California Press.

O'Neil, Brian E. 1974. *Epistemological Direct Realism in Descartes' Philosophy*, Albuquerque, University of New Mexico.

Pariente, Jean-Claude. 1985. *L'Analyse du Language à Port-Royal*, Paris, C.N.R.S. Éditions de Minuit.

Raconis, C. F. d'Abra de. 1651. *Tertia pars philosophiae seu physicae, quarta pars philosophiae seu metaphysicae. Totius philosophiae, hoc est logicae, moralis, physicae et metaphysicae, brevis et accurata, facilique et cara methodo disposita tractatio*, Lugdunum [Lyon], Irenaeus Barlet.

Read, Stephen. 2015. Aristotle and Łukasiewicz on Existential Import. *Journal of the American Philosophical Association*, 1, 535–544.

Read, Stephen. 2017. *Aristotle's Theory of the Assertoric Syllogism*. https://philarchive.org/archive/REAATO-4v2.

Spade, Paul Vincent. August 29, 1985. *A Survey of Mediaeval Philosophy*, Version 2.0.

Stroud, Barry. 1984. *The Significance of Philosophical Scepticism*, Oxford, Clarendon Press.

Suárez, Francisco. 1856–1878. *Opera omina*, Paris, Ludovicum Vivès. Editio Nova, D. EM. André.

William of Ockham. 1974 [ca. 1323]. *Ockham's Theory of Terms: Part I of the Summa Logicae*, Notre Dame, IN, University of Notre Dame.

William of Ockham. 1980. *Ockham's Theory of Propositions (Part II of Summa Logicae)*, Notre Dame, IN, Notre Dame University Press.

William of Ockham. 1981. Reportatio. In: Etzkorn, Girard J. (ed.) *Opera Philosophica et Theologica*, St Bonaventure, NY, Franciscan Institute.

William of Sherwood. 1937. *Introductiones in logicam*, Munich, Sitzungsberichte der Bayerischen Akademie der Wissenschaffen, Phil. hist. Abteilung. Grabmann, Martin (ed.).

Yolton, John. 1975. Ideas and Knowledge in Seventeenth Century Philosophy. *Journal of the History of Philosophy*, 13, 145–166.

Appendix

This Appendix contains technical material relevant to each chapter placed here because of its formal character. Definitions are provided of some technical ideas introduced informally in the text, as well as reconstructions in algebraic or model theoretic terms of various parts of the *Logic*'s theory that may be of interest to formal logicians. The section on Chapter 4 also contains an introduction to the theory of the syllogism, which is familiar to historians of logic and is assumed in the discussion, but which is unfamiliar more generally to historians of philosophy and modern logicians.

Chapter 1. Background Concepts From Algebra

Definitions

<B, $\leq$> is a *partial ordering* iff $\leq$ is a reflexive, transitive, and antisymmetric binary relation on B.

If <B, $\leq$> and <B', $\leq'$> are partial orderings, then a function f from B into B' is *monotonic* iff, for any $x, y \in B$, if $x \leq y$ then $f(x) \leq' f(y)$; *antitonic* iff, for any $x, y \in B$, if $x \leq y$ then $f(y) \leq' f(x)$; and B is *dual to B' relative to f* iff f is 1–1, onto, and antitonic.

Theorem

If <B, $\leq$> and <B', $\leq'$> are dual, then for any $x, y \in B$, $x \leq y$ iff $f(y) \leq' f(x)$.

Definitions

In a partial ordering <B, $\leq$> *the greatest lower bound* of $\{x, y\}$, which is referred to as $glb\{x, y\}$ and $x \vee y$, if it exists, is the $z \in B$ such that $z \leq x$, $z \leq y$, and for any $w \in B$, if $w \leq x$ and $w \leq y$, then $w \leq z$;
the least upper bound of $\{x, y\}$, referred to briefly as $lub\{x, y\}$ and $x \wedge y$, if it exists, is the $z \in B$ such that $x \leq z$, $y \leq z$, and for any $w \in B$, if $x \leq w$ and $y \leq w$, then $z \leq w$.

$<B, \wedge>/<B, \vee>$ is a *meet/join semi-lattice* iff B is closed under a binary operation $\wedge/\vee$ that is associative, commutative, and idempotent.

An ordering relation $\leq$ on a *meet/join* semi-lattice B is defined as follows: $x \leq y$ iff $x \wedge y = x / x \vee y = y$.

Theorems

If $<B, \wedge>/<B, \vee>$ is a *meet/join semi-lattice*, then $<B, \leq>$ is a partial ordering.

$<B, \wedge, \vee>$ is a *lattice* iff, $<B, \wedge>$ and $<B, \vee>$ are *meet* and *join* semi-lattices.

$<B, \wedge, \vee>$ is a lattice iff, $<B, \leq>$ is a partial ordering closed under $\wedge$ and $\vee$.

Definitions

0 is *the least element* of a lattice B iff, $0 \in B$ and for any x in B, $0 \leq x$, $0 \wedge x = 0$ and $0 \vee x = x$;

1 is *the greatest element* iff, $1 \in B$ and for any x in B, $x \leq 1$, $1 \wedge x = x$ and $1 \vee x = 1$.

A (*rooted*) *tree* Tr is a partially ordered structure $<T, \leq, 0>$ such that for any $t \in T$,

{$x | t \leq x$} is totally ordered by $\leq$,
every subset of {$x | x \leq t$} has a $\leq$-first element, and
0 (the *root* of Tr) is the unique $\leq$-least element in T.
An element t of T is *a leaf node* of Tr iff, for any element t' of T, if $t \leq t'$ then $t = t$.

Chapter 3

A First-Order Language With Gradable Monadic Predicates

A first-order language may be extended to include non-classical negations and companion expressions as follows. Relative to a first-order language, let M be a distinguished one-place *mass predicate*, R a distinguished two-place *comparative adjective predicate*, and $A_{-n}, \ldots, A_0, \ldots, A_{+n}$ a distinguished series of *gradable adjectives* (one-place predicates). Let the set of *gradable predicates* T be the set of gradable adjectives closed under the one-place operators $\sim$ and $\neg$. Let *un* be a one-place operator on gradable adjectives. A first-order structure is any $<D, \Im>$ such that

1. D is a non-empty set and $\Im$ an interpretation function on predicates;
2. $\Im(M) \subseteq D$;
3. $\Im(R) \subseteq D^2$ is a connected preordering (reflexive and transitive);

4. there is a distinguished partition $\{\Im(A_{-n}), \ldots, \Im(A_0), \ldots, \Im(A_{+n})\}$ of $\Im(M)$ such that $y < x$ for any m such that $-n < m \leq +n$, for any $x \in \Im(A_m)$, and for any $y \in \Im(A_{m-1})$;
5. $\Im(\sim T) < \Im(T)$ and $\Im(T) < \Im(\neg T)$; and
6. for any m such that $0 < m$, $\Im(un - A_m) = \Im(A_{-m})$.

Proclus' Tree Structure of Emanation and the Great Chain of Being

The following is a reconstruction of the tree of emanation posited by Proclus in the *Platonic Theology*.[1] What is relevant here is the role of privative negation in determining a linear order of causation and perfection, a ordering that reappears in a more Aristotelian form in the *Port Royal Logic*.

By a *privative structure* ("the emanation of hypotheses from the One") is meant some $<N, T, \leq, \sim, 0>$ such that

N is an infinite set ("the stages of Being");
0 (the *One*) is in N;
$<N, \leq, 0>$ is an infinite finitely branching tree rooted in 0 such that for any m in N, such that the finite set $<m>$ of the $\leq$-immediate descendants of n is well-defined (for every n in N there is a unique m such that $n \leq m$, and there is no x such that $n \leq x$ and $x \leq m$);
$T = \{t \mid \text{for some } m \text{ in } N, t = <m>\} \cup \{0\}$ is a partition of N ($<m>$ is called a *taxon*, and m is called its *monad*; the taxa in T are the "hypotheses" of Being);
$\sim$ is a one-place 1–1 operation (called *privative negation*) such that for each taxon $<m>$ in T,

there is a unique $n \in <m>$ (called the $\leq$-greatest element of $<m>$) such that $\sim$ is defined for all elements of $<m>$ but n;
for all n in $<m>$, $\sim n$ is in $<m>$;
there are no "$\sim$-loops" in $<m>$ (there is no series $n_1, \ldots, n_n$ such that for all i and j, $n_{i+1} = \sim n_i$ and $n_1 = \sim n_n$).

The *least element* of a taxon t is that n such that there is no m in t such that $m = \sim n$. Since every node of N is in a taxon headed by a monad, it follows that the privative negation operation is well-defined for every node in the taxon except the least elements. A "linear" order (i.e. a total or connected partial order) on all the nodes of the N, the so-called *Great Chain of Being*, which we may call $\leq_{GCB}$, is definable as the transitive closer of that $\leq^*$ such that $m \leq^* n$ iff ($m \leq n$ or $\sim n = m$).

---

[1] See *Martin 2001*.

Theorems

1. $\leq_{GCB}$ is a total ordering.
   If $\sim n$, $\sim\sim n$, and $\sim m$ are well-defined,
2. $n \leq_{GCB} \sim n \leq_{GCB} \sim\sim n$;
3. $n \leq_{GCB} m \to \sim n \leq_{GCB} \sim m$.

The intensifier that Proclus called *hypernegation*, symbolized by ¬, is the inverse of privative negation: $\neg n = m$ iff $\sim m = n$. Proclus' conversion of the tree of emanation into the linear chain of Being is essentially the same as that which converts the family tree of the British royalty into the linear order of royal succession.

Auroux' Axiomatic Reconstruction of the Structure of Ideas in the *Logic*[2]

Sylvain Auroux has proposed the following axiomatic reconstruction of the *Logic*'s structure of ideas. E is the set of ideas, $<$ is an ordering relation on E, Π and $+$ are binary operations on E, and $-$ is idea negation. $<$ is a strict set inclusion on comprehension-sets. Π and $+$ are abstraction and restriction, respectively, interpreted as set intersection and union respectively on comprehension-sets.

$<E, <, +, \Pi, ->$ is such that

1*. $<$ is irreflexive, asymmetric, and transitive.
2*. $\exists x, y, \ldots, q \in E \ x\Pi y\Pi y\Pi \ldots = q$
3*. $\exists x, y, \ldots, z \in E \ x - y - \ldots = z$
4*. $\exists x, y, \ldots, z \in E \ x = y + \ldots + z$
5*. $\forall v, w, x, y, z \in E$
    $v = w + x + y \land z = x + y. \to v = w + z$
    $v = w + z \land z = x + y. \to v = w + x + y$
6*. $\exists x, y, z, \ldots, q \in E. \ x - y - \ldots - q = z \leftrightarrow x = x + y + \ldots + q$
7*. $\forall x, y, z, \ldots, q \in E. \ q \notin \{x, y, z \to.$
    $x\Pi y\Pi z \ldots = q \leftrightarrow. X = q + r \land y = q + t$
8*. $\forall x, y, z, \ldots, q \in E. \ x, y, z, \ldots, q$ are all distinct $\to$
    $w = x + y \ldots + z \to w < x \land w < y \land \ldots$
9*. $\forall x, y, z, \ldots, q \in E. \ x\Pi y\Pi z = q \to x < q \land y < q \land z < q \land \ldots$
10*. $\forall x, y. \ x < y \leftrightarrow x + y = x$
11*. $\sim \exists y \forall x. \ x - x = y$

Analysis

The axioms are not sufficient to ensure the structure is complemented, or that Π and $+$ are associative and commutative. Since the structure

---

[2] Auroux 1982, p. 89. See the discussion in *Martin 2016*.

need not be complemented, idea negation, represented by —, may not be relative complementation. Axioms 1*, 2*, 4*, 5* and 10* determine a minimal ordering and impose some lattice structure if $x \leq y$ is defined $x + y = x$ and $x \Pi y = y$.

- Axiom 1* ensures that < is a strict partial order.
- Axioms 2* and 4* say in effect that the operations Π and + are non-empty.
- Axiom *5 is unnecessary because, as formulated, it holds by the substitutivity of identity.
- Axiom 10*, which is formulated in terms of a strict order, is false as it stands in a lattice because $x + x = x$ yet $\sim(x < x)$. What is probably intended is $x \leq y \leftrightarrow x \wedge y = x$, which ensure that a more restricted idea is lower in the order. Restriction, which is represented by +, would then be a meet operation if the structure were a lattice. A unique minimal idea, i.e. a most restricted idea, if it existed, would be a least element.
- Axioms 8* and 9* impose some lattice structure. 8* requires that the value of + is a lower bound (not necessarily a greatest lower bound) and 9* that the value of Π is an upper bound (not necessarily a least upper bound).
- Axiom 3* ensures that — is non-empty.
- Axiom 11* appears to say that there is no idea with an empty comprehension.
- Axiom 6* and 7* affirm that there is an abstraction to z from x if, and only if, there is a parallel deconstruction by restriction to x from z.
- Axiom 7* seems to be missing existential quantifiers. It should read:

$$\forall x,y,z,\ldots,q \in E.\ q \notin \{x,y,z,\ldots\} \rightarrow .\exists r,t,s,\ldots, x\Pi y \Pi z\ldots$$
$$= q \leftrightarrow .x = q + r \wedge y = q + t \wedge z = q + s \ldots.$$

Axiom 6* describes essentially the same relation but in terms of negation:

$$\forall x,y,\ldots,z \in E. x,y,\ldots,z \text{ are distinct} \rightarrow (x{-}y{-}\ldots{=}z \leftrightarrow x{=}y\Pi\ldots\Pi z)$$

Here $x{-}y$ appears to represent the idea formed from x by removing the modes definitive of y. $x{-}y$ would then, however, be $x + y$. Perhaps what is intended is the Boolean definition of relative complementation: $x{-}y = x \wedge {-}y$. If ideas formed a Boolean algebra and complementation were well-defined, the ideas necessary for Axiom 6* would be provided by complementation: $(x \wedge y) = z \leftrightarrow x = z \vee {-}y$.

The axiom set is not sufficient to ensure a Boolean algebra or a complemented lattice, but is consistent with both. In sum, Auroux reconstructs the *Logic*'s ideas as forming a pre- or proto-Boolean structure. The *Logic*'s privative negation, which is quite different from Boolean complementation, supports principles like Axioms 6* and 7*, and does not require the maximal and minimal elements of Boolean complementation.

A Formal Reconstruction of the Ontology and Mental Language in the Logic

Definitions

The following is a formal reconstruction of the *Logic*'s structure of ideas and associated ontology. It is intended to capture in formal language the structure described in Chapter 3, showing in part that the *Logic*'s semantic theory is consistent and structurally interesting.

A *Port Royal Ontology* is an 8-tuple <*Souls,Bodies,Differences,Accidents,Substantives,Adjectives,Essences,Inheres,Being*>, such that

> *Souls* ∪ *Bodies* = *Substances*
> *Differences* ∪ *Accidents* = *Modes*,
> *Substantives* ∪ *Adjectives* = *Ideas* = *Terms*
> *Souls, Bodies, Differences*, and *Accidents* are pairwise disjoint,
> *Substantives* and *Adjectives* are disjoint subsets of *Accidents*;
> for some finite natural number r [the number of ranks in the tree of Porphyry], the cardinality h of *Differences* is $(2r) - 1$
> *Being* ∈ *Differences*;
> *Essences* is the least set S such that
>
>> $E^1_1 = \{Being\}$ is in S
>> For any E^n_m, if $n < h$ and E^n_m is in S, then
>> there are d and d' in *Differences* such that
>> $d \neq d'$
>> for any E^j_k, if $j < n+1$, $k < (2m) - 1$, then $d, d' \notin E^j_k$, and $E^{n+1}_{(2 \cdot m)-1} \cup \{d\}$, $E^{n+1}_{2 \cdot m} \cup \{d'\}$ are in S;
>
> *Inheres* is a relation from *Modes* to *Substances* such that
>
>> for any s in *Substances* there is a unique element E of *Essences* and a unique subset A of *Accidents* such that
>> for any d in E, and any a in A, d and a inhere in s and
>> for any substances s and s', if for every difference d and every accident a, d and a inhere in s if and only if d and a inhere in s', then $s = s'$;
>
> *Ideas* ⊆ *Accidents*;
> if i is in *Ideas* and i inheres in s, then $s \in$ *Souls*;
> there is a one-to-one correspondence f between *Ideas* and a subset of the power set of *Modes*;
> the range of f is *IntentionalContents*;
> if i is a substantive then $f(i)$ is *the comprehension* of I;
> If i is an adjective, then $f(i)$ is *the secondary signification* of I;
> for any i, if $f(i)$ is in *Essence*, then i is a substantive and is called a *species*;

228 *Appendix*

for any two ideas i and j, $i \leq j$ iff $f(i) \subseteq f(j)$.

Sig is the mapping from *IntentionalContents* to *Substances* $\cup$ *Modes* such that for any $c \in$ *IntentionalContents*, $\text{Sig}(c) = \{m \mid \text{for any element } m \text{ of } c, m \text{ inheres in } x\}$.

Sig($f(i)$) is the *SignificanceRange* of i and let SR be a function that maps ideas to their significance ranges: $\text{SR}(i) = \text{Sig}(f(i))$;

for any i and j in *Ideas*, i is *inferior* to j if and only if $\text{SR}(i) \subseteq \text{SR}(j)$;

$\{j | j$ is inferior to $i\}$ is the *extension* of i in *Ideas*;

the set of all extensions = *Extensions*;

Ext is the function that maps ideas to their extensions: $\text{Ext}(i) = \{j | j$ is inferior to $i\}$.

Let g be the function that maps sets in the range of SR to subsets of Ideas as follows $g(\text{SR}(f(i))) = \{j | \text{SR}(j) \subseteq \text{SR}(i)\}$.

Theorems

$\text{Ext}(i) = g(\text{SR}(f(i)))$;

$\langle \textit{Ideas}, \leq \rangle$ $\langle \textit{IntentionalContents}, \subseteq \rangle$ are isomorphic partially ordered structures;

f is a monotonic isomorphism from *Ideas* to *IntentionalContents*;

$\langle \text{Range}(\text{SR}), \subseteq \rangle$ and $\langle \textit{Extensions}, \subseteq \rangle$ are partially ordered structures;

g is a monotonic isomorphism from the domain of SR to *Extensions*;

SR is an antitonic many-one mapping from *IntentionalContents* to its range;

for any i in *Ideas*, $\text{Ext}(i) = g(\text{SR}(f(i)))$;

Ext is a many-one antitonic mapping from *Ideas* to *Extensions*.

Ideas are not dual to *Extensions*;

$\langle \textit{Essences}, \subseteq, \textit{Being} \rangle$ is a finite binary branching tree rooted in $\{\textit{Being}\}$.

Chapter 4

The Syllogistic

This section sets out in a brief form the elementary definitions and results of the syllogistic as found in the *Logic*. Most of the material is standard and would be familiar to students of traditional logic. Some of the *Logic*'s idiosyncrasies are noted in passing. What is sketched is a formal reconstruction of the *Logic*'s presentation in Part III.

Syntax

There are four (categorical) propositional forms:

the universal affirmative, every S is P, which is called an *A proposition*;
the particular affirmative, some S is P, called an *I proposition*;

the universal negative, no S is P called an *E proposition*; and
the particular negative, some S are not P, called an *O proposition*.

The first term of a proposition is its *subject*, and the second its *predicate*. A *syllogism* is a three-line series of categorical propositions, of which the first two are called its *premises* and the third its *conclusion*, such that:

> the predicate of the conclusion, called *the major term*, is contained in the first premise, called *the major premise*;
> the subject of the conclusion, called *the minor term*, is contained in the second premise, called *the minor premise*; and
> there is a third term shared by the major and minor premises, called *the middle term*.

A syllogism is defined here as an argument consisting of three propositions, but it may also be understood as a conditional sentence with a conjunctive antecedent, or as a two-line argument.[3] If S represents the minor term, P the major, and M the middle, there are four possible arrangements of terms in a syllogism, which are called *figures*:

> MP,SM,SP, *the first figure*;
> PM,SM,SP, *the second figure*;
> MP,MS,SP, *the third figure*; and
> PM,MS,SP, *the fourth figure*.

A syllogism is uniquely identified by specifying its *mood*, which is defined as the syllogism's figure together with the propositional form of each line (A, E, I, or O).

Semantics

A *standard interpretation* is a function that assigns to each term a non-empty set in a Boolean algebra and to each proposition a truth-value *true* or *false* as follows:

> an A proposition is *true* iff the referent of the subject is a subset of the referent of the predicate;
> an I proposition is *true* iff the intersection of the referents of the terms is non-empty;
> an E proposition is *true* iff the referents of the terms are disjoint; and

---

3 Lukasiewicz argues that Aristotle considered syllogisms to be sentences, but Corcoran contends that they are arguments. See *Lukasiewicz 1957* and *Corcoran 1972*. Formally the two interpretations are equivalent. See *Martin 1997*.

an O proposition is *true* iff the complement of the referent of the predicate relative to that of the subject is non-empty.

In the *Logic*, those sets that are assigned to terms are called extensions and are defined as the set of ideas inferior to that term. The truth-conditions are normally understood in terms of inclusion and exclusion relations on sets, as stated above. As explained in Chapter 4, however, the *Logic*'s own conditions are subtler and are formulated in terms of the distributional properties of terms.

The standard logical relations that make up the so-called Square of Opposition are defined as follows. One proposition is said to be *subaltern* to another iff in any interpretation the first proposition is true only if the second is also. Two propositions are *contrary* iff there is no interpretation in which both are true, and *subcontrary* iff there is no interpretation in which both are false. Two propositions are *contradictory* iff in any interpretation when the one is true the other is false, and conversely.

A syllogism (whether considered as a sentence or an argument) is *valid* iff in any interpretation in which the premises are true the conclusion is true.

Metatheorems

every S is P and *no S is P* are contrary.
some S is P and *some S is not P* are subcontrary.
every S is P and *some S is not P* are contradictory, as are *no S is P* and *some S is P*.
some S is P is subaltern to *every S is P*, as is *some S is not P* to *no S is P*.
There are 24 valid moods, six in each figure, which are listed below with their mnemonic names. Of these the *Logic* fails to explicitly mention the five below that are underlined:

First Figure: AAA (*Barbara*), EAE (*Celarent*), AII (*Darii*), EIO (*Ferio*), <u>EAO (*Celaront*)</u>, AAI (<u>*Barbari*</u>);
Second Figure: EAE (*Cesare*), AEE (*Camestres*), EIO (*Festino*), AOO (*Baroco*), <u>AEO (*Camestrop*)</u>, <u>EAO (*Cesaro*)</u>;
Third Figure: AAI (*Darapti*), EAO (*Felapton*), IAI (*Disamis*), AII (*Datisi*), OAO (*Bocardo*), EIO (*Ferison*);
Fourth Figure: AAI (*Bramantip*, incorrectly named *Babari* in the *Logic*), AEE (*Calentes*), IAI (*Dibatis*), EAO (*Fespamo*), EIO (*Fresison*), <u>EAO (*Camelop*)</u>.

The five underlined moods are not included among the valid moods in the *Logic*. They are so-called indirect moods, in a sense defined below.

Metatheorem

The following rules preserve validity—if the inputs of the rule is valid, so is the output:

> *metathesis* (abbreviated M; in the *Logic* it is called *vult transponi*): if a syllogism is valid, so is the syllogism in which the major and minor premises are switched;
> simple conversion (*conversio simplex*; abbreviated S; in the *Logic* it is called *vult simpliciter verti*): if a syllogism is valid, so is the syllogism like it except that the subject and predicate of an E or I proposition are reversed;
> conversion *per accidens* (abbreviated P; in the *Logic* it is called *vero per acci*) has two forms: if a syllogism is valid, so is the syllogism like it except that either the subject and predicate of an I or O premise are replaced respectively by the predicate and the subject of an A or E proposition, or the subject and predicate of an A or E conclusion are replaced respectively by the predicate and the subject of an I or O proposition;
> *per contradictionem* (abbreviated C; in the *Logic* it is called *per impossible duci*): if a syllogism is valid, so is the syllogism like it except the contradictory of the conclusion replaces one of the premises and the conclusion is replaced by the contradictory of that premise.

If syllogisms are regarded as arguments these rules should be regarded as "epitheoretic" because they specify relations among arguments. If syllogisms are regarded as conditional sentences, they are rules that relate sentences to sentences.

A syllogism s_2 is *directly deducible* from s_1 iff s_2 follows by one of the four rules from s_1. A syllogism s_n is *deducible* from s_1 iff there is a finite series of syllogisms $s_1, \ldots, s_n$ such that for any $I < 1$, s_{n+1} is directly deducible from s_n. Traditionally, these rules were applied to form a reverse series proceeding backwards from what is deduced to what it is deduced from: s_n was said to be *reducible* to s_1 iff s_n is *deducible* from s_1.

Metatheorems

> <u>Soundness.</u> *Barbara* and *Celarent* are valid moods, as are every syllogism deducible from them by the four rules above.
> <u>Completeness</u> ("Reduction" of the valid moods to *Barbara* and *Celarent*). Every valid mood is deducible from *Barbara* and *Celarent* by the four rules above.

The *Logic* does not set out the traditional reductions, but doing so is an elementary exercise.

232 *Appendix*

The *Logic*'s first edition describes the traditional reduction method by which the valid moods are, in effect, deduced from *Barbara* and *Celarent* by means of the four rules.[4] The mnemonic names encode how to reduce a valid mood in the 2nd, 3rd, or 4th figure to a valid mood in the 1st figure, and, in turn, the valid 1st figure moods to *Barbara* or *Celarent*. The letters A, E, I, and O indicate, in order, the form of the three propositions that make up the syllogism (major premise, minor premise, conclusion); the initials B, C, D, and F indicate the 1st figure mood with the same initial letter to which the syllogism is to be reduced; M indicates that the reduction applies the rule *metathesis*; S indicates that the reduction applies *conversio simple* on the preceding line; P indicates that the reduction applies *conversio per accidens* on the preceding line; non-initial C indicates that the reduction applies *per contradictionem*. The other letters are meaningless. *Celaront, Barbari* (AAI in the first figure), *Camestrop, Cesaro*, and *Camelop*, which are the five valid moods the *Logic* does not explicitly mention, are so-called *indirect moods* in the sense that they are reducible to another valid mood of the same figure with the same initial letter by the application of the two conversion rules to the conclusion of the syllogism being reduced.

First-Order Abstraction of the *Logic*'s Truth-Conditions for Categorical Propositions

Motivation

Here first-order logic is employed to show more formally that the *Logic*'s truth-conditions of Part II are abstracted from medieval supposition theory. The technique makes use of a translation function, called * below, that assigns to each categorical proposition a first-order equivalent. Because the syllogistic incorporates an assumption of existential import (that the extension of every term is non-empty), the first-order translation makes this assumption explicit. The rationale for the existential assumption is discussed in Chapter 6.

Definition. * is the function from categorical propositions to first-order formulas:

Categorical Proposition   **First-Order Translation**

$ASP^* = \exists x Sx \wedge \forall_S x \exists_{PS} y \, (x = y)$

$ESP^* = \sim\exists x Sx \vee \forall_S x \forall_P y \, (x \neq y)$

$ISP^* = \exists x Sx \wedge \exists_{PS} x \exists_{SP} y \, (x = y)$

$OSP^* = \sim\exists x Sx \vee \exists_S x \forall_{SP} y \, (x \neq y)$

---

4 *LAP* III.8, Arnauld 1993, p. 204, B 156.

A categorical proposition and its translation are equivalent in a precise sense:

> **Theorem.** For any first-order model structure $\langle D, \mathfrak{I} \rangle$, there is a syllogistic structure $\langle D, \subseteq, \cap, \emptyset \rangle$ and syllogistic interpretation $\mathfrak{I}'$ such that for any term T, $\mathfrak{I}'(T) = \mathfrak{I}(T)$, and for any categorical formula F, $\mathfrak{I}(F) = \mathfrak{I}'(F^*)$. Conversely, for any syllogistic structure $\langle D, \subseteq, \cap, \emptyset \rangle$ and any syllogistic interpretation $\mathfrak{I}$ over that structure, there is an $\mathfrak{I}'$ such that $\langle D, \mathfrak{I}' \rangle$ is a first-order model, $\mathfrak{I}'$ is the restriction of $\mathfrak{I}$ to the terms of the syllogistic, and for any categorical formula F, $\mathfrak{I}(F) = \mathfrak{I}'(F^*)$.

Because the quantifiers are "generalized" conjunctions and disjunctions, the translations are, in effect, transformations into first-order notation of a proposition's "preferred instantiations" as defined in Chapter 4. This fact can be made explicit in first-order model theory by means of suitable substitutional interpretations, which literally interpret the quantifiers as generalized conjunctions and disjunctions. Let $F[c_1, \ldots, c_n]$ be a first-order formula containing the constants $c_1, \ldots, c_n$, and let $F[c/v]$ be the result of substituting the constant c for all free occurrences of v in the first-order formula F.

> **Definition.** A first-order interpretation $\mathfrak{I}$ is *substitutional* iff
>
> $\mathfrak{I}(\forall v F) = T$ iff, for any constant c, $\mathfrak{I}(F[c/v]) = T$; and
> $\mathfrak{I}(\exists v F) = T$ iff, for some constant c, $\mathfrak{I}(F[c/v]) = T$.

The first-order translations of categorical propositions accordingly have a substitutional interpretation.

> **Theorem.** In any first-order substitution interpretation $\mathfrak{I}$:
>
> $\mathfrak{I}(\forall_s x \exists_{ps} y (x = y)) = T$ iff $\forall_{\mathfrak{I}(S)} \mathfrak{I}(c) \exists_{\mathfrak{I}(S) \cap \mathfrak{I}(P)} \mathfrak{I}(c')(\mathfrak{I}(c) = \mathfrak{I}(c'))$
>
> $\mathfrak{I}(\forall_s x \exists_p y (x \neq y)) = T$ iff $\forall_{\mathfrak{I}(S)} \mathfrak{I}(c) \, \forall_{\mathfrak{I}(P)} \mathfrak{I}(c')(\mathfrak{I}(c) \neq \mathfrak{I}(c'))$
>
> $\mathfrak{I}(\exists_{ps} x \exists_{sp} y (x = y)) = T$ iff $\exists_{\mathfrak{I}(P) \cap \mathfrak{I}(S)} \mathfrak{I}(c) \exists_{\mathfrak{I}(S) \cap \mathfrak{I}(P)} \mathfrak{I}(c)\, (\mathfrak{I}(c) = \mathfrak{I}(c'))$
>
> $\mathfrak{I}(\exists_{sp} x \forall_p y (x \neq y)) = T$ iff $\exists_{\mathfrak{I}(S)} \mathfrak{I}(c) \, \forall_{\mathfrak{I}(P) \cap \mathfrak{I}(S)} \mathfrak{I}(\mathfrak{I}(c)(\mathfrak{I}(c) \neq \mathfrak{I}(c'))$

Let it be assumed, as in some medieval semantics, that there are constants that name all the individuals in the extension of the formula's first-order predicates. The truth-conditions are then equivalent to conjunctions and disjunctions of instances. These conjunctions and disjunctions are the first-order versions of a proposition's "preferred instance."

234 *Appendix*

Theorem. In any first-order model $\langle \Im, D \rangle$ in which $\Im$ is a substitutional interpretation and there are sets of constants $\{s_1, \ldots, s_n\}$ and $\{p_1, \ldots, p_m\}$ such that for every element d of $\Im(D)$, there is some s_i in $\{s_1, \ldots, s_n\}$ such that $\Im(s_i) = d$, and for every element d of $\Im(P)$, there is some p_i in $\{p_1, \ldots, p_m\}$ such that $\Im(p_i) = d$, the following hold:

$\Im(\forall_s x \exists_{ps} y(x = y)) = T$ iff $\Im((s_1 = p_1 \lor \ldots \lor s_1 = p_m) \land \ldots \land (s_n = p_1 \lor \ldots \lor s_n = p_m)) = T$

$\Im(\forall_s x \exists_p y(x \neq y)) = T$ iff $\Im((s_1 \neq p_1 \land \ldots \land s_1 \neq p_m) \land \ldots \land (s_n \neq p_1 \land \ldots \land s_n \neq p_m)) = T$

$\Im(\exists_{ps} x \exists_{sp} y(x = y)) = T$ iff $\Im((s_1 = p_1 \lor \ldots \lor s_1 = p_m) \lor \ldots \lor (s_1 = p_1 \lor \ldots \lor s_1 = p_m)) = T$

$\Im(\exists_p x \forall_{sp} y(x \neq y)) = T$ iff $\Im((s_1 \neq p_1 \land \ldots \land s_1 \neq p_m) \lor \ldots \lor (s_n \neq p_1 \land \ldots \land s_n \neq p_m)) = T$

These results entail the theorem below, which captures the Cartesian abstraction of truth-conditions from the entailments of ascent and descent. It lists on the left a proposition's Cartesian truth-conditions and on the right its equivalent, under medieval expressive assumptions, in terms of conjunctions and disjunctions of instances.

Theorem. In any first-order model $\langle \Im, D \rangle$ in which $\Im$ is a substitutional interpretation and there are sets of constants $\{s_1, \ldots, s_n\}$ and $\{p_1, \ldots, p_m\}$ such that for every element d of $\Im(D)$, there is some s_i in $\{s_1, \ldots, s_n\}$ such that $\Im(s_i) = d$, and for every element d of $\Im(P)$, there is some p_i in $\{p_1, \ldots, p_m\}$ such that $\Im(p_i) = d$, the following hold:

$\forall_{\Im(s)} \Im(c) \exists_{\Im(s) \cap \Im(P)} \Im(c')(\Im(c) = \Im(c'))$ iff $\Im((s_1 = p_1 \lor \ldots \lor s_1 = p_m) \land \ldots \land (s_n = p_1 \lor \ldots \lor s_n = p_m)) = T$

$\forall_{\Im(s)} \Im(c) \forall_{\Im(P)} \Im(c')(\Im(c) \neq \Im(c'))$ iff $\Im((s_1 \neq p_1 \land \ldots \land s_1 \neq p_m) \land \ldots \land (s_n \neq p_1 \land \ldots \land s_n \neq p_m)) = T$

$\exists_{\Im(P) \cap \Im(s)} \Im(c) \exists_{\Im(s) \cap \Im(P)} \Im(c) (\Im(c) = \Im(c'))$ iff $\Im((s_1 = p_1 \lor \ldots \lor s_1 = p_m) \lor \ldots \lor (s_n = p_1 \lor \ldots \lor s_n = p_m)) = T$

$\exists_{\Im(s)} \Im(c) \forall_{\Im(P) \cap \Im(s)} \Im(\Im(c)(\Im(c) \neq \Im(c'))$ iff $\Im((s_1 \neq p_1 \land \ldots \land s_1 \neq p_m) \lor \ldots \lor (s_n \neq p_1 \land \ldots \land s_n \neq p_m)) = T$

Chapter 5. The Syllogistic Proof by Herlinus and Dasypodius of Euclid's Proposition 19, Book I

Below is the reconstruction into syllogisms by Herlinus and Dasypodius of the proof from Euclid's *Elements* of Proposition 19, Book I.[5]

---

5 The text in *Herlinus 1566* reads:

> Propositio XIX. Ut triangulus aliquis angulum quemvis habuerit maiorem: ita etiam maiorem habebit eam lineam rectam, quae illum angulum subtendit. Syllogismi quinque.
>   *Primus*. Quicunque triangulus habet duo aequalia latera: is habet etiam duos angulos inter se aequales, quos aequalia illa latera subtendunt. Trianguli αβγ habet latus αγ aequale lateri, αβ. Ergo, Trianguli αβγ angulus αβγ, est aequalis angulo αγβ. *Explicatio*. Maior est propositio quinta. Minor est *hypothesis*. Solutio obiectionis.
>   *Secundus*. Si trianguli αβγ, latus αγ, est aequale lateri αβ: erit etiam angulus αβγ, aequalis angulo αγβ. Sed angulus αβγ, non est aequalis angulo αγβ, quia maior. Ergo,

To be proved:

In any triangle the side opposite the greater angle is greater.

Euclid's Proof (Heath translation *Euclid 1956*):

> Let ABC be a triangle having the angle ABC greater than the angle BCA. I say that the side AC is greater than the side AB. If not, either AC equals AB or it is less than it. Now AC does not equal AB, for then the angle ABC would equal the angle ACB, but it does not. Therefore AC does not equal AB. Neither is AC less than AB, for then the angle ABC would be less than the angle ACB, but it is not. Therefore AC is not less than AB. And it was proved that it is not equal either. Therefore AC is greater than AB. Therefore *in any triangle the side opposite the greater angle is greater*. QED.

The reconstruction of Euclid's proof by Herlinus and Dasypodius consists of a series of five arguments, which they call syllogisms:

> **First.** Whatever triangle has two equal sides also has two angles, which adjoin two equal lines. Triangle $\alpha\beta\gamma$ has a side $\alpha\gamma$ equal to $\alpha\beta$. *Ergo*, the angle $\alpha\beta\gamma$ is equal to the angle $\alpha\gamma\beta$.

Exposition

Major: Every triangle with equal sides has the angles at the base that are equal (Prop 5).
Minor: Triangle $\alpha\beta\gamma$ has a side $\alpha\gamma$ equal to $\alpha\beta$ (hypothesis).
Conclusion: In triangle $\alpha\beta\gamma$, angle $\alpha\beta\gamma$ is equal to $\alpha\gamma\beta$.

Trianguli $\alpha\beta\gamma$, latus $\alpha\gamma$, non est aequale lateri $\alpha\beta$. *Explicatio.* Maior est nota ex syllogismo primo. Minor est *hypothesis*. *Obiectio secunda.* Quid si triangulus $\alpha\beta\gamma$, latus $\alpha\gamma$, sit minus latere $\alpha\beta$. *hypothesis.* Fingamus igitur trianguli $\alpha\beta\gamma$, latus $\alpha\gamma$, esse minus latere $\alpha\beta$. *he apodeixis.* *Tertius.* Ut trianguli latus aliquod fuerit maius: ita maiorem etiam angulum subtendet. Trianguli $\alpha\beta\gamma$, latus $\alpha\beta$, est maius latere $\alpha\gamma$. *Ergo*, Trianguli $\alpha\beta\gamma$, angulus $\beta\gamma\alpha$, est maior angulo $\alpha\beta\gamma$. *Explicatio.* Maior est propositio decima octava. Minor est *hypothesis*. *Solutio obiectionis.* *Quartus.* Si trianguli $\alpha\beta\gamma$, latus $\alpha\gamma$, est minus latere $\alpha\beta$, erit etiam angulum $\alpha\beta\gamma$, minor angulo $\alpha\gamma\beta$. Sed angulus $\alpha\beta\gamma$, non est minor angulo $\alpha\gamma\beta$, maior enim. *Ergo.* Trianguli $\alpha\beta\gamma$, latus $\alpha\gamma$, non est minus latere $\alpha\beta$. *Explicatio.* Maior est nota ex syllogismo tertio. Minor est *hypothesis*. *Quintus.* Trianguli $\alpha\beta\gamma$, latus $\alpha\gamma$, vel est aequale lateri $\alpha\beta$: vel est minus eo, vel maius. Sed trianguli $\alpha\beta\gamma$, latus $\alpha\gamma$, non est aequale lateri $\alpha\beta$, neque item minus latere $\alpha\beta$. *Ergo*, Trianguli $\alpha\beta\gamma$, latus $\alpha\gamma$, est maius latere $\alpha\beta$. *Explicatio.* Maior est nota per se. Minoris pars prior est conclusio syllogismi secundi. Posterior est conclusio syllogismi quarti. *To symperasma.* Triangulus $\alpha\beta\gamma$, habens angulum $\alpha\beta\gamma$, maiorem angulo $\alpha\beta\gamma$, habet etiam latus $\alpha\gamma$, maius latere $\alpha\beta$. Ut igitur triangulus &c. *hoper edei deixai.*

Second. If in triangle αβγ, side αγ is equal to side αβ, then the angle αβγ is equal to angle αβγ. But the angle αβγ is not equal to angle αγβ because it is greater *Ergo*, in triangle αβγ, αγ is not equal to side αβ.

Exposition

Major: Every triangle with equal sides has the angles at the base that are equal (Prop 5).
Minor: The angle αβγ is not equal to angle αβγ (hypothesis).
Conclusion: αγ is not equal to side αβ.

In the triangle αβγ, let the side αγ be less than the side αβ.

Third. Whatever side of a triangle is greater has an opposite angle that is greater.

In triangle αβγ, side αβ is greater than side αγ. *Ergo*, in triangle αβγ, angle βγα, is greater than angle αβγ.

Exposition

Major: In any triangle the angle opposite the greater side is greater (Prop 18).
Minor: In triangle αβγ, side αβ is greater than side αγ. (hypothesis)
Conclusion: In triangle αβγ, angle βγα, is greater than angle αβγ.

Fourth. If in triangle αβγ, side αγ is less than side αβ, the angle αβγ is less than angle αγβ. But αβγ is not less than angle αβγ. *Ergo*. In triangle αβγ, side αγ is not less than side αβ.

Exposition

Major: If in triangle αβγ, side αγ is less than side αβ, the angle αβγ is less than angle αγβ (third syllogism above).
Minor: In triangle αβγ, angle αβγ is not less than angle αβγ (hypothesis).
Conclusion: In triangle αβγ, side αγ is not less than side αβ.

Fifth. In the triangle αβγ, the side αγ is either equal to, greater than or less than side αβ. But in triangle αβγ, the side αγ, is not equal to side αβ nor less than it. *Ergo*, in triangle αβγ, side αγ is greater than side αβ.

Exposition

Major: In the triangle αβγ, αγ is equal to, greater than or less than αβ (*per se* true).

Minor: αγ is not equal to, greater than or less than αβ (second syllogism above). αγ is not less than αβ (fourth syllogism above).
Conclusion: In triangle αβγ, side αγ is greater than side αβ.

Triangle αβγ, which has the angle αβγ greater than the angle αγβ, also has the side αγ greater than the side αβ. Thus, in any triangle the side opposite the greater angle is greater. QED

The proofs appears valid and probably would be accepted as a proof of Euclid's proposition by a modern mathematician. The arguments, however, are not syllogisms in the strict sense. The propositions in the arguments do not conform to syllogistic grammar because they express relations that are not expressible in the syllogistic subject-predicate grammar. To demonstrate that their arguments are not syllogisms, it is sufficient to formalize one in first-order logic as an example. The first syllogism in the series in first-order logic would look like this:

$\forall xyz(T(xyz) \wedge E(xzxy). \rightarrow E(xyzxzy))$

$T(\alpha\beta\gamma) \wedge E(\alpha\gamma\alpha\beta)$

$\therefore T(\alpha\beta\gamma) \wedge E(\alpha\beta\gamma\alpha\alpha\beta)$

The argument is valid, but the formulas express relations and are written in a syntax that is much richer than envisioned in the *Logic*'s Part III.

References

Arnauld, Antoine and Pierre Nicole. 1993. *La Logique ou d'Art de Penser*, Paris, Librairie Philosophique J. Vrin. Clair, Pierre and François Girbal (eds.).

Auroux, Sylvain. 1982. *L'Illuminismo Francese e la Tradizione Logica di Port-Royal*, Bologna, CLUEB.

Corcoran, John. 1972. Completeness of an Ancient Logic. *Journal of Symbolic Logic*, 37, 696–702.

Euclid. 1956. *The Thirteen Books of Euclid's Elements*, New York, Dover. Heath, Thomas L. (translator).

Herlinus, Christian and Conrad Dasypodius. 1566. *Analysis Geometricae sex libroroum Euclidis. Elementum Primum VIII*, Strasbourg, Iosia Richelius.

Lukasiewicz, Jan. 1957. *Aristotle's Syllogistic*, Oxford, Clarendon Press.

Martin, John N. 1997. Aristotle's Natural Deduction Reconsidered. *History and Philosophy of Logic*, 18, 1–15.

Martin, John N. 2001. Proclus and the Neoplatonic Syllogistic. *Journal of Philosophical Logic*, 30, 187–240.

Martin, John N. 2016. Privative Negation in *the Port Royal Logic*. *Review of Symbolic Logic*, 9, 23.

Index

abbreviations 48, 50–51, 176, 178
abstraction 2–3, 12, 14, 36–37, 42, 50–51, 64, 68, 71–72, 76n6, 77–79, 79n9, 80–81, 81n10, 82–85, 91, 98n47, 106, 112n3, 118, 129–130, 135–136, 148, 153, 180, 189n6, 194, 225–226, 232, 234
acknowledgments 3, 61, 119, 137n39, 139, 170, 214
adjectives 36, 39, 41, 43, 46–48, 48n18, 49–53, 55–57, 63, 69, 72, 86–87, 92, 94–95, 97, 97n44, 98, 98n46, 101, 103–105, 110, 172, 179, 186, 214, 223, 227; *see also* connotative terms
analysis 2, 4, 7, 11, 41–42, 47, 78, 95, 110, 114, 126, 129, 135–136, 139–140, 148–155, 157–165, 165n26, 166, 168, 172, 180–181, 191, 197, 202, 213, 217n63
Andrade-Lotero, Edgar 141n48
Anicius Manlius Severinus Boethius 80, 81n10
Aristotle 3, 7, 9–10, 18, 39, 45, 48, 52, 56, 56n31, 61, 66, 90–94, 96, 98–99, 111–113, 136–137, 139, 151, 155, 155n9, 157–158, 160, 162, 165n26, 167, 167n28, 169–170, 173, 175, 178, 178n65, 181, 188, 190–191, 195n14, 196, 198, 200–201, 207, 207n44, 208, 208n45, 211, 213, 216–217, 229n3
Arnauld, Antoine 1, 5, 6n2, 9, 12, 14, 14n11, 15, 17, 23n25, 25–26, 28–29, 31, 33–35, 39–40, 44, 46, 59, 81n10, 100–101, 103n56, 111, 113, 118n22, 125, 130, 131n32, 132, 134, 136–137, 137n39, 139, 145n54, 148, 154, 165n26, 166, 181, 184–193, 199n22, 200, 232n4; *see also* abbreviations
Ashworth, E. J. 69n58, 199n23, 217n63
Auroux, Sylvain 1n1, 54n27, 65, 65n49, 75, 75n5, 76n6, 89n28, 91n32, 98n47, 193n12, 225, 225n2, 226

Barbara 109n1, 118n20, 131, 135, 144–146, 159–160, 162, 166, 230–232
Becerra, Edward Samuel
Bocheński, I. M. 139n45
Brown, Deborah 18n16, 185n2
Buckner, Edward 139n47

Cajetans, Thomas De Vio 59n37
Carnap, Rudolf 128, 128n30
categorical propositions 1–2, 4–5, 7, 11, 41, 43, 50, 58, 60, 65, 65n48, 66, 75, 88, 89n28, 104, 109–111, 111n2, 112–115, 118, 120–121, 123, 125–126, 128–129, 133–135, 139–140, 143, 181, 193–194, 197–198, 205, 207, 216–217, 217n63, 218, 228–229, 232–233
Celarent 109n1, 118n20, 131, 135, 145–146, 230–232
completeness *see* soundness and completeness
comprehension structure 35–36, 40–42, 42n6, 46–47, 50–55, 57, 59–60, 63–66, 68, 72n3, 75–76, 84, 89n28, 91, 98n47, 102, 104–106, 112, 145, 164–165, 172–173, 175, 179, 214, 217n63; *see also* definition; intentional content; secondary signification

Index   239

Conimbricenses 81, 81n10, 178n67
connotative terms 4, 43, 47–51, 53, 56, 62n43, 175; *see also* adjectives
containment principle 1–2, 4, 109–110, 138, 138n42, 139–141, 143, 143n49, 144–146
contingency 64, 124n27, 136–137, 137n38, 194; *see also* contingent truth
contingent truth 2, 5, 21, 23n25, 25n28, 55, 64–65, 68–69, 149, 175, 181, 184, 193–194, 196, 203–204, 207, 218
Corcoran, John 118n21, 138n42, 229n3
Cronin, T. J. 29n41, 31n43

d'Abra de Raconis, C. F. 30
definition *see* nominal definition; real definition
demonstration *see* synthesis
denominative terms 50
de Rijk, Lambertus Marie 116nn16–17, 197n18
Descartes, René 2, 4–5, 9, 11, 14n11, 15, 20n18, 22, 22n23, 23, 23n25, 24, 24n27, 25, 25n28, 27, 52, 58, 66–67, 67n52, 68, 68n55, 77–78, 81, 85, 107, 117n17, 148, 158, 163n22, 166, 166n27, 167, 167n29, 168, 168nn33–34, 169, 169n38, 185n2, 191, 199n22, 204, 204nn36–37, 205, 210–213, 215, 219; *see also* Abbbriviations
dici de omni 2, 139, 143–144
Dominicy, Marc 75, 75n5, 76n6, 91n32, 98, 98n47, 103n56, 189n6
Doyle, John P. 22n22, 132n34
Dutilh Novaes, Catarina

essential definition *see* real definition
essential truth 16, 19–21, 23nn25–26, 25n28, 26, 55, 68, 76, 149, 151, 167, 171, 193–196, 201–207, 217–218
Eustachio de S. Paulo 31, 31n43, 81, 81n11, 82, 101n52, 117n17, 136n36, 178n67
existential import 2, 4–5, 23n26, 25n28, 64, 68, 69n58, 149, 181, 184, 193–197, 199–201, 204–205, 207, 217, 217n63, 218, 232
extension 2–7, 14, 33, 35, 36n53, 37, 39, 41–42, 42n6, 43–44, 44n10, 45–46, 51–53, 57–61, 62n43, 63–66, 68–69, 71–72, 72n3, 73–756, 76n6, 77, 79, 85–90, 98n47, 102, 104–106, 109–110, 114, 125–126, 131, 131n31, 132–143, 145–146, 163, 166, 168–169, 172, 172n49, 173, 179–181, 194, 197, 205, 207, 217, 217n63, 218, 228, 230, 232–233

false idea 4–5, 23, 28, 35, 64, 66–67, 67n52, 68, 68n55, 69, 79n9, 83, 110, 175, 184, 186, 194–195, 207, 210–211, 213–216, 217n63
Fonseca, Petrus 29, 29n41, 30–31
formal logic 1–2, 4, 7, 105, 109, 117, 149–150, 163, 168–170, 193; *see also* syllogistic; synthesis

Garber, Daniel 14n11

Horn, Laurence R. 98n46

ideas: idea structure 76, 90, 106; identity conditions 36–37, 42n6, 52, 71; *see also* ontology, dualism
intentional content 2–4, 9, 15, 29, 32, 35–36, 36n53, 37, 40–42, 44, 46–47, 50–52, 57, 60, 63, 66, 68, 71–73, 76, 83, 85–87, 89n28, 90, 103–106, 109, 145, 148, 166, 172, 172n49, 178–181, 184–186, 188, 191, 214–215, 217–219

Jacuzzo, Leonard 138n42
Jespersen, Otto 99n48
Joachim, H. H. 91n33
John Buridan 12n8, 13n10, 45n12, 49n20, 61n41, 81n10, 84n14, 85n16, 86n20, 90n31, 100, 100n50, 101n51, 116nn16–17, 120, 120n23, 122n25, 123n26, 139n44, 158, 158n12, 176n57, 176n60, 197n18, 199, 199n24, 212n54
John Duns Scotus 16n12, 58n36

Keenan, Edward 134n35
Kneale, William and Martha Kneale 59–60, 60n39, 117, 117n19

Leibniz, Gottfried Wilhelm 4, 44, 74, 74n4, 117, 117n20, 118n22, 137n39, 165, 165n26, 166

240 Index

Lenzen, Wolfgang 74n4
Lovejoy, Arthur Onchen 96, 96n43
Lukasiewicz, Jan 139, 139n46, 229n3

Malebranche, Nicolas 5, 13, 13n10, 19, 25–26, 26nn29–30, 27, 27nn31–33, 28–29, 32–35, 184–185, 185n2, 187–190
Martin, John N. 6n3, 65n48, 71n1, 90n29, 94n39, 97n44, 99n49, 111n2, 118n21, 131n33, 141n48, 184n1, 185n2, 217n62, 224n1, 225n2, 229n3; see also acknowledgments
mental language 2–4, 20, 26–28, 36, 39, 43, 47–50, 52, 85–87, 99, 103, 109, 175–176, 179, 184, 213, 217n63, 219, 227; see also adjectives; categorical propositions; substantives
method: rules 117, 146, 148–156, 158–159; see also analysis demonstration; synthesis
modal logic 206, 206n42
monotonic quantifiers 132, 135
Morris, Charles W. 39, 39n1, 112
Moss, L.

Nadler, Steven M. 14n11, 26n30, 77n7, 185n2
necessity 21, 24, 45, 137n38, 162
Nicole, Pierre 1, 6n2, 9, 12, 14–15, 17, 23n25, 39, 44, 46, 59, 81n10, 100, 111, 113, 125, 130, 134, 136, 139, 148, 154, 166, 181, 184, 186, 193, 200, 204; see also abbreviations
nominal definition 4–5, 37, 39, 39n3, 50, 56, 110, 148–149, 167–168, 175–178, 181
Normore, Calvin 16n12, 185n2

objective being: as modes of the soul 11, 14, 26, 42, 52, 68, 82, 83, 191n9; in perception 3, 5, 25, 188, 191n9; medieval view 51, 83
ontology: dualism 10; perceptual parsimony 3; predicables and species 3, 10, 52

Pariente, Jean-Claude 60, 60n40, 71, 71n2, 89n28, 112n3, 217n63
Pasnau, Robert 13n10

Porphyry of tree 2, 54, 60, 76, 84, 97–98, 105, 151, 206, 227
possibility, double and single-sided 136–137, 137n38
primary signification 47
Proclus 94–95, 95n40, 96, 96nn41–42, 97, 97n44, 98, 105, 153n6, 224–225

real definition 5, 10, 15, 47, 53, 55–56, 65, 77, 84, 167, 171–177, 179, 181, 205–207, 218
reduction: complex to categorical syllogisms 110; dyadic to monadic relations 106, 223; valid moods to Barbara and Celarent 109n1, 118n20, 131, 135, 145–146, 231, 232; see also containment principle; dici de omni
relation 2, 6, 10, 13, 16–17
religious faith 5, 192, 219
restriction: determinative 85, 87, 90; explicative 4, 86, 88, 90, 214

second intention, terms of 47
secondary signification 47, 50–51, 57, 60, 63, 84, 172–173, 175, 179, 214, 227
sensation 2–3, 5, 11–12, 14, 32, 32n46, 33–36, 65–66, 68, 77, 80, 82–84, 149, 170, 174–175, 181, 184–186, 188–194, 208, 215–216, 218–219
significance range 44–46, 55, 66, 71–76, 87, 100, 105–106, 136, 194, 217–218, 228
signification 47, 50–51, 57, 60, 63, 84, 172–173, 175, 179, 214, 227; see also primary signification; secondary signification; significance range
soundness and completeness 135
Smith, Robin 90n29
Spade, Paul Vincent 48n16, 196n17, 212n54
Stencil, Eric 10n1, 137n39
Suárez, Francisco 13, 13n10, 19–20, 20n19, 21, 26, 29, 33, 197, 200, 200nn26–27, 201, 201nn28–30, 202–203, 203nn34–35, 204–205, 205n39, 207, 210, 214
substantives 4, 36, 39, 44–, 46, 51–52, 69, 186, 227

supposition 2, 7, 110–111, 112n3, 118–126, 128–129, 133, 139, 199, 212, 212n54, 213, 232
syllogistic: rules 1–2, 115, 126, 138, 168; *see also* soundness and completeness
synthesis 2, 4–5, 7, 95–96, 150–154, 157–158, 160–161, 163–166, 169, 172, 181, 207

Tachau, K. 13n10, 18n16
Thomas Aquinas 11n7, 13n9, 153n7, 157n10, 208n48, 210n49
Thompson, Michael 61n42
Toletus, Franciscus 18–19, 19n17, 22, 59, 59n37, 117n17
topics 110, 148–149, 153, 160–161, 195
truth: correspondence theory 1–2, 5, 19, 44–45, 75, 203; *see also* contingent truth; essential truth

truth-conditions 1–2, 4, 7, 40n4, 41, 44, 46, 58, 60, 65, 65n48, 66, 68, 75–76, 88–89, 89n28, 104, 109–112, 121n24, 124n27, 128–137, 139–140, 146, 149, 181, 184, 193–195, 205, 207, 216–217, 217n63, 218, 230, 232–234

validity 1, 4, 10, 107, 111, 116, 119, 136, 138–139, 145–146, 198, 231

Wahl, Russell 71, 71n2
Wells, Norman J. 20n18, 29n40
William of Ockham 12n8, 17, 17nn13–14, 48n16, 99n49, 157n11, 188n5, 197n20, 198n21, 199n22, 212n54